Cities and Water

Cities and Water

A Handbook for Planning

Edited by ROGER L. KEMP

McFarland & Company, Inc., Publishers
Jefferson, North Carolina, and London

Library of Congress Cataloguing-in-Publication Data

Cities and water : a handbook for planning /
edited by Roger L. Kemp
p.   cm.
Includes bibliographical references and index.

ISBN 978-0-7864-3469-5
softcover : 50# alkaline paper ∞

1. City planning — United States — Handbooks, manuals, etc.
2. Cities and towns — United States.
3. Water-supply — United States.
4. Water use — United States.
5. Urbanization — Environmental aspects.
6. Strategic planning — United States.
I. Kemp, Roger L.
HT167.C482   2009   307.1′2160973 — dc22   2008042238

British Library cataloguing data are available

Front cover image ©2008 Shutterstock

Manufactured in the United States of America

*McFarland & Company, Inc., Publishers
Box 611, Jefferson, North Carolina 28640
www.mcfarlandpub.com*

To Anika,
the Best and the Brightest!

Acknowledgments

Grateful acknowledgment is made to the following organizations and publishers for granting permission to reprint the material contained in this volume.

American Planning Association
Congressional Quarterly Inc.
Hanley Wood Business Media
International City/County Management Association
Island Institute
Land and Water, Inc.
New Hampshire Local Government Center
The Next American City Inc.
Penton Media
Scranton Gillette Communications
The Trust for Public Land
Urban Land Institute
Worcester Business Journal
World Future Society

Table of Contents

Part III. The Future

Preface

Citizens, nonprofit organizations, and local public officials, in increasing numbers, are embracing innovative water and wastewater management practices. These practices serve as vehicles to improve the quality of life in inner-city, suburban, and rural areas in communities throughout the nation. Public officials especially are learning that they have the municipal power to improve many aspects of their city's environment and economy by using proper management practices for their water and wastewater. Not only can they improve existing conditions on water-related issues, but they can have a profound influence on future growth patterns within their respective political jurisdictions. The contemporary best practices examined in this volume are quickly becoming a way of life in progressive communities throughout the country.

The types of modern water and wastewater management practices evolving in our communities include measures that promote proper practices relative to the creation, protection, preservation, and restoration of our water resources, including our wastewater. How we treat water and wastewater are critical to the growth of developed and undeveloped pieces of land in all cities and towns throughout the nation. The essence of the water and wastewater related projects contained in this volume in each of these four categories is briefly highlighted below.

- "Creation" water and wastewater planning and management practices involving those development regulations and public works projects that will lead to the establishment of desirable, livable, and healthy downtowns, neighborhoods, and suburbs, including our water resources, the systems that manage our wastewater, and the creation of wetlands areas, all of which are critical components to the growth of communities. Adequate water resources are essential for the economic growth of communities in all geographic locations of our nation.

- "Protection" water and wastewater planning and management practices include those development regulations and public works projects that create measures to safeguard the water resources and wetland areas in our downtowns, neighborhoods, and suburbs from possible man-made deterioration and destruction. Protecting our nation's streams and rivers, as well as their wetland areas, is critical to a healthy environment. Likewise, the proper management of our country's wastewater, including its recycling into a positive water resource, is critical to citizens living in our urban environment.

- "Preservation" water and wastewater planning and management practices impose regulations, and positive public works projects, that facilitate the preservation of a community's water resources and wetland areas, including the proper treatment of wastewater, which will become a valuable water resource in the future. Evolving preservation practices focus on improvements to the natural environment in our urban, suburban, and rural areas. Preservation efforts may have their highest payoff in suburban and rural areas because of the past negative management practices of water and wastewater resources in urban areas over the years.

• "Restoration" water and wastewater planning and management practices focus on regulations, public works projects, and projects that will restore water resources (including placing wastewater into this category), due to either faulty, lax, or no regulations in the past, all of which have led to the deterioration of the natural environment relative to the retainment, processing, treatment, and use of water. Restoration projects have primarily focused on inner-city areas and their neighborhoods, secondarily in the suburbs, and lastly in those rural, and undeveloped, portions of land remaining in our communities.

This volume is divided into four sections for ease of reference. The first section introduces the reader to the rapidly evolving field of "cities, water, and the future." The second section, and by design the longest, includes numerous case studies, or best practices, on how cities and towns, as well as their nonprofit organizations and public officials, are taking positive measures to create, protect, preserve, and restore our country's water resources, which are essential to not only the economic growth of our nation but also the quality of life in cities and towns throughout the country. The third section focuses on the future of communities and their water resources and examines firmly established positive trends that will improve the management of our water resources during the coming decades. Section four includes several appendices to promote a greater understanding of this new field.

Based on this conceptual schema, the four sections are examined in greater detail below.

• *Cities and Water.* Chapters in this section examine the relationship of people, water, and the urban environment; America's aging water-related infrastructure; evolving water regulations and land use management trends; and contemporary measures being undertaken to safeguard and protect America's wetland and watershed areas. Chapters 5 and 6 focus on modern measures being undertaken to protect our nation's drinking water resources, and the direct and essential relationship between the existence of water resources and economic growth. The bottom line is that the existence of a quality water supply, including how water is contained, treated, recycled, and used, is critical to our country's economic growth. These chapters provide the framework and background against which the best practices in this field have emerged in America's cities and towns in recent years.

• *The Best Practices.* The various cities and towns examined in this section, including the states in which they are located, as well as highlights of the evolving best practices for the management of water-related issues, are listed in alphabetical order. These case studies represent *an important and significant research effort* to obtain a body of knowledge on the best practices available in the dynamic and still evolving field of water-related management practices in our nation's municipal levels of government. The best practices section includes nearly 40 local governments, 24 states, one province, and two countries — primarily the United States, but also one case study in Canada, because of its proximity to the United States.

Cities —

Allenstown	Ayer
Aurora	Baltimore

Boston
Bradenton
Bradley Beach
Charleston
Charlotte
Chicago
Cleveland
Delphos
Fort Worth
Halifax
Houston
Jacksonville
Kansas City
Lakewood
Las Vegas
Los Angeles
Miami
Moscow

New Orleans
Philadelphia
St. Augustine
St. George
San Francisco
Santa Barbara
Santa Monica
Scottsdale
Toledo
Salt Lake City
Santa Fe
Seattle
Streamwood
University Place
Washington
West Des Moines
Yorklyn

States —

Arizona
California
Colorado
Delaware
Florida
Idaho
Illinois
Iowa
Louisiana
Maine
Maryland
Massachusetts

Missouri
Nevada
New Hampshire
New Jersey
New Mexico
North Carolina
Ohio
Pennsylvania
South Carolina
Texas
Utah
Washington

Province —
Nova Scotia

Countries —
Canada   United States

Selected Best Practices —
Improvements to wastewater treatment processes
Preservation and protection of the public water supply
Conservation and regulation of the public water supply

Revitalization and protection of inner-city harbors and waterways
Use of citizens and nonprofit organizations to clean up waterways
Construction of public recreation areas along bays, rivers, and streams
Restoration and protection of beach shoreline areas
Restoration of stream and wetlands corridor areas
Expansion of future municipal water resources
Improvements to water quality and water quality infrastructure
Removal of levees to reconnect waterways to neighborhoods
Improvements to harbor water quality
Improvements to the management of stormwater
Reconstruction of wetland areas
Restoration of the urban habitat
Regional flood control mitigation measures
Elimination of neighborhood drainage problems
Renewal of inner-city rivers and waterways
Restoration of nature to improve rivers and watershed areas
Restoration of inner-city parks and their waterways
Cleaning of contaminated sites to restore riverfront areas
Creation of new wetland areas to offset urban growth patterns
Acquisition of private property to ensure public access to water areas
Wetlands preservation and mitigations programs for public and private properties
Enhancement of water quality through the use of stormwater pollution prevention plans
Restoration and protection of beachfront coastline areas
Working with citizen groups to restore rivers and streams, as well as their nature corridors
Letting mother nature guide future stormwater management practices

Reclamation, recycling, and reuse of waste-water

Use of smart growth planning practices to improve water quality

Removal of pollutants from rivers to improve water quality

Multi-agency cooperation for the treatment of water-sensitive land areas

Improvements to the quality of public drinking water

Conversion of river and watershed areas into parks and open spaces

Protection of public and private buildings in floodplain areas

- *The Future.* The third section of this volume examines trends in our cities and towns, as well as societal changes taking place in them, primarily the public's concern for their environment, including their rivers, streams, watersheds, and how contaminated water is treated and recycled. Specifically, chapters examine the relationship between growth and the availability of water, public and private citizen movements to reclaim rivers, and Smart Growth and its benefits on a community's water resources. Chapters 49 and 50 focus on the new trend of restorative development and the changing relationship between cities, water, and people to the future of our urban environment. This section examines the trends in our nation as related to water issues, how citizens and nonprofit organizations are focusing on these issues, and how municipal public officials are responding to water-related issues to improve the quality of water resources within their respective communities.

- *Appendices.* Since this is a dynamic and evolving field, several appendices are included to enhance the reader's understanding of this subject, as well as to facilitate research that readers may undertake to seek additional information from the many municipalities listed in the best

practices section, as well as improve their general understanding on the subject of cities and water. The first two appendices, A and B, are a list of abbreviations and acronyms and a glossary of terms for the new field of water and water-related planning and development. Appendices C and D are a national periodical bibliography for this field, and an international water webliography, which contains a listing of websites from professional and research organizations throughout the world that focus on water-related resources and issues. Appendices E and F are a regional resource directory, which includes a listing of the websites for each local government included in the best practice section, and a national resource directory, which lists all of the professional associations and research organizations in the United States that relate to, or focus on, water-related resources and issues.

The various case studies, or best practices, presented represent state-of-the-art practices on how cities and towns as well as nonprofit organizations and local public officials are using new water and wastewater management practices to revitalize America's inner cities, neighborhoods, suburbs, and rural areas to restore and enhance the natural environment upon which our communities depend for their very existence. All of these modern water and wastewater planning and management practices represent additional tools and techniques within the traditional fields of planning, public works, and water resource management. These best practices will assist citizens, nonprofit organizations, and local public officials throughout the nation as they attempt to improve the environment during the coming decades.

The various case studies, or best practices, contained in this volume are typically applied in a piecemeal and incremental fashion in cities and towns throughout America. For the most part, citizens, nonprofit organizations and local public officials are preoccupied with existing projects and issues within their respective communities. They do not have the time to find out what other neighboring cities and towns are doing in these areas, let alone what other communities are doing throughout the nation. For this reason, the various case studies, or best practices, contained in this volume represent an important codification of knowledge in the new and rapidly evolving field of cities and water.

This reference work assembles, for the first time, materials based on a national literature search and makes this information available to citizens, nonprofit organizations, and public officials throughout the nation. The goal of this volume is to help educate citizens, as well as their public officials, on how to use these new planning and development practices to improve their quality of life, as well as to facilitate the restoration of nature within their respective communities.

If additional information is desired to follow up on any of the best practice case studies contained in this volume, every local government contained in this section is included in the regional resource directory (Appendix E). Additional information can be obtained from this directory by contacting the chief elected or appointed official in those cities and towns listed via the contact information contained on their respective websites. Important state, regional, and national resources are brought together for the first time in the national resource directory to assist readers with becoming informed about the evolving field of municipal governments and their water-related resources and issues.

Many hours were spent researching this subject, and the editor hopes that the information contained in this volume will assist local public officials, citizens, and leaders of municipal organizations as they attempt to make sense out of, and cope with, the water and wastewater related issues in their communities. The future of America's cities and towns depends upon the proper management of our bays and harbors, river and streams, as well as their respective watershed areas. Citizens not only expect, but demand, that prudent measures be adopted and implemented to ensure that future growth will not negatively impact, but help create, protect, preserve, restore, and positively impact America's valuable water resources.

Roger L. Kemp
Meriden, Connecticut
December 2008

CHAPTER 1

People, Water, and the Urban Environment

Michael Burger

Diane Easley lives in Nelson County, population 14,000, just south of Charlottesville, Virginia. Big pieces of land were once used to grow tobacco here, but all that remains of this agricultural heritage is some dairy farming and a small lumber industry. The growth industries here now include a ski resort, second homes, and speculation on land ready to accommodate more second homes. It is a prototypical exurb in transition. Charlottesville has been creeping closer for a decade. And if fears of living in a nearby target city like Washington, D.C., intensify following another 9/11, Nelson County's permanent population could double overnight. Already, the population in some parts of the county is growing at ten percent per year.

To retain the area's tony charm — and its water quality — Easley and other residents are trying desperately to keep sprawl at bay.

The construction of new roads and bridges has led to soil erosion and siltation of rivers and streams, and an informal survey of groundwater tables revealed some potential contamination in shallow wells. The equation is simple and common: more houses and roads create more impervious surfaces and human uses; these in turn increase the rate and amount of polluted runoff into rivers and streams, deteriorating the water quality.

Just a few years ago, the forty-something Easley was not by her own account an environmental activist. She was not even especially political. But when the University of Virginia received a "small watershed" grant from the U.S. Environmental Protection Agency to develop a pilot program in her area, she started showing up at meetings. She has since taken charge and expanded what was a 5-person citizen task force into an 80-person organization, the Friends of the Rockfish Watershed, and is now spearheading a campaign to make water quality a top priority in Nelson County.

The campaign represents a change in the way people respond to clean water issues. While much of the modern environmental movement is built on lawsuits and top-down enforcement of federal and state statutes and permitting programs, Easley and groups like hers, known as community watershed organizations, take a more collaborative, bottom-up approach. Their strategy, essentially, is to mobilize individual citizens to participate more directly in the lawmaking process.

Originally published as "Environment: A Watershed Moment: A New Urban Environmental Movement Is Born," *The Next American City*, Vol. 2, No. 4, February 2004. Published by The Next American City Inc., Philadelphia, PA. Reprinted with permission of the publisher.

"We're extremely local and governed by what people that live here want," Easley says.

More than 2,000 groups adopting similar approaches have materialized across the country, and many more are in various stages of formation. Through these organizations, some half million people participate in activities that range from tree planting and river bank cleanups to canoe and kayak trips to public education in schools and parks. In recent years, these watershed groups have taken on a more political bent. A changing legal landscape has raised their profile, and they've become more vocal in city, county, and state legislatures by participating in a collaborative form of decision-making called watershed management planning.

Easley and her friends of the Rockfish Watershed, for instance, have built informational kiosks in local parks and tried to raise general awareness of the issues surrounding water quality by sponsoring events and programs. But they have also sat at the negotiating table with county officials, local business interests, individual farmers, scientists, and engineers to draft a "watershed management plan" for 258 square miles of land that drains into the James River at Howardsville. Like many such plans, it employs clustered zoning — bunching together new developments on small parcels of land in order to preserve parts of the natural landscape in large open spaces — in conjunction with conservation easements — covenants that forbid any future building on these open spaces. These practices help to preserve vital habitats and maintain agricultural uses. The management plan would also, for the first time, regulate area stormwater-drainage systems and require buffer zones free from development along stream banks. Finally, the plan encourages local monitoring of water quality by citizens groups.

The local county government has responded by incorporating various elements of the draft into its Comprehensive Plan and its zoning ordinances. Easley and her group have thus managed to infuse water quality concerns into local politics without having to sue anyone.

The Challenge of Urban Watershed Management

Easley's success with the cooperative watershed planning model of regulation may not translate to all locales, however. Watershed management planning in a metropolis is a different beast than in exurban or small city environments. The politics are more complex, and environmental concerns compete against a slew of other social problems for top billing. The city of Baltimore, for instance, "has a horrible history of trashing the environment," says Richard Hersey, executive director of the Herring Run Watershed Association. "It's the legacy of our industrial background, these contaminated lands and waters. Up until three years ago [and the election of Mayor Martin O'Malley] we couldn't even get the environment onto a list of city's critical urban ills."

But watershed management planning also represents a potentially fresh angle from which to approach urban environmental problems. According to Hersey, watershed management planning is integrally connected with open space preservation, "brownfield" (industrial site) redevelopment, and remediation of Superfund sites. He believes that an adequate citywide plan in Baltimore could help retire 200 to 600 acres from the development market, and integrate that land with restored streams returning to the river's headwaters.

Baltimore is divided into three watersheds — Herring Run, Jones Falls, and Gwynns Falls. As with many urban rivers and streams, much of the water is buried under the city's infrastructure, making it difficult to access, never mind manage, says Christel Marie Cothran, program director at the Jones Falls Watershed Association. And even if Baltimore could map out a vision for the city's watersheds, integrating it into zoning ordinances and comprehensive plans would prove difficult. "I don't really know where the system breaks down, but I think it breaks down everywhere in Baltimore," says Hersey.

Jurisdictional boundaries that have no

relation to watershed boundaries pose particular difficulties. Surrounding Baltimore County has developed a watershed management plan, and has been acknowledged as one of the most aggressive counties in the state in pursuing its design. The plan, however, does not include anything inside the Baltimore city line. The city, in turn, has looked at its three primary watersheds and wants to develop plans for each. Predictably enough, the city and county are acting on different sets of facts, and for any number of institutional reasons have difficulty communicating, although they have at least signed an agreement to cooperate on the issue.

Ultimately, the success of watershed management planning depends on community buy-in, and there are quite simply many differing interests in Baltimore that may prove contentious — at least 8 universities, 8 golf courses, and 26 private schools, for instance, as well as all of the building owners, homeowners, and tenants. "We are trying to work with them to think about ways to change land use practices," Cothran says. Her group has been trying to promote the use of rain barrels — to collect rainwater and prevent it from overwhelming the stormwater system — and bayscaping, which uses native plants in gardens and yards to reduce the amount of pesticide and fertilizer likely to enter waterways.

New Front Lines for Clean Water

Watershed groups have become more prominent in the last half-decade because they are particularly well-adapted for solving a set of problems that environmental law is now addressing after decades of neglect. Since the 1972 Clean Water Act, the United States has most successfully reduced pollution from "point" sources — the end of sewage and industrial pipes. But more than half of all the nation's water pollution comes from "nonpoint" sources, such as urban and agricultural

runoff and discharge from storm sewers, construction sites, and logging operations. Pollution from these sources accounts for nearly all the sediment deposition and the vast majority of nitrogen and phosphorous reaching the nation's waters. In fact, the U.S. Environmental Protection Agency and many states have reported that nonpoint source pollution is the primary reason a high percentage of the nation's waters remain unswimmable and unfishable. Yet, because the problem is so diffuse and difficult to regulate, it remains largely outside the reach of federal and state authorities.

But many cities now have no choice but to deal with it. The Clean Water Act's monstrously-named Phase II National Pollutant Discharge Elimination System (NPDES) Stormwater Program requires operators of municipal storm sewers in urbanized areas with populations under 100,000 to start controlling polluted stormwater runoff, most of which can be attributed to nonpoint source pollution. The patterns of urban and suburban sprawl that accompanied the economic boom of the 1990s increased the number of local governments subject to the regulations even while they made the nonpoint problem worse. "The 1990s were a crazy time for development," says John Rozum, the national network coordinator for Nonpoint Education for Municipal Officials (NEMO), a confederation of programs that educate local decision-makers on the connection between land use and water quality. "You had people buying all these houses, developing all this stuff. Now we're looking at it, and thinking, is this really how we want to be?"

The problem is particularly acute around the Chesapeake Bay, which does not meet the federal clean water standards — in regulatory lingo, the region is a "non-attainment area." The EPA has given the Chesapeake Bay Program, an agency shared by the Bay's watershed states of Maryland, Virginia, and Pennsylvania, until 2010 to clean it up. If the Bay Program fails, the feds will force the states to significantly tighten their regulation of both point and nonpoint pollution sources. The states are loath to take on this Total Maximum Daily Load program. They would have to calculate how much pollution each water body that feeds into the Bay could absorb and then divvy that load among all the players who need or want to discharge into it. The process would be technically challenging and politically terrifying. Under the auspices of the Bay Program, the states are making great efforts to clean up the Bay and avoid regulating daily loads. Maryland, Virginia, and Pennsylvania have each committed to work with local governments, community groups, and watershed organizations to develop and implement watershed management plans in two-thirds of the Bay watershed by the year 2010.

The Chesapeake Bay states have taken different approaches to meeting their commitments, but watershed groups play a role throughout the region. In Maryland and Virginia, watershed management planning is mostly done at the county level, with some participation from state agencies, community watershed organizations, and individual landowners. By contrast, in Pennsylvania watershed management planning is an entirely grassroots affair, where community watershed organizations develop plans with little government oversight. Despite their prominence, the groups have a strained relationship with Bay Program personnel's "perception of local 'friends of' groups that they are limited in scope and competence." The disdain works both ways: "The Bay Program people are ... often perceived as people that live in ivory towers and are asserting their values into local communities," says Steve Talley, watershed coordinator at the Canaan Valley Institute, a nonprofit group that works in West Virginia and Pennsylvania.

An Undefined Future Role

Watershed management planning and other collaborative approaches to environmental decision-making are now being championed not only by progressives and liberal pragmatists, but also by Interior Secretary Gail Norton and other proponents of deregulation and private rights. Ambiguities in the current watershed planning process have temporarily brought together forces that want very different outcomes from the process. It remains uncertain, for instance, whether these plans create the enforceable regulations that environmentalists want or merely encourage the voluntary efforts by businesses and citizens that conservatives often promote. It also remains unclear just who is beholden to them, and what impact they actually have.

How these watershed planning processes turn out will determine whether this new trend becomes primarily an educational tool, or a new kind of political force for the environmental movement. The Canaan Valley Institute's Talley thinks of watershed management planning in broad, educational terms, "The fundamental essence of watershed management planning," he says, "is really nothing more than an effort to get local folks to differently value natural resource conservation." Tom Schueler, executive director of the Maryland-based Center for Watershed Protection, stakes out the alternative perspective; he derides what he calls "pleasant structures"— voluntary programs that spur citizen participation — and thinks that watershed activists need to push full force into local legislatures, and into the law, as the Friends of the Rockfish have. "A lot of people just want to get people to talk and think that's going to be enough," Schueler says. "I think we need to raise a little hell."

CHAPTER 2

America's Aging Water-Related Infrastructure

Lori Burkhammer

The problems may be hidden underground, but sooner or later they will surface. America's water and wastewater systems are crumbling, and there is not enough money to repair them. A commitment on all levels is required to fix it; however, policymakers in Washington are failing to provide much-needed support. Are local governments prepared to pick up where the federal government has left off?

In February, the Bush Administration proposed cutting the Clean Water State Revolving Fund (SRF) — the nation's biggest source of funding for sanitation and watershed management systems — by 37 percent in its fiscal year (FY) 2006 budget. If approved, the cut would continue a steady decline of federal support for the program, decreasing its overall budget from $1.3 billion in FY 2004 to the proposed $730 million in FY 2006.

Although the administration plans to keep the Safe Drinking Water Act SRF, which supports the construction of drinking water purification facilities, steady at $850 million, both amounts are still far below the annual needs of water and wastewater utilities. The severe lack of federal funds reaches deep into the pockets of local communities. "To keep up with growth demands, local resources are being stretched," says Jim Canaday, engineer-director for the Alexandria Sanitation Authority in Alexandria, Va. "A reduction in federal support does not help local municipalities deal with increasing treatment requirements, unfunded mandates and other issues."

Professional and advocacy groups have identified the country's aging water and wastewater infrastructure as a top concern. In March, the Reston, Va.–based American Society of Civil Engineers gave water and wastewater systems D-minus grades in its "2005 Report Card for America's Infrastructure." One month later, American Rivers, an environmental group based in Washington, released "America's Most Endangered Rivers of 2005."

Because of its high sewage content, the Susquehanna River — which flows through New York, Pennsylvania and Maryland — was listed as the most endangered and declared a public health threat. The report notes that some of the sewage in the river is untreated because aging pipes cannot deal with increased flows from residential and commercial devel-

Originally published as "The Invisible Problem," *American City and County*, Vol. 120, No. 5, May 2005. Published by Penton Media, Overland Park, KS. Reprinted with permission from *American City and Country* magazine. Copyright 2005, Penton Media, New York, NY.

opment, let alone the sudden increases during storms. As a result, sewer overflows bypass the treatment plants and pour into the rivers.

Failure to address the condition of water and wastewater infrastructure could lead to more sewer overflows, water pollution, disease outbreaks and possibly a loss of jobs. For instance, since 1988, more than $23.5 billion in federal investment from the Clean Water SRF has been leveraged into approximately $46 billion in clean water projects, resulting in the creation of 47,000 jobs. If funding shortfalls continue, that economic benefit could be threatened.

Worse yet, given funding demands for more visible programs, such as health and education, water does not appear to be a priority for the federal government. "Unfortunately, water and the environment doesn't even make the top 10 in terms of issues that [decision-makers] are concerned about in Washington," says Tim Williams, director of government affairs at the Alexandria, Va.–based Water Environment Federation (WEF). "They're concerned about Medicare and Medicaid costs, homeland security and [the] No Child Left Behind [Act]."

How Bad Is It?

In hundreds of municipalities across the United States, pipes, water treatment facilities, sewer systems and wastewater treatment plants — many built between 1900 and World War II — need maintenance, rehabilitation or repair. Water and wastewater utilities are responsible for more than 800,000 miles of water pipe and more than 600,000 miles of sewer line, according to the U.S. Government Accountability Office. At one-third of the utilities, one in five pipelines are nearing the end of their useful lives. At one in 10 utilities, half or more of the pipelines are in a similar state. Moreover, rapidly growing communities are placing increasing demands on water resources and risk not meeting those needs because of insufficient pipelines and treatment facilities for drinking water and wastewater.

To fix all the problems, wastewater utilities need to spend between $331 billion and $450 billion, while water utilities need to spend between $154 billion and $446 billion, according to the U.S. Environmental Protection Agency (EPA), the Congressional Budget Office and Water Infrastructure Network. Additionally, the Congressional Budget Office estimates that rural and urban systems lose 20 percent or more of their water through leaky pipes; and nationally, the projected costs of revitalizing and expanding water systems range from $485 billion to nearly $1.2 trillion.

With growing demand and dwindling resources, city managers and plant operators find themselves in a difficult position. "There is no doubt that water and wastewater services help protect public health and the environment, but the water quality community is in an unsustainable position," says Robert McMillon, former Fort Worth, Texas, assistant water director and a past president of WEF. "We are faced with a mandate to protect water resources with aging, capacity-limited or nonexistent infrastructure assets, and diminishing financial resources and commitments. Locally, and across the nation, we need to determine where the funding will be found."

How Did We Get Here?

In the early to mid–1800s, sewers were installed to take care of storm water and basic waste removal, with many sewers designed, built, owned and maintained by private individuals or companies. Adjacent cities eventually took them over, making them publicly owned.

Around the same time, people recognized that community health could be improved by discharging human waste into the storm sewers for rapid removal. Development of municipal water-supply systems and household plumbing brought about flush toilets and the beginning of modern sewer systems. By 1910, there were approximately 25,000 miles of sewer lines in the United States.

However, during the first half of the 20th century few municipalities and industries treated wastewater. Instead, untreated urban wastewater was discharged the least expensive way: directly into the closest water body, a practice known as "disposal by dilution." Wastewater was handled that way because of virtually non-existent regulations, little scientific knowledge of negative ecological and health-related effects, and lack of construction funding.

The New Deal provided federal monies in the 1930s to bolster state efforts in occupational safety and health, with a greater focus on water quality and pollution control. And in the late 1940s, as water and wastewater treatment became a widely accepted necessity, the federal government became directly involved in water pollution control. Passed in 1948, the Federal Water Pollution Control Act — the first federal clean water law and precursor to the 1972 Clean Water Act (CWA) — was signed into law. The act primarily appropriated federal monies for surveys, studies and construction of publicly owned treatment works.

In the 1950s and 1960s, the U.S. government provided funds for constructing municipal waste treatment plants, water pollution research, and technical training and assistance. Despite those efforts, expanding population and industrial and economic growth caused pollution and health difficulties to increase. Because of the growth in the 1970s, huge public investments were made in roads, sewers, water lines and power grids. The environment, however, paid a price, bringing about the greatest public outcry on water quality — and corresponding legislative and executive response — in U.S. history.

The public's emphasis on the environment helped create Earth Day in April 1970, followed by the creation of EPA later that year. In October 1972, Congress enacted CWA, which committed the federal government to water quality standards, controls and funding at unprecedented levels. The federal government invested more than $72 billion to build sewage treatment works and related facilities during the 1970s and 1980s. The Clean Water SRF eventually replaced the construction grant funds.

"Even with the federal grants program, local governments still paid most of the construction costs during the '70s and '80s," Williams says. "Unfortunately, the rate structures that many cities adopted during that time, which are still in place today, are only adequate to pay for annual operating costs and maintenance. For various reasons, local governments have not budgeted for [infrastructure] replacement. And although there is a strong argument for federal investment, most agree that local governments will end up with the biggest share of the cost."

What Can Be Done?

While water and wastewater utilities currently are facing an unprecedented financing challenge, history is repeating itself in the call for federal, local and individual investment. More than eight in 10 Americans believe that clean and safe water is a national issue that deserves federal investment, according to a recent poll of 900 adults, conducted jointly by Republican and Democratic polling firms Luntz Research Companies and Penn, Schoen & Berland Associates.

The water quality community agrees. There is a growing consensus to develop a strategy for overall infrastructure sustainability, including investments on local and federal levels. That would include a greater commitment first from local legislators, followed by a significant increase in federal investment. "Without a significantly enhanced federal role in financing and wastewater infrastructure, critical investments will not occur," McMillon says. "Failure to meet these needs over the next

20 years risks the environmental, public health and economic gains achieved under the Clean Water Act."

Before that can happen, however, the main players must be educated. "Overall, there appears to be a general understanding of the infrastructure issue," Williams says. "However, considering the magnitude of this problem, [water quality professionals] need to be more proactive in educating public policy makers, local legislators and the general public about the implications of not making investment a priority."

As a result, WEF is rolling out a public education campaign this fall to re-educate residents about the importance of clean drinking water and safe sanitation services. "We believe that when the facts are presented to the public, they will support spending for clean water," Williams says.

Utilities and ratepayers already are working together to share the financial burden of repairing their water systems. Using alternative funding options such as low interest loan programs combined with gradual rate increases, cities such as Alexandria, Va., have supported capital improvements and facility upgrades.

In 1996, the Alexandria Sanitation Authority (ASA) was required to perform a $350 million treatment plant upgrade. After exploring all financing options, ASA realized that rates would have to nearly double during the first five years of its rate increase program. By the end of the fifth year, the typical residential bill for wastewater services would have risen by 85 percent. After that, residences would see a series of lesser rate increases to complete construction and address normal operations. ASA was able to generate public support, minimize opposition and lessen the impact on ratepayers through careful financial planning, educating key stakeholders and securing low-interest revolving fund loans and a Virginia state grant.

"The success of ASA's rate increase program is a real-life demonstration of the validity of and need for a robust Clean Water State Revolving Fund," Canaday says. "The availability of the revolving fund loan program will, over the life of the loan, save ASA's ratepayers tens of millions of dollars in interest payments."

While Alexandria's success is not an isolated example, neither are the incidents in Poughkeepsie, Des Moines or Baltimore. Without local and federal action, an increasing number of infrastructure failures will be grabbing headlines and forcing the hidden problem to the surface. Because the federal commitment is waning, the question becomes whether local government leaders will be satisfied to struggle with the symptoms of their failing systems or make water and wastewater infrastructure a top priority.

CHAPTER 3

Water Regulations and Land Use

Jon D. Witten

The Safe Drinking Water Act (SDWA) remains one of the federal government's most aggressive attempts at managing land use at the local level of government. Although certainly not billed as a land use control statute, the SDWA, particularly as revised in 1996 with the creation of the so-called "SWAP" (source water assessment program), set in motion a process by which local governments and suppliers of drinking water are encouraged to take proactive steps, including but not limited to the regulation of private property to protect drinking water resources.

This latter point — the regulation of private property to fulfill a public purpose — remains controversial, even though zoning and land use controls have become a staple of virtually every metropolitan and suburban community across the nation.

This chapter highlights key provisions of the SDWA, particularly the "SWAP" and then concludes with an abbreviated menu of the zoning techniques available to local governments as they seek to fulfill the goals and requirements of the SWAP initiative.

Federal Safe Drinking Water Act

Section 1453 of the 1996 SDWA Amendments requires states to develop comprehensive State Source Water Assessment Programs, commonly referred to as SWAPs. Each state is required to submit to U.S. EPA a SWAP that includes the following four components:

- Delineation of the source water protection area: that portion of a watershed or groundwater area that may contribute contamination to the water supply;
- Identification of all significant potential sources of drinking water contamination within the protection areas identified above. The resulting contamination source inventory must describe the sources (or categories of sources) of contamination either by specific location or by area;
- Determination of the water supply's susceptibility to contamination from identified sources. The susceptibility analysis can be either an absolute measure of the potential for contamination of the water supply or a relative comparison between sources within the protection area; and
- Distribution of the source water assessment results to the public.

Originally published as "Protecting Drinking Water Resources Under the Source Water Assessment Program," *The Commissioner*, Winter 2001. Published by the American Planning Association, Chicago, IL. Reprinted with permission of the publisher.

The SWAP requires information pertaining to drinking water supplies be developed, and not that the supplies necessarily be protected. In other words, despite going to great lengths to require states and local governments to "do the right thing" with respect to resource protection, the protective actions are left solely to state and local governments. And, despite some examples of aggressive state actions, the vast majority of public water supplies in the nation are reliant on the steps taken by local governments.

Step One: Source Water Protection Areas:

A source water protection area is the watershed or groundwater area that may contribute pollution to the water supply. The purpose of the source water protection area delineation is to establish priority focus areas for the source water assessment, described in Component 2.

Public water supplies that rely on surface waters must include in their delineated areas the entire watershed upstream of the water supply's intake structure, up to the state's border with another state or jurisdiction.

In addition, surface water based public water supplies must include in their delineations the impacts of groundwater upon the surface water resource. This requirement is tricky. The source water protection areas must include both surface watersheds and ground water recharge areas (so-called zones of contribution or wellhead protection areas) to public surface water supplies.

Step Two: Contamination Source Inventory:

A contamination source inventory is an inventory — identification — of all present and potential sources of drinking water contamination within the source water protection area described above. Potential sources of contamination are historical (they existed in the past and still pose a threat to drinking water), current (they exist today) and future (they could exist in the future according to the local comprehensive plan, local regulations governing land use and/or market forces).

Contaminants of concern include a wide range of "raw" water contaminants regulated under the Safe Drinking Water Act including those that may present a threat to public health such as viruses and bacteria.

The contamination source inventory must include a clear description of the sources of contamination (or categories of sources) either by specific location or by area. And as noted above, these descriptions must include past, present and future sources. This latter requirement is of great importance to public officials planning for the future protection of drinking water resources. The contamination source inventory will allow public officials to focus — prioritize — their efforts with respect to drinking water protection. By knowing where likely contamination sources are, local officials can pinpoint and target their labor and dollar resources efficiently and with high probabilities of success.

It is important to note that groundwater and surface water supplies are threatened in different ways and by different contaminants. Surface waters are vulnerable to contamination from both runoff and groundwater infiltration. Runoff of contaminants from the surface areas in a watershed, either near a drinking water supply intake or in upstream tributaries can cause contamination. Similarly, contaminated groundwater can recharge streams or lakes.

Groundwater can become contaminated through infiltration from the surface, injection of contaminants (e.g. septic systems and injection wells) or by naturally occurring substances in the soil or rock through which it flows. Depending upon the hydrogeologic setting, contaminants in ground water may migrate far from the source and pollute water supplies thousands of feet, even miles away.

Step Three: Susceptibility Determinations:

The third required component of a SWAP is the susceptibility determination: the determination of the susceptibility of the water supply to each contaminant source identified in Component 2. U.S. EPA has encouraged susceptibility determinations for several years, arguing that they are useful for decision making with regard to prioritizing management decisions. The thinking goes something like this:

City A has identified 22 contaminant threats within the watershed to its primary surface water reservoir. These threats include past, present and potential future contaminant sources. The susceptibility determination provides the City with additional information, essentially a relative risk ranking of which of those threats are the most imminent versus the least likely.

While this prioritization of actions may, at first glance, appear economical (the City has limited resources and cannot solve all 22 problems at once), each of the 22 threats are real and each must be dealt with. In other words, while the City may seek to remediate or fix the most menacing of threats immediately and postpone the others until a future date, the City must nevertheless respond to all 22 contaminant sources. This point is underscored by the sheer complexity, particularly with respect to drinking water derived from groundwater resources, of the movement of contaminants within the subsurface.

For example, U.S. EPA and several states have recommended that local governments focus on a "time of travel" priority for contaminants. This approach views those contaminants that are closest to a drinking water well to pose the greatest threat; those furthest away posing a lesser threat. Unfortunately, this approach presumes that contaminants will flow uniformly through the subsurface: essentially a race through the aquifer, the closest getting to the well first. But few groundwater environments are uniform and over-reliance on time of travel may minimize the threats of contaminant sources distant from pumping wells. Again, the point is simply that the susceptibility determination should not lead to an ignorance of distant threats: all known and foreseeable contaminant sources must be responded to in order to adequately protect drinking water supplies.

Step Four: Publicizing the SWAP Results:

States are required to publicize the results of their SWAP efforts to individual municipalities. The publication requirement can take several different forms, but is intended to be in "plain-language" and must include maps of the delineated source water protection areas and the sources of contamination described in the contaminant source inventory.

It is important to note that the four components described above amass and assess data relative to public drinking water supply protection. The next, and perhaps most important step is left to the state's respective local governments.

Prior to reviewing a handful of the zoning tools available to local governments in the pursuit of drinking water protection, it is worth noting that local governments may have a legal obligation to protect public drinking water resources from contamination.

This obligation stems from tort law: the body of law defining civil actions and responsibilities of private individuals and, more recently, public agencies. While a more lengthy discussion is beyond the scope of this article, it is worth remembering that a local government's failure to protect a drinking water supply from a known contamination threat may be tantamount to negligence, establishing liability to an injured consumer of contaminated water.

Generally speaking, negligence liability of a municipal government is dramatically reduced where it can demonstrate that it acted reasonably — took reasonable steps — toward the protection of drinking water resources. Adoption of the following techniques is a good start toward protecting drinking water resources.

Local Regulatory Options for Protecting Drinking Water Resources

It should be noted at the outset that there are two broad categories of techniques available for protecting drinking water supplies. They are best divided into regulatory and non-regulatory approaches. The following discussion focuses solely on the former and within this category, solely on zoning techniques. (Note, however, that local governments have had success with a variety of other regulatory controls as well as non-regulatory approaches, including land acquisition, best management practices and public education).

With few exceptions, the following zoning tools are available to local governments throughout the nation. Each has proven successful in the protection of drinking water supplies.

Using Zoning Controls to Protect Drinking Water Supplies

Zoning is a household word in some portions of the nation. In others, the concept of zoning remains an affront to private property rights and represents government intrusion at its worst. As for the protection of drinking water supplies, however, zoning remains one of the most appropriate and successfully used regulatory techniques available and one that even the most reluctant community needs to consider.

There are many variations of zoning regulations that are used to protect drinking water supplies. They include:

Overlay districts. A zoning overlay district is the marriage between the source water protection area(s) and zoning (or other land use) regulation. Given the requirement that all source water protection districts must be mapped and the information made available to each municipality, few excuses exist for not linking the delineation to a regulatory program. Moreover, the adoption of an overlay district allows the municipality to expand both its regulatory and non-regulatory protection efforts in the future. The areas of concern are mapped, made official through the adoption process and remain available for the public to view and identify as areas of special concern.

Large lot zoning. Perhaps the most controversial of the techniques used, large lot zoning is straightforward. Its goal is to minimize the numbers of dwellings and thus impervious surfaces associated with residential development. When applied in areas of a community without advanced wastewater treatment facilities, large lot requirements reduce the number of septic systems and associated bacteria, viruses and household contaminants. The controversy stems from the debate as to whether large lots contribute to (or in fact, define) sprawl and whether large lot zoning is equitable given the shortage of affordable housing nationwide. Nevertheless, within a source water protection area, fewer lots, dwellings and associated impacts is generally better.

Performance standards. This technique remains my favorite. It is based upon the assumption that a drinking water resource has a threshold beyond which its ability to function deteriorates to an unacceptable level (as dictated by statute or public acceptance). Adoption of performance standards allows a municipality to establish limits to development density, type and location within a source water protection area. By articulating the protection area's carrying capacity (the threshold limit of contaminants) the municipality can regulate development such that the capacity is not exceeded. The opposite approach, of course, allowing development without regard to the drinking water supply's carrying capacity, ultimately and inevitably leads to the degradation of the water supply.

Transfer of development rights. Given the requirements for identifying source water protection areas and susceptibility assessments, local governments are now in an ideal position to embrace and begin to use transfer of development rights to protect drinking water supplies. TDR has been used successfully throughout the nation to protect water supplies.

Development agreements. Another of my favorites, development agreements are contractual and binding agreements between a landowner and governmental agency that establish the rules for the development of land. Development agreements require both parties to adhere to the public hearing and meeting process, but typically can lead to development approval with greater public benefits than would be associated with the typical project. In that regard, development agreements often allow the municipality to achieve greater protections for drinking water supplies than would otherwise be possible under the standard development and permit review process.

In exchange, the land owner/developer can often secure protections from future zoning changes and obtain permitting support from various public departments and commissions thus ensuring approval in shorter than normal time periods.

Using SWAP Information to Protect Drinking Water Supplies

Over the next two years, all states will have completed the four components of the Source Water Assessment Plans described above. This information will be made available to every county, city, town, reservation and parish in the nation. It is left to these jurisdictions, however, to use the information contained in the SWAPs to protect drinking water supplies. While some states may mandate certain levels of land use controls, it is likely that most of the protection efforts will need to occur at the local level of government.

The use of an array of zoning techniques, such as the ones discussed in this publication, might provide the most immediate protection from a range of drinking water contaminants.

CHAPTER 4

Protecting Our Watersheds

Jonas Sipaila and William McCully

Meeting the current national, local, city and watershed rules and regulations poses the greatest challenge in storm water management practices. Civil and water resources engineers must address widely varied problems, including rate control, water quality, water conservation and flood protection. However, in spite of the extremely different issues, current best management practices (BMPs) typically focus on one narrow, specific problem; these BMPs lack the versatility to address diverse storm water challenges.

At the same time, present day BMPs face obstacles raised by the centuries-old philosophy and historical model for storm water management that treats storm water as a waste product. This waste product model has resulted in the physical establishment of "slope" and runoff and the simultaneous construction of curb and gutter, catch basins, manholes, pipes and conveyance systems that exist solely for moving storm water quickly and efficiently to its final dumping ground. Therefore, a storm water movement, rather than management, system exists.

Problematic Paradigm

Unfortunately, this movement paradigm has created its own problems. For example,

water in motion increases its kinetic energy, translating into a growing erosive force that not only moves sediments, pollutants and trash material from initial surfaces, but also creates destructive downhill power.

Particulates and debris moving toward the catch basin initially enter the below-ground pipe, then start restricting the catch basin openings, momentarily reducing the open area. Diversionary devices merely stage the pollutants for entry during subsequent higher-flow events or, through by-pass, move the water mass with increasing energy to a lower collection device. However, plugged piping or volume miscalculations ultimately lead to system collapse and failure.

The answer to storm water management does not include creating bigger and more expensive storm water management systems. Rather, it means changing our philosophy and methods to implement true water management systems that actually prevent and treat storm water pollutants.

Before pollution issues arose as significant, the curb-and-gutter systems served as convenient conduits to clean the immediate environment. Routinely hosing down driveways and walkways, flushing street traffic accident spills and debris to the nearest catch basins, spraying streets with street washing equipment and allowing rain to clear away

Originally published as "Ready for a Paradigm Shift?" *Storm Water Solutions*, Vol. 4, No. 2, April 2007. Published by Scranton Gillette Communications, Arlington Heights, IL. Reprinted with permission of the publisher.

waste seemed inconsequential. However, the process of cleaning the immediate environment simply transferred pollutants to larger bodies of water; it also assumed that environmental responsibility was irrelevant.

As population densities increased, so did impermeable surfaces. While engineering reconstruction kept up with water movement strategies, water pollutant dumping overwhelmed natural cleaning cycles, and pollution issues rose to the forefront.

Evolving BMPs

Current BMPs have evolved toward crafting devices that filter and capture floating debris or gross visible pollutants. These devices include catch basin inserts, traps, filters, vortex cyclone flow devices, in-line diversion screens, manhole baffles, and capture screens and floating barriers at final discharge points. Even though gross pollutants account for the largest volume of contaminants from storm events, this pollutant category actually has the least amount of biological impact on the final receiving bodies of water. In general, the devices work as efficient debris removers in light storm water flows, but larger flows overwhelm them and they have to rely on the built-in by-pass features.

These BMPs provide add-on improvements to existing curb-and-gutter systems, but they clearly fail to attempt to address, much less change, the foundational philosophy of such systems. Another problem involves the necessity of a higher maintenance cleaning and servicing schedule for these sorts of devices. Finally, though the eventual collection and disposal of these wastes improve aesthetics, these devices do little to prevent the inflow of phosphates or nitrates to ponds, streams, wetlands and lakes.

Storm water detention and retention structures in the form of National Urban Runoff Program (NURP) basins became a BMP standard to address the collection of sed-iment pollutants, the primary source of soil phosphates. In theory, slowing down incoming water to manmade ponds would allow some of the particulate matter to settle at the pond bottom, letting only slower and less contaminated surface flows continue to the major receiving waters. Surface debris could be skimmed off while the soil sediments settle.

While this BMP has become, mostly by regulation, a current state-of-the-art requirement for storm water mitigation, by nature the model creates a long list of spinoff problems; indeed, it is questionable that this BMP actually adds to the environmental equation of improving the terminal receiving bodies of water. Numerous problems with basins have been documented, but some in particular are worth noting: The basins are expensive to build and to maintain; they hog real estate; they stir up material during construction; they pose liability hazards; they are aesthetically unappealing; they create a mosquito-breeding habitat; they attract nuisance geese; they provide minimal recharge to groundwater; and they promote the re-suspension of pollutants.

If the ecological goal in storm water management is the reduction of pollutants that initiate algae blooms and consequential oxygen deprivation in the primary recipient bodies of water, then the focus in storm water management must be the reduction of nitrates and phosphate sources. Unfortunately, BMPs that tend to augment conventional curb-and-gutter water movement systems cannot mitigate the reduction of these contaminants and, in some cases, actually contribute to the increase of these contaminants.

Understanding Contaminants

Before we can advance true storm water management and treatment BMP systems, we must understand the nature of these two main storm water contaminants.

Nitrates. Nitrates (NO_3^-) are the negative anions of a broad spectrum of basic chemical compounds commonly identified as sodium nitrate, ammonium nitrate, potassium nitrate, calcium nitrate, nitric acid, etc. Most nitrate compounds are soluble in water and therefore will travel anywhere that water goes. Holding a negative charge, they can travel great distances in soil, which by nature also carries a net negative charge. So, they can relocate to groundwater formations or larger bodies of water great distances away from the original point. Once formed, no non-biological chemical reaction in soil can precipitate or neutralize the compound. Nitrate movement and biological absorption become part of the planet's nitrogen cycle.

Nitrate production is ubiquitous in storm water runoff because of excessive fertilizer application leaching, formation in rain from thunderstorm events and washings of surfaces exposed to automobile exhaust. Because nitrates are so highly soluble and negatively charged, an effort to control nitrate pollution by conventional curb-and-gutter systems cannot happen; water movement itself must actually be controlled.

Phosphates. The primary source of this group of nutrients is a natural rock mineral called phosphorite. It consists largely of calcium phosphate and is used as a raw material for the subsequent manufacture of phosphate fertilizers, phosphoric acid, phosphorus and animal feeds. While commercial grade deposits can be found in Florida; North Carolina; Tennessee; California; Wyoming; Montana; Utah; Idaho; Northern Africa; and Russia, some level of phosphate is universally present in all soils of agricultural quality (soils with the ability to grow plants whether they are weeds, turf or commercial crops).

The planet's soils can be categorized as a percentage and combination of three particle size primary components: sand, silt and clay. All three particle components are derived from weathered rock and reflect the chemical characteristics of the many rock composition minerals, including the phosphorus-bearing mol-

ecules. Phosphorus molecules, unlike the negatively charged nitrate molecules, have a net positive charge and as such bind themselves quickly to the negatively charged soil particles. While nitrates readily move with water as compounds in solution, phosphates generally only move as "riders" on soil particles.

Sands (0.05 to 2 mm) by nature are larger particles and are primarily composed of quartz crystals. Therefore, there is less surface area or physical affinity for phosphates to attach as compared with the larger surface area and negative charges available on silt (0.002 to 0.05 mm) and clay (< 0.002 mm) particles. Effective BMPs for phosphate pollution control must integrate three source areas as phosphate control equates to the control of erosion and relocation of soil particles:

1) Prevention of soil erosion;
2) Sedimentation and removal of settleable solids formed as sands and silts; and
3) Prevention of movement of suspended solids in the form of clay particulates, generally known as "muddy" or "turbid" water.

Some current BMPs can effectively settle sands and silts but cannot handle brown muddy water where the majority of phosphates reside. Specialized high-volume, pump-activated mechanical filters can make an attempt on "muddy water" in limited volumes, but high operating expense, frequent breakdown and service needs make these systems not a viable solution to storm water pollution problems.

Silver Bullet BMP?

True storm water management involves a change in design philosophy and methods. Who wants to cause a paradigm shift within the storm water industry? Is there a silver bullet BMP that can apply to all or most site designs?

Imagine a BMP that:

• Effectively prevents passage of sediments and thus phosphates from moving downstream;

- Allows for effective biological absorption, de-nitrification and use of nitrates;
- Allows for effective storm water volume reduction by allowing infiltration to recharge the groundwater;
- Prevents infiltration in areas where it is undesirable due to soil contamination;
- Changes the way storm water is treated, used and reused;
- Filters, treats, stores and uses storm water as a valuable resource rather than a byproduct necessary to deal with as quickly as possible;
- Uses a simple design, therefore eliminating complicated maintenance;
- Allows the uptake of dissolved nutrients and other organic chemicals;
- Harvests storm water for irrigating landscaping and lawns, thus requiring 50 to 85% less water for irrigation;
- Becomes modular in form and works as a lineal BMP along county roads and highways;
- Cools and reduces the temperature of storm water runoff;
- Provides water quality treatment to the first flush and larger storm events with the possibility of having no outflow; and
- Accommodates a retrofit conversion of a wet to a dry detention pond with under-drain system.

Until now, these benefits have appeared as only a lofty goal for one BMP. One versatile BMP, however, the EPIC System, has taken this new approach to storm water management.

The system is based on a combination of the oldest of technology, a sand filtration system, and a patented and proprietary device that controls subsurface water flow. The system is an underground irrigation, drainage, storm water harvesting and storage management system. It captures and stores storm water as soon as it flows over the system. The system can turn green space, shoulders, side slopes and ditch slopes into a storm water management system. It captures and quadruple filters sheet flow and storm water runoff and slowly releases the excess downstream in a controlled manner.

System and Philosophy

In 1985, Jonas Sipaila, now of Rehbein Environmental Solutions, Inc., crafted the basic idea of the system. While visiting a construction site one day after a rain storm, Sipaila noticed a large pile of sand wicking up water from an adjacent puddle. This led to a 14-year study and refinement of Jonas' innovative idea: to utilize a proven, reliable medium — sand — therefore taking advantage of first-century physics to solve 21st-century problems associated with irrigation and drainage. By combining the concepts of subsurface irrigation, subsurface drainage and the capillary movement of water through sand from nearby water sources, Sipaila invented and received a patent in 1999 for the first pipe designed specifically for contact with sand. Other subsurface systems have always had problems with clogging, thus hampering their effectiveness, but Jonas' invention has eradicated those problems.

Essentially, the system is a passive subsurface irrigation and drainage system that uses capillary physics and gravity to deliver water and nutrients to plants and to move water through an interconnected series of chambers and pans. The low pressure and greatly reduced water volume means less energy is needed to move the water.

A simple explanation of how the system works: Rather than allowing water to run off any type of surface — parking lots, roofs, driveways, football fields — the gravity-based system (essentially a network of underground reservoirs) captures and filters storm water runoff at its source and stores the water for irrigation.

By using a layer of porous sand beneath the surface of the turf, the system draws and filters water to an underground storage area created through the combination of chambers, pans and PVC pipes. From this, water can then be wicked up through the same sand to the plant roots, thus taking care of all irrigation needs.

Therefore, while relying on zero moving parts and on an efficiency of 100%, this single product provides superior drainage, irrigation and storm water management benefits to a water resources industry hungry for real solutions.

CHAPTER 5

Safeguarding Our Drinking Water

Stephen Goudey and Laura Tipple

Infrastructure managers are under pressure from state regulators to deal with an issue that is getting press and popping up in mail from concerned citizens: How will the latest generation of wastewater contaminants affect water sources, and what can we do about it?

The issue is how "micro constituents"— emerging contaminants such as endocrine disrupting chemicals (EDCs)— impact environmental and human health.

EDCs, which have been detected at trace concentrations in waters around the world, interfere with hormonal processes and alter the way organisms reproduce and develop. They also affect the function of the thyroid and immune and nervous systems. Many are pharmaceutical products, such as contraceptives and hormone-replacement drugs, which are non-degradable, persistent, and effective even in small quantities. When these compounds flow from the sewage-treatment system into the effluent outlets of city systems, they have unwelcome effects.

Estrogen Effect

EDCs first came to public attention in the 1990s when it was discovered that downstream of some municipal effluent discharges, the fish population exhibited an abnormally high percentage — more than 90% in some cases — of females. Further investigation found that estrogens in the wastewater from a variety of sources were a major cause of the phenomenon.

Under directives from the 1996 Food Quality Protection Act and 1996 amendments to the Safe Drinking Water Act, the EPA established the Endocrine Disruptor Screening Program (EDSP) in 1998. This program aims to use assay methods to identify chemicals that have the potential to interact with the endocrine system and to determine the endocrine-related effects caused by each chemical.

In turn, regulators are asking wastewater treatment plant managers to monitor for substances such as EDCs in their effluent. Estrogenic compounds are among the first EDCs in many jurisdictions to move toward regulation. One reliable, accessible testing tool uses genetically modified yeast that can bond to estrogens, producing an enzyme that can be measured. Even tiny amounts of estrogens cause the yeast to react reliably, forming a robust test system.

But the challenge lies beyond estrogens. Some 4000 substances, many of which will ultimately be flushed into our environment, are registered daily with the Chemical Abstract Service of the American Chemical Society. Scientists lack the technology and resources to meas-

Originally published as "Fish Stories," *Public Works*, Vol. 3, No. 11, October 2007. Published by Hanley Wood Business Media, Chicago, IL. Reprinted with permission of the publisher.

ure the effects of all these potential contaminants, particularly from exposures to substances below analytical detection limits (quantities that exert an effect but are too low to measure).

Other compounds, such as those found in many plastics and naturally occurring substances, can mimic estrogens. Therefore, new formulations of such common household products as laundry detergent could likewise have unintended effects upon release into the aquatic environment.

Uncertain what to measure, plant managers usually consult a testing laboratory. The lab comes back with a long list of compounds to test for, a costly and ineffective way to predict the future effects of these substances. And some may have little environmental impact. Consider the range of EDC compounds for which one city recently asked a laboratory to test:

- Pharmaceuticals (48 drugs)
- Metals
- Steroid hormones (12 analytes)
- Alkyphenol, ethoxylates, and carboxylates
- Phthalate esters
- Brominated flame retardants
- Chlorinated dioxins/furans
- Brominated dioxins/furans
- Congener specific PCBs
- Organochlorine pesticides
- Bisphenol A.

Instead of testing for the presence of a limited range of compounds, it's more effective to ask what effect, if any, the effluent has on organisms in the receiving environment. Effects-based testing removes the guesswork and focuses on what really matters: the impact on the living creatures exposed to the substances.

Test Process

Effects-based testing involves exposing organisms to effluent, measuring the effect of that exposure, performing fractionation, and retesting the fractions.

The fractionation procedure uses conven-tional wastewater treatment technologies such as aeration, filtration, manipulation of pH, and solubility in water. One effluent sample is turned into 24 fractions to isolate compounds based on their physical/chemical properties. Then all fractions are tested, and the fractions with the greatest effect are analyzed.

The effects of the different fractions are totaled and compared to those in the unfractionated effluent to determine recovery and identify potential synergistic and other interactive effects. Once the substance has been identified, and if it's commercially available, it can be added back into the effluent as a final confirmatory step.

Estrogenic compounds are an example of the utility of an effects-based investigation. We know these compounds turn male fish into females, so the measurable effects include changes to the appearance of the fish and production of an egg yolk protein in the blood (vitellogenin). If these effects aren't found, it can be deduced that no effective levels of EDCs are present in the effluent stream.

If the effects are found, the next stage is to corroborate them with faster, inexpensive tests that require less volume, such as the yeast assay. The sample is subjected to a routine fractionation procedure to isolate the responsible estrogens from compounds, including other estrogens, that aren't causing the effect. Once isolated, the compounds are more easily identified and managed.

The cost of conducting this type of testing to confirm the presence of EDCs in an effluent, including the initial confirmatory test, fractionation, retesting of fraction, chemical analyses, and reporting typically ranges from $15,000 to $25,000. The lower cost is for identifying conventional contaminants; the higher cost covers using mass spectra to identify chemicals not previously isolated and recognized.

For wastewater managers, the return on investment comes in peace of mind, pre-emptive compliance with pending and future regulations, and potential savings from not having to commission a lab to identify unknown compounds.

CHAPTER 6

The Relationship of Water to Growth

Richard M. Stapleton

The near-record snows that blanketed the eastern United States this past winter left regional reservoirs brimming and water supply managers smiling. For the first time in years, stressed water systems were at full capacity, and for most, the drought emergencies that had become annual events in recent years are fast becoming bad memories.

Ironically, for drinking-water-supply people, that's the downside. There is, after all, nothing like a drought to make people appreciate water. "We have what we call the 'hydro-illogical cycle,'" quips hydrologist Paul K. Barten. "It goes from drought to concern to rainfall to apathy." Barten, a researcher at the University of Massachusetts, is working with the Trust for Public Land on a two-year project funded by the U.S. Environmental Protection Agency to demonstrate the effectiveness of using land conservation and forest management to protect drinking water sources.

All Open Space Is Not Equal

"Last year's drought raised a lot of people's awareness of our reservoir system," says Don Outen, natural resource manager with the Baltimore, Maryland County Department of Environmental Protection and Resource Management, which manages water supplies for the city and surrounding county. "It gave us validation that protecting source waters is important."

Protecting source water means protecting the watersheds from which drinking waters flow. Baltimore County was visionary about land protection. In the mid–1970s, 60 percent of the county's land was down-zoned — meaning that fewer housing units could be built on it — and today 85 percent of the people live on just one-third of the county's land area. Recognizing the link between water quality and land conservation, the county has protected some 33,000 acres of open space in reservoir watersheds. Even so, development pressures are mounting. Don Outen's job is to prioritize land for protection.

"Is all forest cover equal?" he ponders. "That's the key question." The positive relationship between forest cover and water quality is well established, but the question is key because there is more forest at risk than there is funding to protect it. "How much forest cover do you need in a watershed?" Outen asks. "It's all intuitive right now."

Originally published as "Water, Water Everywhere...," *Land & People*, Vol. 15, No. 1, Spring 2003. Published by The Trust for Public Land, San Francisco, CA. Reprinted with permission of the publisher.

Intuitive watershed protection, it turns out, has been getting it wrong. For decades supply managers have been protecting the forest at the reservoir shoreline and along the banks of main feeder streams, while ignoring the upland forest that covers tiny headwater streams. That thinking, Outen says, needs to be flipped. "The best forest," he says, "is a large forest with minimal human disturbance, located on headwater stream systems."

Headwater streams, the first small rivulets that gather in swales or flow out of marshland, account for 50 percent of the total stream-miles in a watershed. This means that by the time they converge to become babbling brooks, these smallest streams already carry the pesticides, fertilizer, septage, and other runoff from 50 percent or more of a reservoir's watershed.

Armed with this knowledge, TPL moved quickly when rumblings of development threatened the largest privately held tract of forestland in the Gunpowder Falls watershed. The woods, encompassing nearly 300 acres and stitched with small streams, were home to three youth camps run by local service organizations, which had been serving urban and suburban youth since the 1930s. But skyrocketing land values at a time when the camps faced increasing costs and dwindling resources put the forest and the drinking water it protected at risk.

Working with the Gunpowder Valley Conservancy, a Baltimore County conservation organization, TPL negotiated conservation easements that protect the forest in perpetuity. At the same time, they give the camps an endowment that not only covers operating costs but also provides scholarships for disadvantaged youth. Private foundations supplemented state and county conservation funding for the easements.

The Reservoirs You Cannot See

While dried-out reservoirs are a stark reminder of the need to protect surface water supplies, the more important, long-term supply concerns may be out of sight, beneath the ground.

Groundwater is the technical term for water beneath the surface of the earth. It is nature's storage tank, feeding the springs that bubble forth from hillsides to replenish surface water supplies. When groundwater levels fall, streams dry up. Deeper in the earth, groundwater may pool in layered aquifers that can underlie vast portions of the United States. Groundwater provides more than 40 percent of the nation's drinking water, and groundwater recharge is critical to that supply.

People studying water supply have discovered that greater demand — more people who need water — is just part of the linkage between development and groundwater supply. "Development," says TPL's Caryn Ernst, "prevents groundwater recharge." Indeed, one of the reasons the reservoirs filled so quickly this spring is that so much land is covered by hard surfaces — roofs and driveways, streets and parking lots — that divert rainfall into streams and storm-water systems and prevent it from soaking into the ground. Rain that does not soak in to recharge the groundwater flows quickly to the sea and is lost.

As manager of the Source Water Stewardship Project for the Trust for Public Land, Ernst helped select the four watersheds being studied by Paul Barten. "The Metedeconk River," she says, "was an obvious candidate."

Located in Ocean County on New Jersey's pine-forest coastal plain, the Metedeconk River watershed is small, covering just 70 square miles, but beset by problems such as residential and road development, lack of forest management, and nonpoint source pollution — all problems typical of drinking-water-supply watersheds.

"The drought last year put huge stress on the Metedeconk system," says Leigh Rae, director of TPL's New Jersey Field Office. "There was not only less water to drink, there was less water to dilute the pollutants running off the land." Those trying to address the

Metedeconk's problems ran up against a common roadblock — lots of official players, with one hand often not aware of what the other is doing.

"A lot of municipalities and counties have developed open space plans," Rae says, "but they are not integrated." On the Metedeconk, for instance, Ocean County and Jackson and Brick townships all wrote independent development plans, despite the fact they share the same river and the same underlying groundwater. "Encouraging a regional perspective," Rae concludes, "could be our most important achievement."

It cannot come soon enough. With critical properties at risk, TPL is already forging cross-township partnerships. Working with Jackson and Freehold townships, Ocean County, and the state, TPL negotiated two deals covering numerous individual properties totaling more than 1,700 acres. The aggregate land, at the headwaters of the Metedeconk, protects the drinking-water supply of three downstream municipalities. This acreage is being added to the adjoining Turkey Swamp Wildlife Management Area, nearly doubling its size.

Because of last summer's drought and the problems it underscored, New Jersey moved to designate the Metedeconk a Category One watershed, providing more protection from development and giving it preference for open space funding. "TPL's study will provide better information about what land needs to be protected," Rae says. "And it will give us better tools for presenting our case to potential funders."

Holding Ground in Connecticut

Ironically, while water systems in most states are trying to purchase additional watershed land, some utilities in Connecticut are selling theirs off. The situation is complicated; the sell-off is in part an unintended consequence of federal regulations requiring that

reservoir drinking water be filtered. Filtration costs money; one way to raise that money is to sell off land, and Connecticut's privately held water companies had no shortage of "excess" property to market.

Water company land holdings are classified based on proximity to and potential impact on public drinking-water supplies. Land located distant from active drinking-water supplies can be sold with few restrictions. The key word here is "active." Many companies, rather than invest in upgrading marginal reservoirs, have chosen to abandon them. Once they are out of active service, the surrounding land can be sold. In its 1997 study, *An Ounce of Prevention,* the Trust for Public Land Connecticut Field Office reported that some 21,000 acres of water-company-owned lands — an area nearly as large as the entire Connecticut State Parks system — was liable to be sold for development.

"The drought raised a critical question," says TPL Project Manager Elisabeth Moore. "What if we need these reservoirs in the future? We need to think about future drinking-water supply." While the drought's impact has made people more concerned about surface water supplies, Moore says that the real issue in Connecticut, as in New Jersey, is the water beneath the ground. "Those excess properties may very well be the recharge zones for aquifers." Aquifers cut across topographical lines and can underlie more than one watershed. "There is very little mapping of aquifers," Moore cautions, "and a watershed doesn't necessarily capture an aquifer."

There's more: TPL's study found that even Connecticut's largest water companies own, on average, only 25 percent of their active watersheds, with smaller companies owning far less. Although protecting open space around active water supplies is key to protecting the quality of their water, the companies are making no effort to expand their holdings of primary watershed.

The TPL report, and the media coverage it triggered, brought a pledge from Connecticut Governor John Rowland to spend $166 million over five years to protect watersheds and open space. Continued efforts by TPL led to passage of an act providing tax credits to companies selling land for conservation. Since 1997, TPL's Connecticut Watershed Initiative has protected nearly 2,000 acres buffering active and potential sources of drinking water in communities spanning the state, and in 2001 the state announced plans to protect more than 15,000 acres of water-company-owned land in a single acquisition.

Connecticut is not alone in finding that large tracts of open space, long thought to be safe from development, are suddenly at risk. North Carolina's Gaston, Lincoln, and Mecklenburg counties, which encompass the Charlotte-Gastonia metropolitan area, are home to Mountain Island Lake, created in 1924 by a Duke Power Company hydroelectric project. While the lake was created to generate electric power, it also became a natural source for the region's drinking water. More than half a million people today drink Mountain Island Lake water — water so pure that since moving its drinking-water intake from South Fork River to the lake, the city of Gastonia has been saving $200,000 a year in water treatment costs.

Watershed protection efforts began in the 1970s, and today most of the lake's eastern side is protected by the Mecklenburg County Park and Recreation Department. But until recently much of the open space on the western shore was still owned by Duke Power. Lands that were no longer needed for power generation were transferred to the company's real estate development arm, Crescent Resources.

With both open space and the quality of their drinking water at risk, conservation groups, including the Trust for Public Land, created the Mountain Island Lake Initiative,

dedicated to preventing development along 80 miles of lakeshore and some 250 miles of tributary streams. With an initial $6.15 million grant from North Carolina's Clean Water Management Trust Fund, TPL worked with Gaston and Lincoln counties and a consortium of municipal governments to purchase 1,231 acres along six miles of the lake's western shore from Crescent Resources.

That was in 1998. Since then, parcel purchases and conservation easements have nearly met the initiative's goal of protecting 80 percent of the lakeshore. "But we also need to protect the tributaries," says Bill Holman, executive director of the Trust Fund. "And with smaller tracts and more owners, that's going to be difficult."

Gaining Understanding, Setting Priorities

Difficult, but not impossible. "There is overwhelming public support for protecting watershed lands," says TPL's Caryn Ernst. "We find that support in all our public polling, and we have seen it in ballot issues all across the country." And setting priorities is becoming easier as new understanding — about forest cover and the value of headwater streams — is coupled with powerful mapping tools that, says Paul Barten at the University of Massachusetts, "can finally let us identify the most important sites to protect."

With development inexorably pushing into farmland and forest, setting priorities is a constant issue for water supply managers. Spring runoff may have filled the reservoirs, but summer already looms. "And we know," Barten says, "that the next drought is somewhere just down the road."

PART II: THE BEST PRACTICES

CHAPTER 7

Allenstown, NH, Improves Its Wastewater Treatment Process

Ray Gordon

Clean water is essential for all life. We rely on it for cooking, drinking, bathing, cooling off on a hot day and, yes, even for removing our bathroom waste streams. We often don't think about where our waste goes when we flush the toilet, and many would rather not think about its fate. However, 80 percent of all New Hampshire residents depend on on-site treatment for their wastewater. This means that their wastewater undergoes treatment in their septic tank before it is discharged into the ground to the leaching field for further treatment, before becoming part of the groundwater.

The proper maintenance of on-site septic systems is important to protecting New Hampshire's water resources. The responsibility for the maintenance of individual septic systems belongs with the property owner. However, many residents are unaware of what is required to properly maintain these systems. Septic tanks should be inspected annually and pumped every two to three years. Unfortunately, many septic system owners become educated through the costly process of dealing with a failed septic system that backs up into their basement. Failed septic systems are a

threat to public health and the environment. The primary cause of failed septic systems is failure to pump the tank.

Not all failed septic systems are immediately identified and can release their pollution for years before they are detected. Nutrient, chemical and microbiological contamination is introduced to the water. The Granite State Designers and Installers Association has identified failing septic systems as one of the primary causes of non-point pollution in New Hampshire coastal areas. ("Non-point pollution" is generally defined as pollution caused by sources other than pipe or direct discharge to surface waters.)

As a municipal official you might think that the disposal of septic tank waste (septage) is the responsibility of the homeowner or the free market. But the truth is that New Hampshire state law places municipal responsibility for septage disposal on the town or city. RSA 485-A:5-b requires municipalities to either provide or assure access to septage disposal for their residents. If a municipality does not own a facility, then access is assured through written agreements with another facility or municipality. Most towns and cities are in com-

Originally published as "Septage Disposal: Municipal Responsibility Is the Key to Clean Water," *New Hampshire Town and City*, Vol. XLIX, No. 9, October 2006. Published by the New Hampshire Local Government Center, Concord, NH. Reprinted with permission of the publisher.

pliance with this statute; to check on your community's status visit http://des.nh.gov/wwe/DisposalMap/SEPTWeb.pdf.

Septage disposal in New Hampshire is primarily dependent upon wastewater treatment plants, as illustrated by the accompanying chart. In 2005, 77 percent of New Hampshire septage was disposed at wastewater treatment plants (both in and out of state). For communities that do not have a wastewater treatment plant, this means that they have to rely on neighboring cities and towns to provide septage disposal capabilities.

Presently many of the state's wastewater plants are nearing their design capacity. Once this point is reached, wastewater plants may restrict septage disposal to only municipalities with signed agreements. This is a situation that could cause waste from towns that do not have agreements to be diverted to facilities further away.

The proximity to treatment plants is important as it can lower the costs to transport the waste, making treatment more affordable to residents. In turn, residents will then be more likely to maintain and pump their septic tanks regularly. However, New Hampshire does not have enough capacity to treat all of its own septage; 27 percent of this waste goes to out-of-state wastewater treatment plants for disposal. In addition to the increased costs to transport and dispose of the wastes, septage disposed out-of-state removes at least $1.5 million a year from New Hampshire; instead of funding local wastewater treatment plants that serve New Hampshire communities, these monies end up subsidizing wastewater facilities in neighboring states.

This financial aspect is one that has been recognized by a few New Hampshire municipalities in recent years. As an example, the Allenstown wastewater treatment plant has begun to accept septage from all over the state. The tipping fee that is collected has helped to fund a full time staff person at their treatment plant and additional monies are being saved for future plant upgrades. This small town would find it difficult to afford plant upgrades without the septage revenue generated through tipping fees.

Technical Assistance and Grants

The New Hampshire Department of Environmental Services offers technical assistance and grant funds to help municipalities comply with their septage disposal responsibility. The grant funds will pay for up to 50 percent of the eligible costs to acquire and construct septage treatment facilities or to upgrade existing wastewater treatment plants to increase capacity for septage disposal. The technical assistance includes assisting municipalities to secure written agreements to assure access to septage disposal for their residents.

As a municipal official, your efforts to establish a good agreement with another municipality to secure septage disposal capacity can benefit both the environment and your community. Your residents will benefit from a secure, economical, local disposal outlet that will encourage them to maintain their systems. The disposal outlet will receive the benefit of the tipping fee for the septage, which will help fund the facility, whose goal is to protect the environment by providing clean water.

CHAPTER 8

Aurora, CO, Preserves and Protects Its Water Supply

Amy Kimball

The American population continues to shift from cold, wet, Eastern cities to the dry, warm West: Phoenix is threatening Philadelphia's rank as 5th-largest city, and Austin's population recently surpassed Baltimore's. Every person that moves to Los Angeles, Tucson, or Las Vegas means local governments have to use money and political muscle to secure that much more water. As big public works projects like Los Angeles' Owens River Aqueduct — made famous in the movie *Chinatown*— become rarer, Western cities increasingly look to nearby farmers with long-standing water rights to quench their thirst.

Looking to Farms for Water

Aurora, Colorado, a booming Denver suburb, entered 2005 with its reservoirs at drought levels, just as it had done the previous three years. The city has difficulty supporting the water needs of its current population — and expects another 200,000 people in the next five years, raising the population to a half-million.

Aurora's thirst has decimated the agricultural community 150 miles to the south, in the Arkansas River Valley Farming belt centered on Rocky Ford, Colorado. Over the last 50 years, Aurora has slowly bought up the water rights from the irrigation ditch there that watered thousands of acres of cantaloupes and grains.

Stan Fedde and his family have been farming in Fowler, a 1200-person town outside of Rocky Ford, for more than 100 years. The Otero Canal, a manmade tributary of the Arkansas, provides most of the Fowler farmers with their water through a series of irrigation systems.

Fedde still resents Jimmy Carter's grain embargo against the Soviet Union, which sent grain prices plummeting in 1980. Though the embargo is long past, the downturn it initiated for area farmers has not yet abated. Corn prices are at an all-time low, and wheat is not doing much better. As in most parts of the country, small farmers are forced to operate more and more on credit. The ever-growing debt that farmers face makes selling out an appealing option, especially when there is always a willing buyer in the form of towns like Aurora. The farmers' water rights are more valu-

Originally published as "Selling Water Instead of Watermelons: Colorado's Changing Rural Economy," *The Next American City*, Vol. 3, No. 8, April 2005. Published by the The Next American City Inc., Philadelphia, PA. Reprinted with permission of the publisher.

able than their land and can often bring a farmer enough money to pay off the debts he has amassed over the years. Even the best crop year can't offer money like that.

The sale of water rights and farmland, however, threatens a way of life; it endangers the plans of those who want to stay like Fedde, who is not about to let four years of serious drought end his family's farming legacy. One can hear the tense reserve in his voice when he says, "we hate to see farmers sell out." As one farm after another closes, the area's landscape and economics change. One-third of the Arkansas River Valley's historic agricultural land has now reverted to grasslands as farmers have sold their water and land. With these farmers gone, many businesses in Rocky Ford have not been able to sustain themselves, thus endangering the other farmers.

The farmers have a habit of wintertime gazing at the snow pack on ski slopes for indications of the next growing season. The custom has taken on heightened significance in recent years: a heavy spring thaw not only determines the fate of the remaining farmers' crops; it also signifies how much of a drought Aurora and other Denver suburbs will likely have, and thus how hard they will bargain for water rights.

A New Lease on Life for Colorado Farmers?

Now Fedde and his fellow farmers have a new opportunity to hold on to their farms, their towns, and their way of life. Last March, Aurora began a program to lease water rights, rather than buy them, as a temporary solution to the severe drought.

This solution may seem obvious, but legal precedent banning short-term water agreements formerly stood in the way. A recent court reversal of this ban has allowed Aurora to begin offering short-term leases. Under this arrangement, farmers are paid for their water on a per-acre basis at a rate that is deter-

mined by historical average crop prices. In most cases, farmers leased a fraction of their total water rights and continued planting the rest. Fedde, for example, leased 60 percent of his total acreage this past year, leaving that much of his land unirrigated. With prices last year below the historical average rate and crop yields down, Fedde said this opportunity "helped a lot." His farm staved off what would have likely been major losses.

Aurora has also encouraged a number of practices that make the farmers' use of water more efficient. The city has offered subsidies for farmers to install drip irrigation systems, which result in considerably less evaporation than from other irrigation methods. In the first year of the program, 700 acres' worth of drip irrigation was installed. To protect topsoil in fields left fallow, Aurora also requires contracting farmers to plant a cover crop.

Besides allowing farmers to keep their land and water rights, the lease program allows Aurora to access water much faster than the traditional method of purchasing water rights, according to Doug Kemper, manager of water resources for Aurora. While acquiring full water rights provides the city with long-term water supplies, the acquisition process is time-consuming and expensive. All decisions regarding water rights in Colorado must be heard by a special court, and it frequently takes up to ten years to fully transfer these rights. With the worst drought in 300 years, Aurora did not have any time to waste. The short-term leasing arrangements also saved Aurora from building up water resources that it may not need in non-drought years. Had it been faced with an overabundance of water, Aurora might have felt compelled to plan for an artificially high level of population growth to justify having built a bigger water system. A system of short-term leasing may encourage more responsible growth.

While he's pleased with the new lease agreements, Fedde does not harbor any illusions that Aurora is interested in the well-being of farmers in the long-term. "Realistically, they probably don't care (about us). Their goal is to grow and to get water."

The long-term result of this agreement remains to be seen. One factor unlikely to change is the growing number of people crowding into Colorado and other Western states. And some scientists argue that the recent "drought" is just a return to normal conditions after an exceptionally wet past few centuries. The Arkansas River Valley's farms could keep fading into grasslands if the short-term leases are renewed and renewed until they effectively become permanent. More optimistically, farming communities like Fowler and suburbs like Aurora alike may become less water-intensive and learn to accommodate new growth. In any event, the water rights Western farmers have so long taken for granted are now as much of a market commodity as Rocky Ford cantaloupes.

CHAPTER 9

Ayer, MA, and Other Cities Must Preserve Their Water Supply to Accommodate Growth

Cory S. Hopkins

Could the Central Massachusetts economy dry up? There are plenty of hurdles to economic expansion in Central Massachusetts, most notably the region's high cost of living when compared to areas in the nation's south and west.

But one resource that many take for granted could prove an even bigger hurdle to economic growth locally: the scarcity of plain old H_2O.

The Northeast is generally considered immune from the severe drought issues that plague other parts of the United States.

But per capita water availability in Massachusetts is significantly less than in the arid state of Nevada, according to a 2006 report from the Massachusetts Executive Office of Environmental Affairs and Water Resources Commission.

Drip Dry

Faced with an aging infrastructure, increasing population density and sweeping economic development initiatives — on top of an unusually dry summer — the region's water resources are being taxed as never before, according to state and local officials.

While confident that Central Massachusetts won't turn into a barren wasteland any time soon, planners are stressing smart growth, water reuse and conservation, and targeted infrastructure upgrades to ensure that, quite literally, the well does not run dry.

Development Knocking on the Door

Take the town of Ayer. According to Mike Madigan, Department of Public Works superintendent for the town of 7,300, its single largest user of water is CPF Inc., a bottling plant that uses the town's water to make Aquafina.

The town is permitted by the state to draw 2.5 million gallons of groundwater per day. In order to ensure that the town doesn't exceed its capacity, Madigan says he keeps a "water bank," a running tally of how much more demand the town's system can handle

Originally published as "Water Woes," *Worcester Business Journal*, November 26, 2007. Published by the Worcester Business Journal, Inc., Worcester, MA. Reprinted with permission of the publisher.

without being in danger of outstripping capacity or permitted withdrawal levels.

That total stands at about 300,000 gallons per day, Madigan said. For now, the capacity is sufficient to allow for modest growth in the town.

But if another CPF wants to move to town — which would be a boon for Ayer's tax base — Madigan's stress level would surely go up.

"If someone came knocking on the town's door, another company, another high water user, that's where I would be concerned," Madigan said. "A situation could come up where their needs couldn't be met in the short term, and they'd have to go somewhere else."

Even Devens — the region's savior when it comes to business growth — is facing similar concerns. There, pharmaceutical giant Bristol-Myers Squibb is constructing a massive $750 million manufacturing plant, one that promises to use "enormous amounts" of purified water as part of its manufacturing process, according to Joseph Tarnowski, senior vice president, technical operations, biologics manufacturing and process development at BMS.

Devens is permitted to draw 4.33 million gallons per day. At full build-out and 100 percent capacity, BMS promises to use 1.2 million gallons per day, or more than a quarter of the former Army base's capacity, said Jim Moore, utilities department supervisor at Devens.

Should another large water user come in, capacity could get tight in a hurry.

"If BMS does do 100 percent of what they say they might, unless you limit growth, we may have to expand our capacity in a few years," Moore said.

Aged Infrastructure

Oddly, it's the rural and suburban communities surrounded by the state's abundant water resources that are the ones at the most

risk of running dry, according to Paul Matthews, executive director of the 495/ MetroWest Corridor Partnership, a regional advocacy organization.

Boston has long been the commercial and cultural heart of the state, and as such has always had the resources necessary to invest in and maintain its massive water infrastructure, Matthews said. However Central Massachusetts, largely rural and undeveloped until the past 20 or 30 years, is now experiencing tremendous growth, but has aging or inadequate facilities.

The town of Littleton is a perfect example. Home of the Veryfine juice company, which uses the town's water in its beverage products, the town draws an average of 1.4 million gallons per day for residential, commercial and industrial use, which coincides almost exactly with the town's permitted use, according to Savas Danos, general manager of the Littleton Electric Light and Water Department.

During this summer's drought, when water demand was at its highest, the town regularly drew more than 2 million gallons per day. When one of the town's four wells became clogged with mineral deposits, the other three wells were pushed to keep up with demand, Danos said.

"We got caught this summer with our pants down," said Danos. "We didn't have an opportunity to clean our well screens, and when the summer came, it came with a vengeance. We had to go into an aggressive program of water restriction."

To make sure the town isn't hung out to dry again next summer, Danos is working with the state on preliminary plans to establish a fifth well site in the town, one that would increase capacity. Madigan said Ayer is pursuing a similar course.

Well Wishers

But towns and utilities can't just keep going to the well, as it were, and increasing their permitted capacity every few years. Expanding that capacity not only further taxes the state's water resources, it adds a heavy burden to an already over-burdened infrastructure, Matthews said.

The DEP issues permits for town water use on a 20-year cycle, explained Jennifer Pederson, executive director of the Massachusetts Waterworks Association in Acton, a 1,300-member organization that advocates for water suppliers in the state. Because of that cycle, many communities are now in the process of renewing permits issued in the 1980s under the state Water Management Act. Pederson said new permits may soon come with water conservation conditions attached, which will put unnecessary constraints on economic growth.

If passed, water conservation standards pushed by the state Water Resources Commission would impose mandatory per capita water use caps on towns, in the neighborhood of 65 to 85 gallons per day per capita, Pederson said.

"The thing is, a lot of communities are well below their regulated use as passed in the 80s," Pederson said. "They have enough capacity to bring in businesses, but we fear that by putting these conditions on, they might hinder economic development."

Which isn't to say that the Massachusetts Waterworks Association is against water conservation, or advocates an "if you've got it, flaunt it" approach to water use. Instead, Pederson said, they advocate a best management approach that would allow towns to find out what works for them, with their rates and infrastructure.

Instead of being worried about conserving water, the state should worry more about rising water rates that must fund badly needed infrastructure improvements, said Pederson. Water, traditionally undervalued, is now becoming much more expensive as towns seek ways to fund new wastewater treatment plants and higher-capacity wells, she added.

CHAPTER 10

Baltimore, MD, and Other Cities Revitalize Their Harbor Areas

Guillermo Lopez

Before the 1980 grand opening of Harborplace at the Inner Harbor — the downtown seaport project that reinvented the city's waterfront as a landmark retail, dining, and entertainment hub — Baltimore was a gritty, working-class, port city with an eclectic blend of disconnected ethnic neighborhoods. Its small-town feel and forthright industrial character had earned it the nickname "Charm City," a wry and affectionate sobriquet that was as much a testament to the geniality of its residents as an oblique reference to the city's provincial scale.

However charming it may have been, Baltimore was definitely not an economic powerhouse or a vital urban center. Tourists were not flocking to the Mid-Atlantic city, the housing market was not booming, and crime was on the rise. The increasingly empty downtown heart of the city — suffering population losses as the result of a postwar shift of residents to surrounding counties — fueled the growing perception that Baltimore was an urban dead end.

Harborplace, almost single-handedly, changed all that. Shortly after Harborplace opened, the revitalized Inner Harbor added to its list of attractions the new National Aquar-

ium and a renovated and expanded Maryland Science Center. In the 1990s, Oriole Park at Camden Yards and a new Baltimore Ravens football stadium opened just blocks from the harborfront. Today, the vibrant, thriving waterfront is packed with shops, restaurants, museums, and attractions, with tourists and residents mingling amid street performers, vendors, and tour guides. The resurgent Inner Harbor and its attendant economic boom have inspired substantial peripheral development, with hotels, businesses, and residences springing up downtown and connecting to adjacent neighborhoods — a feverish pace of development that is still accelerating today in places like the nearby Harbor East mixed-use waterfront neighborhood.

What are the cultural, economic, and architectural forces that make Baltimore's Inner Harbor such a powerful economic engine? How do they work? And how does design help create the kinds of public spaces that generate development and inspire economic revival in an underperforming economy? Can design alone make the kind of difference that affects a city and a region?

An optimum public space is vibrant, comfortable, and accessible. It provides natu-

Originally published as "Public Space Design," *Urban Land*, Vol. 65, No. 3, March 2006. Published by the Urban Land Institute, Washington, DC. Reprinted with permission of the publisher.

ral landmarks and intuitive pathways and connectors to frame its activity in ways that invite discovery and exploration. Well-designed public spaces combine intimate nooks with spacious gathering areas; they both stimulate social interaction and allow for private moments and personal reflection.

The fundamental tenet of community design — that public spaces are for people — may seem obvious, but it is too often overlooked. Well-executed public spaces attract people, make them comfortable, and give them a reason to stay and return.

Design can contribute to the creation of public spaces in a variety of ways. Lincoln Road in Miami's South Beach offers an example of how design decisions can change the complexion of a space. For decades a draw for film stars and holiday visitors looking for a nightclub, a movie, or a shopping experience, Lincoln Road succumbed to familiar pressures. By the 1950s, changing demographics, as well as self-contained luxury hotels and resorts that sealed themselves off from the street, had turned the road — once referred to as the "Fifth Avenue of the South" — into a dilapidated shell of its former self.

When Miami Beach architect Morris Lapidus closed seven blocks of the ten-block street to vehicle traffic in 1960, however, the transformation of Lincoln Road began. Though it was not until the 1980s that the area would truly flourish, it was Lapidus's design — a pedestrian promenade lined with retail and entertainment venues — that reflected a true South Beach ethos and set the stage for the radical changes to come. Today, Lincoln Road is considered a Miami landmark once again. Cafés, boutiques, and art galleries line the street, and pedestrians walk amid fountains, sculptures, and bustling sidewalks as they shop and people-watch.

Lincoln Road offers an instructive and stark reminder that the great designs of today generally are echoes of the past. To create compelling public spaces, people need look no further than their own history, where the pub-

---

What Constitutes a Successful Public Space?

The Project for Public Spaces, a New York City–based nonprofit organization dedicated to development and maintenance of public spaces, lists four elements critical to their success:

- activities and uses;
- comfort and image;
- access and linkage; and
- sociability.

---

lic square and main street have served as hubs of social activity and community interaction, allowing residents and visitors to run errands, chat with friends, or grab a bite to eat and a cup of coffee. Such places naturally become hubs of economic activity — centers of attention where performers, merchants, politicians, shoppers, and diners congregate to engage in day-to-day life.

The current global development trend favoring town centers and more integrated outdoor mixed-use projects is an acknowledgment of the important role these spaces play in collective community narratives and of their efficacy in sparking commerce and trade. The architectural design of these spaces should reflect the character and spirit of the local community and display an organic connection to the surrounding physical and cultural environment. The key to designing spaces that can seamlessly incorporate a wide range of commercial, dining, and entertainment elements is to recognize and adhere to certain fundamental design strategies — to apply universal rules appropriate for projects big and small and all over the globe.

Simplicity and clarity are two design elements critical for any public space. Because people do not like to be confused or uncertain, landmarks and waypoints need to be established to break up the space. Some urban projects use individual city blocks to break down a larger space into manageable and discrete components, while still maintaining the long sight lines that unify and define the space. Breaking a development into linked sections gives visitors a chance to approach the project at their own pace and not feel overwhelmed, and to experience a sense of revelation and exploration.

Green space should be used wherever possible. A small park or a row of trees not only softens the architectural landscape, but also provides natural gathering places and anchor points. The village green, a concept as old as villages themselves, evokes that ingrained sense of community that adds to the comforting perception of permanence and livability.

People like to walk, move, and circulate through a space. Street grids, wayfinding materials, and structural elements should be used to create broad frameworks that encourage movement and interaction. Clearly defined starting and ending points, be they traditional anchors or strategically positioned elements like a fountain or plaza, can provide needed structure and spatial context. A seemingly endless expanse of storefronts or entertainment options can actually be too much of a good thing, creating what can feel to the visitor like a daunting challenge and discouraging casual visits.

Elements should be mixed together. While it behooves architects and developers to be sensible in determining their merchandise mix and architectural style — for example, few would think a Dollar Store should be adjacent to a Tiffany's or that a thatched roof belongs on a contemporary frame — there is an inherent energy and excitement in the juxtaposition of differing styles and the availability of a wide range of products, services, and entertainment options.

Ultimately, great design in public areas is about understanding the goals and limitations — as well as the possibilities — inherent in the creation of engaging, occupied spaces. Use of art for art's sake is a noble pursuit, but a counterproductive one when designing public space that must not only accommodate a wide variety of uses, but also encourage them. Public spaces are to be lived in; they cannot, and must not, become museum pieces.

That is not to say that they must be boring or utilitarian. Many of the world's greatest public spaces, from the piazzas of Italy and Las Ramblas in Barcelona to Grand Central Station and Times Square in New York City, are better known for their colorful spirit, artistic energy, and cultural relevance than for their economic power. The animation, color, scale, lighting, cohesion, and physical and natural landscape of a place should work to transform shopping from running an errand to having an experience. As the Walt Disney Company can attest, people will pay more — much more — for an experience.

The financial benefits of successful spaces can be profound, affecting the surrounding infrastructure and boosting a region's economic outlook in a variety of ways. In general, the mechanisms that translate spaces into dollar signs fall into three broad categories:

- **Direct.** A new development can provide initial and clearly measurable benefits. These include revenue generated through the sale of goods and services, higher wages due to an increase in local hiring, and additional monies contributed by new visitors — especially tourists, who can boost local cash flow substantially.
- **Secondary.** A landmark public project can function like a pebble dropped into a pond, sending ripples of complementary development in all directions. Adjacent developments and needed support structures might include additional residential, restaurant, and hospitality options, as well as the presence of vendors and service providers newly positioned to capitalize on the influx of a customer base and income.
- **Intangible.** The intangible benefits of well-designed public spaces, in some ways providing the most important and dramatic influence, are easily underestimated and

often underappreciated. The sense of civic pride, community identification, and improved public perception can be a profound force. This phenomenon can be seen at work in places like Baltimore and, more recently, Detroit, where dramatic downtown projects are encouraging a return to city living.

High-quality design can overcome a host of seemingly insurmountable obstacles. Even in some of the most downtrodden and economically disadvantaged parts of the world, a well-designed public space can be commercially viable and provide a major boost to struggling local and regional economies.

Plaza San Marino, a shopping and entertainment development that opened in 2003 in Guayaquil, Ecuador, illustrates this mechanism in action. The city's new commercial and social hub, San Marino includes upscale fashion franchises, home furnishings outlets, a bookstore/café, and a Tower Records store, as well as restaurants and upscale entertainment venues that include a state-of-the-art 12-screen cineplex with stadium seating. The enclosed galleria surrounded by the outdoor elements of an open leisure center blends tenets of modern town- and lifestyle-center architecture with the handcrafted detail and stylistic influences of distinctive South American design.

Many of the materials used to build the center were locally crafted: artisans hand carved much of the center's concrete, and iron for the detailed handrails was cast on site. Details throughout the space represent reproductions of existing architectural elements in the city, such as cast-iron lamps, kiosks, wrought-iron railings, hand-painted mosaic tiles, and accurate reproductions of traditional marble and stone details. An iconic 110-foot bell and clock tower is the center's landmark feature, giving San Marino a distinctive and instantly recognizable public face. Towers and cupolas, clay roof tiles, and plaster-finished stucco walls lend regional flavor, and intricate Gustav Eif-

fel–inspired ironwork and bold lighting elements provide distinctive structural highlights.

Partly because it provides a feeling of permanence and belonging to the age-old community of Guayaquil, the center draws heavily from its local population of nearly 2 million residents. From roof tile details to the rough-iron railings and fences, San Marino is 100 percent Guayaquil. Even the roof metal structures and skyline call to mind the old town areas of the city, reflecting the history and tradition of the city's architecture.

San Marino provides far-reaching economic benefits to the surrounding Guayaquil community, increasing the revenue stream through tourist and visitor dollars. The project has fostered a sense of civic pride, local and regional identity, and national and international recognition; affirmed local history and culture; and promoted a sense of connection and identification with global development and the modern economy.

In a country where 70 percent of the population lives below the poverty level and the per-capita gross domestic product is $3,200, San Marino posts close to $300 in sales per square foot and is visited by about 800,000 people a month. Places like San Marino demonstrate how design, by creating spaces that promote connection, comfort, and community, can boost a community economically and transcend boundaries.

In Baltimore, the Inner Harbor is viewed as a national landmark — an enduring and instantly recognizable icon that defines both the city's skyline and its storyline. Not only does it capture the spirit of the city, but also it symbolizes the transformation that has led to a booming — and ongoing — economic expansion.

The city is breaking new boundaries — from Best Buy's first-ever downtown location, to new parks, museums, and explosive residential growth adjacent to the Inner Harbor. More than $1 billion of new development is currently planned for Baltimore, and over 11 million tourists and others visit the city annually, contributing nearly $3 billion to the local economy.

The future is bright for public spaces. As more and more cities, towns, and developers begin to appreciate the impact that well-designed public spaces can have on their communities — and their wallets — the more this encouraging trend will become a self-propagating phenomenon. At the same time, as cities and developers move away from the mentality of trying to squeeze out every last square foot of available leasable space and in the direction where the economic benefits of good architectural design will be recognized and embraced, they will be improving the quality of life, as well as the quality of public spaces.

CHAPTER 11

Boston, MA, and Other Cities Use Citizens and Nonprofit Groups to Clean Up Rivers

Tom Arrandale

Back in the summer of 1966, a rock group named the The Standells enjoyed their only major hit, "Dirty Water." The words were inspired by Massachusetts' befouled Charles River, a winding 80-mile-long stream that runs through Boston's high-tech suburbs, separates Boston and Cambridge and empties into Boston Harbor. The Red Sox still play the song to celebrate each home victory in Fenway Park. But the lyrics no longer fit the river itself: Most days, the Charles is safe enough for residents to swim and boat in its waters.

Of course, Cleveland's Cuyahoga River no longer catches on fire, either. All around the nation, water quality has improved since federal and state regulators began enforcing the Clean Water Act of 1972. But there's something more behind the Charles' remarkable comeback: Vigilant citizens, organized along the length and breadth of the watershed, are leading the charge to finish restoring their hometown river to its natural state.

Near Boston, those efforts have been orchestrated by the Charles River Watershed Association, a 40-year-old nonprofit group.

Governance of the densely populated region, with some 900,000 residents, is divided among 35 cities and towns. But arguably no other institution, not even the federal or state government, has done more to clean up what had been one of the country's most polluted urban waterways.

CRWA's executive director, Robert Zimmerman Jr., seems an unlikely prospect to be leading revolutionary changes in protecting the environment. Nevertheless, for the past 16 years, the former prep-school headmaster has been recruiting some 1,200 volunteers to clean up the Charles' banks, organizing annual canoe and kayak races, and training the association's 80 members to sample water quality at 37 sites.

Zimmerman also has bolstered the association staff to include eight engineers and scientists to analyze the results to pinpoint where untreated sewage and tainted storm-water runoff discharges into the Charles. Inside the watershed, "we know more — and we can prove what we know — than governments and their agencies," Zimmerman says. With trustworthy data and broad local support, "you get to sit at the table, and you get listened to."

Originally published as "Confluence of Interest," *Governing*, Vol. 21, No. 12, September 2007. Published by Congressional Quarterly Inc., Washington, DC. Reprinted with permission of the publisher.

The association put its research to use persuading federal and state regulators to crack down on pollution to make the river safe for swimming and boating. The group has also prodded Massachusetts officials to cap groundwater withdrawals by fast-growing towns that threaten to deplete the river's flow. CRWA's credibility demonstrates how citizen-led organizations are stepping up where the federal-state-local environmental partnership most often breaks down and leaves serious threats to fester beyond the effective reach of government control.

Around the country, federal and state officials concede that they'll never command enough money and manpower — or the un-contested political authority — to complete the job of cleaning up America's impaired waters. Nor can local officials be expected to force their constituents to take on the burden of cleaning up rivers or streams when communities many miles downstream will reap the clearest benefits. To make continued progress, "what you need to do is devise new ways to get local citizens engaged in solving the problem," says William D. Ruckelshaus, who served as the U.S. Environmental Protection Agency's first administrator in the early 1970s. "That's what watershed groups are doing."

Local Eyes and Ears

Nearly four decades after EPA was established, federal and state regulators are still puzzling over how to deal with less visible "non-point" pollutants that run off with the rain from farms, ranches, logging operations, construction projects, streets, parking lots, yards, gardens and other sites. Standard top-down regulation by federal and state agencies is too cumbersome — and often too controversial — to effectively manage cumulative threats that literally come from people's backyards. As Ruckelshaus points out, "the same programs don't work for non-point sources; there's just too many of them."

So governments are turning to the grass roots for help. One approach, being tried all over the country, is to work directly with local citizens who organize themselves along natural watershed boundaries instead of by city, county or state lines. Instead of dictating solutions, government environmental officials now sit at the table with businessmen, farmers, ranchers, loggers, hunters, boaters, hikers and others to seek common ground on protecting the watersheds in which they live and work. Governments "have never had and never will have all the resources to do what the public expects and law clearly requires," says Don Elder, director of River Network, a clearinghouse in Portland, Oregon, that assists local groups around the country. "They need eyes and ears in the watersheds."

Carol M. Browner, Clinton's EPA chief, called that "place-based" environmental protection; similarly, the Bush administration's "collaborative conservation" initiative defers to local community efforts to deal with environmental issues as close to the ground as possible. Roughly 6,000 watershed groups are now at work to protect rivers that run through industrial neighborhoods in inner cities as well as blue-ribbon Rocky Mountain trout streams. Some gather once a year for trash pickup drives or a stream-bank restoration work day, but about 3,500 have established formal structures supported by private donations, foundation grants and government fiscal and technical assistance. The Oregon Legislature created and funds groups in all the state's watersheds; Washington State gives watershed-level organizations key roles in implementing growth management and salmon recovery programs.

Some groups operate like conventional environmental advocates, but many prefer to partner with other interests to build community consensus on balancing environmental and economic needs. Their focus goes beyond "not-in-my-backyard" resistance to a single landfill or sewage plant. At both the federal and state levels, environmental authority remains split between natural resource and wildlife conservation departments and pollution-control agencies with much different cultures and responsibilities. While government regulators are still bogged down writing pollution permits and fining violators, many watershed groups are working out common-sense local solutions to meet national environmental goals more effectively — then persuading governments to go along.

Pushing the Envelope

After taking charge in 1991, Zimmerman built the Charles River Watershed Association into a $1.5 million-per-year operation that gets roughly one-third of its funding from EPA, as well as state grants for water quality monitoring and analysis. The association staff "brings strong technical skills, credible science and politically astute advocacy to their work," says John DeVillars, the Clinton administration's EPA regional director for New England who now sits on the CRWA board.

Twelve years ago, DeVillars approved the "Clean Charles 2005" initiative, which committed the feds to working with state and local agencies, the association and other stakeholders. Although the effort fell short of making the river fully safe for swimming within a decade, during that period EPA's scorecard grade climbed from D to B+. In addition to detecting illegal discharges, the association works with state regulators to devise a total maximum daily load (TMDL) limit for nutrients discharged to the river. It surveys the shoreline after heavy rains to target polluted storm water, and is collaborating with federal and state regulators to tighten controls on combined sewer overflows. CRWA "is willing to work with the agencies," says William Walsh-Rogalski, an EPA attorney. "There are times they give us a kick, but it's usually for a good purpose."

Once you look at an entire watershed, Zimmerman notes, you see connections that governments often miss. EPA focuses on water quality, for instance, while state agencies deal with water supplies. To clean up Boston Harbor, EPA and Massachusetts agreed to build the huge Deer Island sewage treatment plant that will collect and treat wastewater from 48 towns for discharge into the ocean. But the region relies primarily on groundwater for drinking, and it is losing 180 million gallons every day that seep through cracked pipes into the centralized sewage system. Zimmerman points out that cleaning up the river won't accomplish much if storm-water systems and leaky sewers keep diverting so much water from the river. In effect, he argues, "we're dewatering eastern Massachusetts with a solution to the Boston Harbor problem. The solution to a symptom is creating an environmental disaster of the first order."

To help stem groundwater losses, CRWA joined with the Boston-based Conservation Law Foundation in a lawsuit that has forced Massachusetts to prohibit town drinking-water systems from pumping more than 65 gallons per person from groundwater wells per day. That success now puts the association at odds with local governments looking to drill new wells to supply growing populations. Franklin, Massachusetts, town manager Jeff Nutting has lived his whole life within a half mile of the Charles, and he once was a CRWA member. He thinks the association went too far by singling out local water utilities in its efforts to restore the watershed. "They have a right to push the envelope, but they don't have to answer to the ratepayers, and we do," Nutting says. "Their goal is to have trout in the Charles, and that will take an act of God in my view."

The way EPA's Walsh-Rogalski sees it, "groundwater recharge is a state issue, and we don't think about it a lot. But Zimmerman is really good at pushing the envelope, in this case to bring recharge and water withdrawals together. It's a good example of how a local watershed group can bridge gaps." EPA New England officials are now encouraging groups along Boston's Mystic River and other heavily urbanized watersheds to emulate CRWA's monitoring and data-collecting model.

Meanwhile, citizen-led efforts in Houston; Portland, Oregon; and Washington, D.C., also are helping to restore degraded river systems. Baltimore and Philadelphia are promoting multi-jurisdictional watershed programs to protect drinking-water sources and manage storm water. Around Birmingham, Alabama, the Cahaba River Society has been working with local governments for 20 years to strengthen sewage treatment and storm-water measures for a watershed that hosts more wild species per mile than any other North American river. The society's board includes engineers, architects and business owners; and Beth Stewart, the director, says the group operates "very much in the consensus model of getting things done."

Two years ago, however, some Birmingham corporations and developers stepped in to stymie local counties' plans for stringent storm-water rules. Stephen Bradley, a public relations consultant there, dismisses the Cahaba River Society as "basically a no-growth group. We don't really trust them." Birmingham business leaders have turned down invitations to discuss their differences, and Stewart says the society is reassessing its consensus-building strategies.

Coffee and Conservation

With rancorous politics and numerous jurisdictions, urban watersheds can be difficult places in which to operate. Rural Western states are even tougher terrain, but in the past 15 years, collaborative groups have sprung up where anti-government sentiments hold sway in some of the region's remote ranching and logging communities.

Montana ranchers, for example, are leading a collaborative campaign to restore the Blackfoot River that Norman Maclean celebrated in his book *A River Runs Through It.*

The Blackfoot drains 2,300 square miles in forested mountains just west of the Continental Divide in lightly populated parts of three Montana counties. By the early 1990s, ineffective federal and state laws left the Blackfoot ecosystem falling apart. Noxious weeds crowded native plants off the range; bull trout and cutthroat trout were disappearing; and Plum Creek Timber Co. was preparing to sell its huge forest holdings to subdivision developers. Ranchers owned crucial wildlife habitat along valley floors, and they were too suspicious of government bureaucracies to cooperate with either federal or state wildlife managers.

Alarmed by talk that Congress could declare the Blackfoot a federally protected Wild and Scenic River, landowners began meeting over pie and coffee at Trixi's Restaurant and Bar in Ovando (population 71). Then they invited government land managers and conservationists to sit in on the discussions. "At first, the government people were there to listen, but as our relationship grew, we started to play more of a role," says Greg Neudecker, a U.S. Fish and Wildlife Service biologist. Eventually, landowners, conservationists, and local federal and state agents formed a nonprofit group called the Blackfoot Challenge to forge mutual strategies for restoring the watershed.

Challenge participants follow what they term "the 80/20 rule," focusing discussions on problems where agreement is likely instead of getting bogged down in battles over a few emotionally charged issues. Now local landowners are working with Trout Unlimited, a national fishermen's group, to stabilize the Blackfoot's banks and restore its naturally flowing character. It's also teamed with Powell County officials to control invasive knapweed and leafy spurge.

With money from Congress and help from the Nature Conservancy, the Challenge also has brokered a precedent-setting purchase of 88,000 acres from Plum Creek Timber. Most will be turned over to the U.S. Forest Service and state agencies or sold to adjacent ranchers. But the group plans to hold on to 5,600 acres to create a community forest reserve as part of a 40,000-acre cooperative conservation area that will be managed for recreation as well as timber production.

In rural areas such as the Blackfoot, environmental agencies may accomplish more "by being good neighbors, versus telling people what to do," Neudecker says. "Native fish numbers in the Blackfoot have rebounded by 400 percent since the effort started. "You've got to have sound biology to do that, and that's strong evidence that collaborative conservation can work," he adds. "We haven't had a lot of hard-core environmental group action in the Blackfoot. That says something about our approach."

Last year, Harvard University's Kennedy School of Government gave the Blackfoot Challenge an award for innovations in government. The award came with a $100,000 grant that this summer funded workshops for similar groups from eight Western states. Montana alone now has 50 watershed organizations, and state regulators and county conservation districts fund efforts to come up with local approaches to complying with federal water-quality standards. On Montana's Big Hole River, ranchers and fly fishermen banded together to revise irrigation rules to keep enough water flowing during droughts to preserve an isolated Arctic grayling population. The group also persuaded conservative commissioners in three counties to enact setback ordinances that keep trophy homes from encroaching on the river's prized trout fishery.

The Bush administration is promoting collaborative community-level approaches to thinning fire-prone national forests. National environmental organizations, however, remain skeptical that collaborative groups are making much lasting progress. Oregon and California watershed groups faltered after their founders moved on to other challenges. Some academics contend that grass-roots, watershed-level cooperation so far has produced more feel-good tales of homegrown cooperative spirit

than measurable environmental improvement. Judith Layzer, an environmental policy professor at MIT, says: "You can't just abdicate to local groups and expect the environment to come out better."

Peer Pressure

William Ruckelshaus, though, is convinced that enlisting local communities in devising on-the-ground solutions will be crucial to further progress. A Seattle resident since 1975, Ruckelshaus is now leading a bold effort to restore Puget Sound's dwindling Chinook salmon runs that the federal government has listed as endangered.

Joined by former U.S. Senator and Washington Governor Dan Evans, King County Executive Ron Sims and other influential leaders, the former EPA director pulled together a nonprofit alliance called Shared Strategy for Puget Sound. The group then persuaded the National Marine Fisheries Service to let the region try drafting its own salmon-recovery plan instead of imposing federally prescribed habitat restoration measures. With Ruckelshaus actively involved, Shared Solutions spent five years working with the sound's 14 watersheds to draft separate plans for repairing salmon habitat in a 16,000-square-mile region. Some sessions got off to "stiff and accusatory" starts, Ruckelshaus recalls, "but then they started to listen to each other." In 2005, the 14 watersheds' separate proposals were wrapped into a 50-year strategy for bringing the Chinook populations back. NMFS approved the plan in January.

"That's huge, almost epic in scale, and it's amazing they pulled it off," says University of Washington professor Craig W. Thomas, who's studied collaborative conservation initiatives around the nation. Washington Governor Christine Gregoire tucked $50 million into the state's budget to begin implementing the salmon plan, and also named Ruckelshaus to head a state Puget Sound Partnership that will coordinate an $8 billion comprehensive cleanup program. Ruckelshaus acknowledges that monitoring plans for salmon recovery efforts remain "embryonic at this stage." Eight watersheds came up with solid plans, but others "need more work," he adds.

There are signs that county commissioners remain reluctant to follow through. But Ruckelshaus is confident that other watershed councils "will put peer pressure on the watersheds that drag their feet." Federal scientists — including Ruckelshaus' daughter Mary, the chief NMFS biologist for Puget Sound salmon recovery — may well have come up with stronger habitat protection in a federally dictated recovery plan. But William Ruckelshaus contends that "if you can't get the local citizens on your side, you're going to spend all your time in court or the state legislature or Congress fighting with them. That doesn't work for anybody."

The Puget Sound Partnership instead applies watershed collaboration on the largest scale ever attempted. "That makes it doubly difficult: It's complicated to think about what's necessary for an entire ecosystem, and you've got all the jurisdictional and social and economic complications to deal with at the same time," Ruckelshaus says. "It takes people who are willing to try new things from a governance standpoint to address this."

CHAPTER 12

Bradenton, FL, Area Prepares Boating Paradise on Its Rivers and Streams

John Osborne

Manatee County, Florida, is truly a canoe and kayak paddling paradise.

The area is blessed with miles of isolated mangrove islands, sandy white beaches, and views of sunsets over the Gulf of Mexico. The county is also home to the Manatee and Braden rivers, and various bays and bayous teeming with wildlife.

In August 2000, with help from the National Park Service's Rivers, Trails, and Conservation Assistance Program, the county was awarded a $25,000 grant from the Florida Department of Community Affairs Coastal Management Program for the development of blueways (canoe and kayak trails). The aim was to develop a series of marked, interconnected blueway trails throughout the coastal and river areas of Manatee County.

Until recently, the county had only one designated and unmarked five-mile blueway. But then the Paddle Manatee project came to fruition. Created at the suggestion of county residents, Paddle Manatee is now a 75-mile marked and interconnected blueway system with accompanying waterproof guidebook that details the county's paddle trails.

According to American Trails, Inc., the National Association of Water Trails, and the National Park Service, there are few marked and mapped interconnected blueways at this scale. The only other physically marked trail this large, also located in Florida, is the 99-mile inside water route from the Everglades to Flamingo, in the southern reaches of Everglades National Park.

More Money, More Paddling

Paddle Manatee is Manatee County's first trails project. Why start with blueway trails? The real reason was grant timing. The original Florida Department of Community Affairs Coastal Management Program grant became available at the very beginning of the county's overall trail planning efforts.

In Florida, coastal waters are publicly owned, making blueways an ideal first trails effort for coastal communities. There are no land acquisition issues as long as there is some public property on the water to serve as a launch point. There are also few if any NIMBY issues because power boaters operate in these waters already.

Originally published as "Blue Ways: What It Takes to Create Canoe and Kayak Trails," *Planning*, Vol. 69, No. 10, October 2003. Reprinted with permission from PLANNING, copyright Oct. 2003 by the American Planning Association, Suite 1600, 122 South Michigan Avenue, Chicago, Illinois 60605, USA.

The original grant was for a limited blueway network on a couple of area waterways. However, when grant funding from the Florida West Coast Inland Navigational District was secured for more markers, the project expanded countywide. This second grant, received in March 2001, was for an additional $25,000.

This extra funding enhanced the trail network by adding about 52 miles to the previously proposed 23-mile network, greatly increasing the connectivity and paddling opportunities and creating a 75-mile interconnected paddle trail network.

This entire effort began in November 2000, when the Citizen Trail Committee hosted a public event, the Citizen Greenways and Blueways Public Input Forum. At this event citizens were asked to mark up maps to show where trails should be located. By the end of the meeting, county waters were completely covered with potential blueways. Residents also provided tips about good fishing spots, bird watching areas, snorkeling spots, and stories about where smugglers and moonshiners used to hide from the revenuers back in the days of Prohibition.

Even information about a ghost town on the river that was unknown to most Manatee County residents emerged from the discussions. Much of this information added local flavor to the Paddle Manatee guide that was eventually published.

The project plan included marking and routing all trails using a global positioning system. Although Paddle Manatee is intended for nonmotorized canoes and kayaks, the blueway trails also share the area waters with power boats. In creating the blueway, the county made every effort to minimize potential conflicts between paddlers, power boat users, and nesting birds. According to John Stevely, a marine extension agent from the University of Florida, "the project provides a window to the natural beauty that few of us are aware exists in our backyard."

During the mapping phase, the routes were paddled in both seasons: summer and non-summer, partly to detect tidal differences occurring at various times of the year. The routes were paddled during several points in the week as well to gauge use by power boats. The key point is that the routes were paddled many times.

Lewis and Clark?

Marking the trails was an experience my colleague and co-paddler Troy Salisbury and I will not forget. For some reason, other coworkers pictured us sipping cocktails in the Florida sun while girls in bikinis did all the paddling. If only that were true.

In fact, we were in the water by 7 A.M., paddled all day to 5 P.M., and then cleaned the gear until about 7 P.M. The next day was spent entering soggy field notes and GPS coordinates into a database. We spent many days on the water with rain, heat, cold, wind, or strong currents. It seemed we were always paddling against the wind and current in both directions.

Some areas we looked at were full of monsters: alligators, snakes, mosquitoes, the infamous Florida no-see-ums, assorted marine life, and a variety of spiders. Troy generally cleared the way of spider webs because he sat in the front seat of my tandem kayak. Some trails had to be cleared of exotic vegetation as we paddled — with spiders and crawling sticks raining down on Troy continuously.

One time we were paddling in open water in Tampa Bay and the wind increased dramatically — and unexpectedly. The wave heights quickly grew to five feet, and a U.S. Coast Guard helicopter hovered overhead to make sure we were not in trouble or just plain crazy for being out there in a kayak.

Then there was the incident with a marine animal as large as a bus that moved underwater so swiftly that its wake came over our bow. Troy has not been the same since. After talking to some of our marine fisheries friends, we decided we must have startled a nurse shark.

You would think two experienced outdoorsmen, one with a little Cherokee blood even, with college degrees in geography, supplied with maps, a compass, GPS, and aerial photographs, would have a tough time getting lost. Some of the areas we paddled had so many small mangrove islands crowded together that none of the above helped.

The only thing that saved us from becoming crab food was blind luck and surveyor tape. Our experience led us to add as much navigational information to the Paddle Manatee guide as possible.

After Troy and I developed a set of draft trail maps, the blueways subcommittee of the Citizen Trail Committee took over. They divided up the blueways and began to research each area. They also paddled the trails. And the trail committee provided valuable assistance in proofreading and editing the draft guide.

Professional assistance came from other agencies. Safety being a major issue, our Chief of Marine Rescue in Manatee County, Jay Moyles, who is also an avid paddler, developed the safety language in the guide. Other details, such as cautionary advice about tide changes and geographic features, and emergency contact information, were added to the guide as well.

The Great Guide Divide

Looking at other trail maps, our trail committee was in a quandary about how to create a usable field guide that would have all the necessary information but could still fit in the front pocket of a PFD (personal flotation device). Most trail maps we found were the fold-up type, with one large map on one side and information on the other; however, these maps are terrible during windy conditions.

Besides, each blueway had unique cultural, historical, and wildlife traits. We collectively decided that a guidebook was the way

to go, one made with waterproof paper and stainless steel staples for durability.

After editing by the trail committee and others, *Paddle Manatee: A Guide to Area Canoe and Kayaking Trails* was completed and printed in time for the Paddle Manatee Kick-Off in September 2001, just before the State Greenways and Trails Month. A prototype paddle marker was unveiled, and related exhibits, displays, and canoe and kayak excursions were made available. Volunteers were recognized for their efforts.

The guide has been extremely well received. Requests arrive via e-mail daily, and copies of the guide are sent all over the country. Press releases have been distributed to a variety of media outlets and periodicals.

According to Tim Ohr, author of a number of books about Florida, including *Florida's Fabulous Natural Places*, "Manatee County was ahead of the curve in creating their county blueway. They have started a pattern followed by several other Gulf coast counties creating all together hundreds of exceptional miles of saltwater and freshwater paddling."

Ten thousand of the guides were printed and almost all have been distributed. Area paddling clubs have sprouted up (there were none two years ago) and have quickly attracted new members. Most new paddlers appreciate the guide because it gives them basic information at no cost.

To further promote Paddle Manatee, a state trail designation from the Florida Greenways Coordinating Council was applied for and received in May 2003. This designation also means the trail system will be promoted by the state of Florida along with other state-designated trail systems.

The county also plans to apply for National Recreation Trail designation through American Trails at some point in the future. Nancy Engel, the executive director of the Manatee Economic Development Council and an avid paddler, also considers Paddle Manatee to be "one more asset we can tout in our marketing efforts."

Learning from Our Mistakes

Here are some recommendations we hope future blueway trail builders will heed.

• Get a copy of required marker permit applications early. This could affect mapping and GPS. Florida Uniform Marker Permit applications require some detailed information, such as direction sign faces.
• Meet with permitting agencies, which can provide many hints that make mapping work easier. Most likely they have done this many times before.
• Meet with trail developers and future trail managers; decide who will maintain the trail system and what should be budgeted for this function.
• Paddle all trails in all conditions, seasons, tides, and times. We made several changes based on tides and suggestions from other paddlers.
• Take lots of pictures. Grantor agencies like to see your progress, and you may be able to write an article about your experience later.
• Make sure mapping software is usable by the final graphic artist. Sometimes UNIX-based GIS systems and MAC-based graphic arts software don't communicate well. Who would have thought about that?

Making Connections

"Paddle Manatee is an impressive waterway trail system, and the longest to be officially designated as part of the Florida Greenways and Trails System," says Marsha Rickman of the Florida Department of Environmental Protection's Office of Greenways and Trails. "In addition to providing enormous opportunities for local paddlers, segments of the system have the potential to serve as an integral part of a circumnavigational trail around the entire state."

Paddle Manatee does just that, marking Manatee County's portion of the state circumnavigational paddle trail envisioned in *Connecting Florida's Communities with Greenways and Trails,* published by the Florida Greenways Coordinating Council in 1998. It is hoped that Paddle Manatee will be replicated by other coastal communities in Florida, furthering the vision of that around-the-state paddle trail.

CHAPTER 13

Bradley Beach, NJ, Restores and Protects Its Beach Shoreline

JoAnne Castagna

It's below 30 degrees on a February day on Bradley Beach in New Jersey. Locals are walking their dogs along the snow covered shore, riding bicycles on the promenade and even sporting wet suits and surfing the ice cold waves.

It was obvious to a group of ear-muffed U.S. Army Corps of Engineers personnel that the residents of Bradley Beach are pining for beach season as they walked along the shore with local and state officials surveying the dune work created by the community.

The residents are also literally pining for beach season. For the past five years they've been donating their used Christmas pine trees to the town to create dunes along the mile long Bradley Beach shoreline to maintain the sand nourishment work completed by the Corps in 2001.

The Bradley Beach shoreline had experienced erosion due to previous storms and was in need of sand nourishment. In July 1999 the U.S. Army Corps of Engineers, New York District began a sand nourishment project on Bradley Beach, in Monmouth County, NJ, as part of the Corps' Sandy Hook to Barnegat Inlet Beach Erosion Control Project.

The Corps contracted Weeks Marine to place 3.1 million cubic yards of sand on the shore, which added over 200 feet of beach front, and to create seven groin notches and four outfall extensions.

"Dune creation was not a part of the Corps' project because they are not needed in this project area for protection because the area has a naturally high backshore. If dunes were needed, the Corps certainly would have added this feature," said Lynn Bocamazo, Senior Coastal Engineer, USACE, New York District, who designed and monitored the completed beach nourishment project.

After the project was completed in January 2001, a local effort arose. The Bradley Beach residents wanted to take an additional step to protect the Corps' work, so they decided to create beach dunes. Beach dunes control beach erosion by limiting wind-blown sand loss.

"We wanted to protect the beach's promenade from future storms and give it a new look, like no other town has," said Richard Bianchi, Operating Supervisor of Public Works for Bradley Beach who designed the

Originally published as "New Jersey Community Pines for Beach Season," *Land and Water*, Vol. 49, No. 3, May/June 2007. Published by Land and Water, Inc., www.landandwater.com, Fort Dodge, IA. Reprinted with permission of the publisher.

dune project and has been a lifelong resident of Bradley Beach.

"We also wanted to block out the noise for sunbathers on our beaches. The only noise that you hear now is the sound of the waves and birds. The dunes also protect beach residents' homes and provides them a beautiful ocean front and privacy."

Bocamazo said, "Bradley Beach is not the first community along the 21-mile area to create dunes. Manasquan Beach and Monmouth Beach created dunes using fencing or dune grass, or a combination of planting and fencing. Bradley Beach is the first to use Christmas trees."

Every January Bradley Beach residents leave their used pine Christmas trees on the curbside where a truck from Bradley Beach Public Works Department picks them up.

So far an estimated 20,000 trees have been used to create a stretch of dunes, 4–9 feet high, along the mile-long oceanfront. This past holiday season an additional 3,000 trees were added.

On the beach the trees are placed on the ocean side of the dune system. They are placed on their sides where they can capture sand blowing inland from the beach and eventually form permanent dunes.

The community is designing the dune system in what is called a saw-tooth design. "Snow fences are being placed on an angle along the promenade side of the dune to support the dune system. This also makes the beach look appealing from the shore side," said Bianchi.

Dune grass is being planted on the dunes. Dune grass serves several ecological functions in terms of the dunes. It helps to stabilize the sand. Structurally, the root system of the plant forms a network beneath the sand. When the grass takes and continues to multiply, it literally holds the dune in place. A dune anchored by a dense growth of beach grass forms a much stronger barrier to storms and wave action. Dense growth also serves to dampen the force of the wind resulting in de-creased removal of surface sand. "When the project began the town planted 50,000 plugs of dune grass on the dunes to keep the dunes anchored," said Bianchi. "We are in the process of receiving a grant for an additional 25,000 to 50,000 plugs of dune grass." The snow fences installed also discourage people from walking on these newly planted areas.

Dune grass serves as habitat for insects and small birds and mammals. The insects often provide food for the birds and mammals. The grass also provides shade and hiding areas during the heat of the day. Thus the grass can provide a critical habitat for the young of these species that breed on the beach.

The Bradley Beach Public Works Department plants the dune grass plugs by inserting a broom handle into the dune to create holes and; the dune grass plugs are placed in these holes, usually there are 5–6 plants per plug. During the Spring and Summer the grass grows upwards and spreads along the dune. During the wintertime, the dune grass dies off and grows downward. Maintenance is minimal. However, dune grass does need to be maintained because it eventually dies off and needs to be replaced every 5–7 years. A sign that the grass is dying off is when weeds, such as ragweeds, are seen growing on the dunes.

The beach dunes have proven to be successful. "The placement of Christmas trees in combination with snow fencing and dune grass has proven to be very effective in capturing windblown sand that results in the growth of the height and width of the dunes," said Bianchi.

The dunes have shown to be beneficial to the environment because they provide a more diverse habitat than just sand alone. "The dunes create a sanctuary for sparrows. They also attract all kinds of insects that all wild birds eat," said Bianchi.

The public also finds the dunes appealing. "Everyone is excited about the dunes. They think it is a wonderful project and they love the feeling of the beautiful dunes and scenery," said Bianchi.

Bianchi adds that the public now has a personal connection with their beach that draws 20,000 residents every beach season. "Their donated trees will be there forever. They don't rot. The residents are now a part of the beach."

Community officials are also very supportive of the project and think it's beneficial to the public. "When you walk through the dunes to get to the beach from the promenade psychologically it provides the illusion that you are leaving one world for another," said Stephen Schueler, Mayor of Bradley Beach who is a strong supporter and the financer for the project. Schueler will be funding the project until 2008, the year the dune project is expected to be completed.

It's this type of community involvement that the Corps likes to see. Bocamazo said, "A proactive municipal public works department is a beneficial addition to any Federal or State beach erosion control project. Bradley Beach is trying to aggressively maintain the sand that was placed there and is an active participant in the project's success."

CHAPTER 14

Charleston, SC, and Other Cities Protect Their Urban Waterfronts

John Buntin

For most people, Charleston conjures up images of grand, antebellum mansions looking out over the Battery toward Fort Sumter and the Atlantic Ocean. Or perhaps "Rainbow Row"— the bright-hued townhouses that line East Bay Street near the old warehouse district. But this handsome city of 100,000 residents is also the home of the sixth-busiest container port in the United States. Therein lies a challenge.

American ports are experiencing an unprecedented shipping boom. Most of the growth has come in the form of enormous cargo containers carrying electronics and consumer products from Asia. In the past decade, container traffic has climbed from 20.5 million to 30.4 million TEUs (twenty-foot-equivalents, the standard measurement for a container unit), and economists expect that number to double by 2020. While West Coast ports have experienced the highest growth rates, East Coast ports such as Charleston, Savannah, Norfolk and New York/New Jersey have also seen their container businesses grow rapidly. As cargo levels have increased, container ships have gotten bigger. Today's behemoths stretch to more than 1,000 feet long and can carry more than 8,000 TEUs. They also require bigger cranes, deeper channels, longer docks, better road and rail connections, and ultimately more land.

Charleston seemed to have the perfect place to expand: sparsely populated Daniel Island, about five miles upriver from downtown. But in 1999, when the South Carolina State Port Authority released the environmental impact report for a 12-berth, 1,300-acre container terminal on the island, it ignited a firestorm of opposition. Environmentalists and neighborhood groups protested the scale of the proposed project, warned of traffic congestion and criticized the logic of the site. To the surprise and dismay of the SCSPA, opponents persuaded the state legislature to prohibit a new terminal facility on Daniel Island.

The South Carolina State Port Authority's bruising battle over Daniel Island reflects a new reality for many port authorities. Agencies that are accustomed to ruling over their waterfront domains with minimal outside interference are now contending with another trend — cities' return to the waterfront. From Boston to Houston to Seattle, local and state officials are struggling to balance ports' traditional activities and need to expand with the desire of residents and developers to use urban waterfronts in other ways.

Originally published as "Pier Pressure," *Governing*, Vol. 18, No. 1, October 2004. Published by Congressional Quarterly Inc., Washington, DC. Reprinted with permission of the publisher.

Even Los Angeles and Long Beach, the nation's two largest port operations, are facing space constraints and new demands to reduce their environmental impact. In the process, officials are grappling with tough questions. What are the advantages of a big container port? When do luxury condominiums make more sense than, say, an intermodal water-to-rail transfer facility? And as residents question the traffic congestion and air pollution that come with working ports, are there ways cities can capture the benefits of ports while minimizing costs?

Growing Pains

Charleston's entire history is rooted in its role as a port city. When the first European settlers landed on the Charleston peninsula in 1670 and established their settlement upriver along the banks of the Ashley River, they were rebuked by investors in London for building too far inland. Duly chastened, they uprooted their small settlement and moved down to the tip of the peninsula. There they established a port that soon made Charleston one of the richest cities in the New World. They also left an architectural legacy that continues to define the city to this day today. Last year, 4.6 million tourists visited the city, generating an estimated $5 billion for the region. To Charleston Mayor Joseph Riley, who has governed the city for 29 years, historical preservation and outstanding design are not just about charm, they're the key to the city's economic vitality.

A short stroll down Queen Street illustrates Riley's point — and highlights the challenges that arise when a water-oriented city meets a working seaport. To the right, a construction crane hovers above the newest low-rise luxury condominium complex. To the left is the headquarters of the South Carolina State Port Authority and behind that, occupying some of the most valuable land in the city, is Union Pier — a parking lot for the BMWs manufactured upstate in Spartanburg. A little further north is the oldest of Charleston's three container-shipping terminals. In 1966, when the Columbus Street terminal began to handle containers, it occupied 11 acres, a tract of land one local paper described as "massive." Today, the terminal covers 78 acres and processes roughly 250,000 TEUs a year, and it's the smallest of Charleston's three terminals.

Because of local opposition, the port of Charleston hasn't been able to build new shipping berths since the mid–1990s, when it inaugurated the 300-acre Wando Welch terminal. Instead, it's had to improve the efficiency of its operations. Although the SCSPA and other ports have managed to boost productivity in recent years, officials insist that only expansion will allow ports to meet the future needs of U.S. exporters and consumers. "The long-term solution is not going to be met by increases in efficiency and streamlined labor costs," says Gerald Ricchio, executive director of the port authority in Bridgeport, Connecticut, and head of the Association of American Port Authorities' economic development subcommittee. "It's going to have to be met through increased capacity of other properties and through the acquisition of land."

The need to expand port operations has put cities, states and port authorities in something of a quandary. On the one hand, waterfront areas are increasingly seen as desirable development locations and port authorities are taking on the role of real estate developers. Along the South Boston waterfront, for example, the Massachusetts Port Authority is redeveloping hundreds of acres of parking lots and lightly used industrial land into luxury hotels and office towers. Others have embarked on even more exotic ventures. Fans of the Cleveland Browns football team park in a garage owned and built by the port of Cleveland. The port of Corpus Christi is constructing a minor league baseball stadium.

On the other hand, a thriving port also generates large numbers of well-paying, blue-collar jobs at a time when such jobs are hard to come by. In 2003, the average wage for fully registered longshoremen was $89,000. In L.A., when the International Longshore and Warehouse Union and the Pacific Maritime Association announced plans to sign 3,000 new longshoremen earlier this year, more than 400,000 applicants responded. Indeed, the port of Los Angeles alone helps sustain more than 260,000 jobs in Southern California — one out of every 24 jobs in the region.

Nowhere has the question of how the port should use its urban waterfront properties been more hotly debated than in Seattle. While most port authorities are independent agencies whose members are appointed by mayors (on the West Coast), counties (in Florida) or governors (further up the East Coast), the Seattle Port Authority's commissioners are directly elected by King County voters. Last fall, Alec Fisken ran against one of the incumbent commissioners on a platform that called for better management and a rededication to traditional maritime uses. One of Fisken's first acts was to lead the charge against a proposal to redevelop one of the city's four major container terminals, Terminal 46, into an 88-acre mixed-use neighborhood with apartments, office buildings, parks, a marina, a cruise ship terminal and perhaps a basketball stadium as well.

While Fisken calls it "a great plan," he also considers the port a kind of insurance policy for the region. "It's important to have those diverse kinds of jobs that pay well and don't require a doctorate in anything," says Fisken. "It's good to keep that mix." In early August, the Seattle Port Commission voted against the redevelopment proposal.

Unappreciated Resource

That ports are an important source of jobs is not in doubt. A 2002 economic impact study found that the SCSPA's port activities supported 280,000 jobs in South Carolina alone. Yet despite these benefits, few communities that surround ports seem to have much enthusiasm for the economic powerhouses docked next door. When the SCSPA proposed to build a new container terminal in the old Navy Yard in the blue-collar city of North Charleston in the mid–1990s, Mayor Keith Summey expressed his opposition by commandeering an armored personnel carrier and declaring "war" on the port.

"The big issue was the effect on the surrounding neighborhoods," Summey says. And while he acknowledged that the project would create some decent-paying jobs for the community, he worried that most of the jobs would go to businesses in other parts of the state, leaving North Charleston with traffic congestion and vast parking lots containing nothing but stacked empty containers. Ultimately, the North Charleston city council passed a resolution barring the construction of a new container port in the city. That's when the SCSPA shifted its attention to Daniel Island.

The back-to-back defeats of both port expansion proposals caught the SCSPA and Charleston's business community off guard. "I think it's fair to say that the port found itself faced with a climate that had changed in ways that were a bit unexpected," says Wilbur Johnson, president of the Charleston Metro Chamber of Commerce.

The SCSPA's insistence on building a massive new terminal "showed a stunning lack of insight and comprehension," says Dana Beach, executive director of the Charleston-based Coastal Conservation League, an environmental group that helped organize the opposition to the Daniel Island project. "Part of it is the culture of the SCSPA," she says. "They have been able to get over the years whatever they wanted. In the 1970s, they fought a big battle over the Wando [Welch] terminal and were able to overcome local opposition. They didn't realize that 25 years had made a huge difference in public attitudes."

SCSPA executive director Bernard Groseclose acknowledges that the residents' demands on the port can be frustrating. "Look around the perimeter of the Wando Welch terminal," he says. "All the land adjoining it was industrial up until the last 10 or 12 years or so. It was gradually rezoned residential, and people started building up to the [port] property line. Then they started complaining, 'Well, gee, could you have a quiet day on Sunday?'"

In 2002, however, the SCSPA finally secured a victory. The state legislature (with an assist from the federal government) made North Charleston an offer it couldn't refuse: In exchange for negotiating an agreement with the SCSPA, the city could have the northern half of the Navy Yard. The parties negotiated an agreement that gave the SPSCA the go-ahead to start work on a new, three-berth container terminal at the south end. Port officials say the new terminal will increase the port's capacity by 20 percent and ultimately generate thousands of new jobs. Mayor Summey is a lot more enthusiastic about a new mixed-use development planned for the old base. "While we didn't want the port, the port was sort of mandated to us," he says. "My job was to get as much for the city as I could from the mandate."

Regional vs. Local Benefits

Charleston isn't alone in having a history of conflict between neighborhoods and ports. In Los Angeles, the San Pedro neighborhood has long contended with heavy traffic congestion and air quality levels that are not merely bad but possibly deadly. The combined ports of Los Angeles/Long Beach emit more pollution than Southern California's top 300 emitting plants and refineries. A 1999 study by the South Coast Air Quality Management District found that residents of the LA port area have a significantly higher risk of cancer than other residents of the region. Many other major ports, including New York, Oakland and Houston, also violate federal air-safety standards. They may be great for the region,

but many residents worry that they are sacrificing their health for another area's wealth.

Increasingly, port authorities are acknowledging these concerns. Jerry Bridges, executive director of the Port of Oakland, says ports not only need to deal with environmental problems, they also need to do more to ensure that the residents of areas around ports receive the benefits that flow from them. "When we look at where ports are situated and how communities are impacted, some of the biggest pockets of unemployment are just outside of the gates of our terminals," says Bridges. "We need to look at ways to bring those unemployed individuals into the industry."

One way to do that is through apprenticeship programs with local labor unions and industry. Another approach that is attracting attention in maritime circles is a strategy pioneered by Charleston's most serious competitor, the Port of Savannah.

A New Focus

Seventy miles south of Charleston lies the Port of Savannah, the country's eighth-largest container port. Like Charleston, Savannah is an historic port city. Unlike Charleston, however, Savannah is not blessed with a natural port. Container ships departing from Charleston's most modern terminal reach the ocean in 90 minutes. In contrast, it takes container vessels roughly three hours to travel 24 miles up the sinuous Savannah River to the Georgia Port Authority's Garden City terminal.

Yet despite this apparent disadvantage, the port of Savannah has experienced explosive growth in its container business over the past five years. Five years ago, Savannah handled 730,000 TEUs. By last year, that number had increased to 1.5 million, a figure that has brought its container business to within a few thousand containers of the port of Charleston.

Moreover, while most of Charleston's trade continues to come from Europe, Savannah has tapped into trade with Asia, which bodes well for future growth.

Some of the GPA's success can be attributed to its location. Unlike the port of Charleston, the Garden City terminal does not compete for space on the urban waterfront. It's located a few miles upriver from downtown Savannah. As a result, it's been able to expand more easily and to build new facilities, notably an intermodal rail-transfer facility where containers can be loaded directly onto trains. However, space to expand accounts for only a part of the GPA's success. More important has been the GPA's economic development strategy.

Of the 360-odd ports in the United States, less than 24 have the capacity to handle significant numbers of shipping containers. Because containers transport valuable cargo and typically require careful and frequent handling, they create the most jobs and spur the most economic activity. As a result, ports compete fiercely for business from the 10 shipping lines that control most of the world's container business. In the past, proximity to major markets, on-dock facilities and prices have determined who fared best in this competition. But beginning in the mid–1990s, Savannah added another variable to the mix — the customer.

The key to Savannah's recent successes is found not along its 7,600-foot dock (soon to be 9,800 feet) but four miles down the road at a windowless, 1.4 million square foot warehouse — the distribution center for Home Depot. In the early '90s, Savannah had struggled with a problem. Because it had comparatively few imports, Georgia exporters couldn't get enough containers to serve their needs. So the port, together with state and county development agencies, set out to attract big customers to the area. Its first major catch was Georgia-based Home Depot. Today, the area around Savannah is home to a dozen major distribution centers, including Pier 1, Target,

Best Buy, Kmart, Lowe's, and the mother of all importers, Wal-Mart.

Targeting customers has given the GPA unusual leverage over the major shipping lines. "The ocean carriers are not picking the port to the extent they used to pick the ports they served," says Doug Marchand, executive director of the GPA. "It's being driven by the big shippers saying, 'If you want my business, you'd better be in Savannah.'" According to GPA officials, the state's focus on end-use customers has generated approximately 20,000 distribution jobs for Savannah area residents. The port's approach means that jobs, not just traffic, are now concentrated in the area.

An Uncertain Future

Savannah's success in attracting customers and then using them to lure Asian cargo and negotiate good deals with the shipping lines is being watched closely by other ports. However, not everyone believes that this approach should be applied to more urban, industrial ports such as Charleston.

"There is an issue of scale here," says the Coastal Conservation League's Dana Beach. "The cost of these new berths is going to approach three quarters of a billion dollars and that does not include infrastructure improvements. The question remains: Is this an investment that is wise for the state to make or are there alternatives, either in Charleston or elsewhere? What are the opportunity costs versus other types of economic development in the region? I think that if we were to look very dispassionately and analytically, we would realize that our port is perfectly adequate as it is and that we'd don't need massive expansion."

SCSPA executive director Bernard Groseclose and other port officials don't share that view. "Clearly, there are communities that are balking at port expansion," says Bridgeport's Ricchio. "Some communities are saying, 'You're so big already, what's the point? Let the cargo be diverted to another port.' That's easy to say if you're a citizen in the area, but if you're running a port and don't want to see your competitive advantage undermined, you're going to be as aggressive as possible in getting and developing that land. To many of us, a water view is not a water use. A residential condominium project with a restaurant on the water is not really the best use of a port property."

For now, the contentious debate has re-ceded to the background in Charleston. The SCSPA's current focus is on the new three-berth container terminal at the Navy Yard. However, Groseclose refuses to rule out the possibility of more berths in the future — an idea that environmentalists and community groups seem certain to resist. Despite calls for ports to rethink their operations, a sea change doesn't seem likely.

CHAPTER 15

Charlotte, NC, Restores Stream and Wetlands Corridor Area

Pete Romocki and Chris Matthews

Project Background

The Little Sugar Creek Environmental Restoration Initiative encompassed a stream restoration, greenway trail development and overall enhancement of a stream corridor through the greater Charlotte, North Carolina metropolitan area. It covered a 15-mile section of Little Sugar Creek running south from Uptown Charlotte to the North Carolina/ South Carolina state line. Phase 2 of this initiative was a joint effort between Mecklenburg County and the EEP known as the Freedom Park Stream Restoration Project. The EEP-funded project was one of the largest of its kind in the state, placing more than 1,500 linear feet of stream on a new alignment as much as 150 feet from its current location. The Little Sugar Creek flows through the entire length of Freedom Park, a distance of more than 4,500 linear feet. Freedom Park is in a highly urbanized setting two miles south of the central business district. The 14-square-mile watershed is virtually built-out, with the only development occurring on in-fill locations. Therefore, urban runoff and storm water are the main contributors to

stream degradation along this section of the creek.

Historical records indicated that Little Sugar Creek was likely channeled and straightened in the early 1900s to improve storm water conveyance and allow urban development to occur on the floodplain. In the 1970s and '80s, the creek was showing signs of instability due to upstream development, so a concrete and grouted rip-rap liner was installed along the banks to provide stability and prevent erosion. The stream remained in this state for the next 25 to 30 years.

In 2002, Mecklenburg County awarded a contract to demolish the concrete banks in preparation for the upcoming restoration project. The demolition ran concurrently with the design and permitting of the channel restoration. In 2003 a restoration of Little Sugar Creek that passes through Freedom Park was commissioned. HDR, the national engineering consulting firm, and a local environmental specialty firm, Habitat Assessment and Restoration Program Inc., were selected to design the project based on past experience in the watershed, availability to devote technical expertise and other resources to this complex

Originally published as "Freedom Park Stream Restoration Project Repair," *Land and Water*, Vol. 50, No. 6, November/December 2006. Published by Land and Water, Inc., www.landandwater.com, Fort Dodge, IA. Reprinted with permission of the publisher.

project and a familiarity that had been formed through previous work with EEP. The team performed an extensive watershed survey, a sediment transport study, a reference reach analysis and a site survey to achieve a permittable and stable design. The final design incorporated natural channel techniques to enhance and create habitat, provide stability, improve water quality, control storm water runoff and provide a more aesthetically pleasing stream ecosystem.

Project Update

Approximately one year after the completion of the initial project some areas were experiencing significant erosion on the stream banks. Specifically, this was occurring at locations where planted vegetation had failed due to nutrient poor soil conditions and where the straw/coconut erosion matting that was used to initially preserve the diverse custom seed mix was no longer in place. The problems developed along areas of the stream banks that were experiencing high shear stress loads from occasional intermittent high volumes of storm water flow. The owner of the project site bought attention to these stream bank areas of concern and the engineer, HDR, took on the task of correcting the deficiencies in the stream bank's design. The original work included installation of root wad sections in high velocity areas. The repair effort of this project only involved some of the original straw/coconut erosion blanketed areas.

The initial design of the stream banks utilized a jute netted coconut/straw erosion blanket to protect the banks from the expected high shear stress loads. This product was selected because of its ability to completely biodegrade. Coconut/straw erosion blankets typically have the ability to withstand shear stresses in the 2.0 to 3.0 pounds/square foot range after being vegetated. Evident after the fact was that flow conditions were exhibiting shear stresses considerably greater than

what banks without vegetation could survive. Typical stream bed erosion protection is accomplished using turf reinforcement mats (TRMs). TRMs are composed of nonbiodegradable materials, usually some type of plastic, and can survive shear stresses of 10 lbs./ft^2 or more after being fully vegetated.

HDR chose not to use TRMs because of the non-biodegradable nature of the product. It can be detrimental to the environment as snakes and other fauna that inhabit riparian areas have been seen getting caught in the plastic matrix, particularly the nettings. HDR has also made it a point to design their stream projects such that the combination of slope and vegetation allow for a stable stream bank. If the soils allow proper vegetative growth and the banks have been constructed properly, based on a thorough examination of the hydraulic pressures in the system, TRMs may not be necessary. The issue at Freedom was that the extremely poor soil conditions prevented the establishment of temporary and permanent vegetation. This was especially true of the woody vegetation which provides a root mass adequate to keep stream bank soils in place during flood events. The banks were thus vulnerable to the high velocity floods that occur in the park with the original erosion materials selected.

The Freedom Park project had strict environmental requirements from HDR to be constructed with materials that were completely biodegradable. This requirement eliminated the option to use traditional TRMs. In the redesign of the failed eroded areas HDR surveyed the marketplace for other available options. Selected was a combination of biodegradable erosion blanket materials. Utilized was a netless excelsior blanket (Curlex Net-Free) and a heavy woven 700 gm./sq. meter coir mat used in combination with each other. The coir mat was installed on top of the netless excelsior and both were anchored down using one foot long wooden stakes approximately every 2 square feet (Ecostakes).

The repair work was completed by a four

man crew in about four days by North State Environmental, Inc. They hydroseeded the cleared banks using a browntop millet variety grass seed. The netless excelsior blanket was then installed onto the seeded banks and finally the heavy woven coir matting was laid down on top of it and staked. The contractor installed the netless excelsior blanket on a large area and had the intention of installing the coir mat over it the next day. Unfortunately a significant storm occurred that evening and damaged the entire area that had been laid. They were able to reclaim most of the netless excelsior fiber, redistribute it and then secure it with coir mat. The lesson learned is to install the coir mat on top of the netless excelsior as soon as possible to prevent damage.

Significant rain had also occurred less than 10 days after the installation and the repaired areas appeared to have held up well during this first test. The site was again inspected six months later again with very good results. Vegetation had become well established and the combination of blanket materials appeared to be doing the trick. In September 2006 the project was once again inspected and found to be surviving well. This was an experimental project for HDR in that it is the first case where a net free product was installed under coir mat as a "composite" solution for a stream bank restoration project. Stream bank restoration projects are unique in that all biodegradable "natural" components are required. It makes erosion control of high shear stress level areas difficult because TRMs cannot be used. The use of Curlex NetFree as a part of a component system for protecting stream banks in high shear stress areas is now part of HDR's arsenal of solutions.

CHAPTER 16

Chicago, IL, Considers Options to Expand Its Future Water Resources

Geoff Manaugh

Too often, urban water management takes place out of sight and out of mind, considered so uninteresting by the general public that only specialists should give it thought. Occasionally, a project comes along — like New York's Water Tunnel No. 3, drilled beneath the city through miles of billion-year-old Grenville bedrock — that captures the public imagination. But water is water — why think about it, as long as it keeps pouring out of the tap? Yet fresh water is almost universally agreed to be "the oil of tomorrow," a phrase that refers not only to water's dwindling supplies, but also to its uneven distribution.

The future of urban water will only become more complex. Rain is an excellent example of a water source that is infrequently considered and more frequently ignored. For the most part, U.S. cities are designed — and paved — to clear rainfall as quickly as possible for many of the problems associated with urban storm events — flash flooding, for example, as water pools on impermeable surfaces.

But storm water can be a resource, provided we build the spaces and tools to capture it. The recent book *Worldchanging: A User's*

Guide for the 21st Century, by Alex Steffen (with a foreword by Al Gore), discusses ways in which cities can reuse or mitigate the effects of storm water. Among these is rainwater harvesting, a passive process that has been around for millennia. Rain simply "runs through downpours into cisterns that store it for use in a variety of applications," including doing laundry, flushing the toilet, and irrigating grass. The "quality of the water," the book says, "can be matched by the role that the water will serve."

The long-term value of this kind of environmental integration should not be overlooked. In April, a U.N. climate panel warned that an altered climate "could diminish North American water supplies and trigger disputes between the United States and Canada over water reserves already stressed by industry and agriculture." The outlook, even for a comparatively "wet" continent like North America, is dire: our future will include "more frequent droughts, urban flooding and a scramble for water from the Great Lakes, which border both the United States and Canada." More efficient — and imaginative — uses of local water supplies will help alleviate future droughts and water wars.

Originally published as "Anchor Institutions: Subplots — Water, the New Oil," *The Next American City*, Vol. 5, No. 15, Summer 2007. Published by The Next American City Inc., Philadelphia, PA. Reprinted with permission of the publisher.

I recently spoke to Martin Felsen of UrbanLab, a Chicago-based architecture firm and national winner of this year's City of the Future Contest, sponsored by the History Channel. For that contest, UrbanLab submitted an ingenious proposal that completely redesigned the infrastructure of Chicago, transforming the city into a kind of living filter — or what might be called a bio-architectural valvescape — creating a highly efficient water treatment plant at a metropolitan scale.

"We wanted to do something that involved the whole city," Felsen said in an interview, "so we immediately started thinking: what's a simple, relatively modest move, whose principles could be easily communicated? And water is basically the reason why Chicago is here. The whole economy here is really based in this water supply." In particular, the supply is Lake Michigan and the rain that falls on the city. (Amazingly, 20 percent of the world's surface freshwater, and 95 percent of America's surface freshwater, is contained in the Great Lakes.)

Referred to as "Growing Water," UrbanLab's project calls for some intriguing hydro-management techniques. First, switching the Chicago River back to its natural direction of flow (it had been reversed once, by the Army Corps of Engineers, in 1900). It would also create a series of "eco-boulevards" — something of a cross between a Venetian canal and an artificial wetland. They would run west to east, from Chicago's suburbs to the shores of Lake Michigan. Each eco-boulevard would function as a giant living machine, treating 100 percent of Chicago's waste and storm water naturally, using microorganisms, small invertebrates (such as snails), fish, and plants. Water thus treated would be domestically re-

used — before, once again, being recycled — or would simply be returned to the Great Lakes biosystem. All in all, it's a fascinating and richly imagined project.

In our last issue, TNAC explored water — specifically, the lack of it in cities like Las Vegas. It's interesting to point out how U.S. hydro-politics connects Las Vegas to Chicago. In a recent *Chicago Reader* article, Michael Miner discussed the future of political control over freshwater from the Great Lakes. When we reach "the day the west runs out of water," he asked, will Las Vegas, Phoenix, L.A., and others come knocking on Chicago's door, demanding water? Miner argues that, as long as the Great Lakes exist, southwestern cities will never truly learn to live within the limits of their natural water supply; the Great Lakes are a kind of psychological crutch, an abettor to addiction. Once water in the desert southwest runs out, we may see a "siege" on Chicago, which holds the keys to interstate access to the Great Lakes.

If the day comes when Las Vegas shows up, cups in hand, political lobbyists in tow, demanding several years' worth of Midwestern water, shouldn't the region do more than simply say no, and instead point to its own imaginative infrastructure of eco-boulevards? This is one of the most important aspects of UrbanLab's plan. What at first appears to be a radical — almost science fictional — re-imagining of Chicago's plumbing becomes the practical reorganization of a whole city according to inevitable future realities. As Martin Felsen suggested, this is how Chicago "could become relevant again — when water has a more urgent, global importance, and Chicago has rebuilt itself to deal with this coming problem."

CHAPTER 17

Cleveland, OH, and Other Cities Improve Their Drinking Water Infrastructure

Nancy Zeilig

America's ailing drinking water infrastructure is like having a crazy old uncle living in the basement. Everyone knows he is there, but no one wants to talk about it. Unless, of course, you are a water professional, and then the problem becomes making people listen.

A nearly universal problem in public works, lack of funding is the major obstacle to addressing infrastructure needs, according to more than 75 percent of the utility employees who responded to a 2004 State of the Industry survey conducted by the Denver-based American Water Works Association (AWWA). "Water utilities are some of the most capital-intensive businesses in the world," says Julius Ciaccia, director of utilities in Cleveland. So while water departments struggle with a crumbling infrastructure, water systems are being continuously used, therefore requiring ongoing improvements.

Cleveland's Division of Water serves 1.5 million people within the city and in 69 surrounding communities. "We spend $60 to $70 million a year — the equivalent of about 5 percent of our fixed assets — on system improvements," Ciaccia says.

Cleveland's extensive water system needs that kind of upkeep. "We've spent more than $1 billion on system upgrades since 1988," Ciaccia says. "If a policy-maker asks me when this program will be done, my answer is: 'If we're doing our job right, it will never be done.'"

Addressing nationwide drinking water infrastructure problems will cost between $250 billion and $300 billion over the next 30 years, according to a 2004 AWWA report, "Dawn of the Replacement Era: Reinvesting in Drinking Water Infrastructure." The rate-paying public ultimately will have to bear that burden, the report says, because utilities cannot count on federal funds financing infrastructure improvement projects. Utilities apparently have taken that advice to heart and are using rate increases, bond issues, capital reserves, streamlined operations, loans, grants and surcharges to fund needed water system improvements.

Priorities for capital projects often vary

by region. In the nation's older cities, especially those in the Northeast and Midwest where pipelines are aging and customer bases are dwindling, distribution system rehabilitation generally is the main concern. In the Southwest, where populations are mushrooming and water resources are scarce, new treatment plants to help expand supplies take precedence. And in California and Colorado where earthquakes and forest fires are ever-present threats, shoring up system vulnerabilities against hazards sometimes heads the infrastructure improvements list.

Upgrading Treatment Plants

Cleveland's Division of Water currently is focusing on a multi-year program to modernize its treatment plants — two built in the early 1900s and two in the 1950s. One plant was upgraded in the 1980s, and the city is spending $750 million to bring the other three up to date.

Funding for the upgrades comes primarily from five-year rate increases instituted in 1990. "Raising rates in five-year increments smooths out the impact," Ciaccia says. "Customers and politicians accept that rates will increase every year but not by much. In 1990, we asked the city council for an annual increase of 8 percent, in 1995 we requested 7 percent annually, and now we're raising rates by only 3.5 percent a year."

Ciaccia says the incremental rate increases allow them to predict what levels of debt they will need to incur. "We look at projections a year at a time. We also got back in the bond market to refinance some debt while interest rates were low." He notes that since the division began using incremental rate increases, Standard & Poor's and Moody's have been upgrading its bonds.

In addition, Cleveland is taking advantage of the Drinking Water State Revolving Fund (SRF). "We've been receiving $20 to $30 million a year in SRF loans lately, and in-

terest on these loans is usually a percentage point less than on the open market," Ciaccia says. "We fund about 20 percent of our annual capital program from cash reserves."

Like aging celebrities, many water distribution systems are undergoing reconstructive surgery, and some water systems spend millions of dollars each year to repair or replace pipelines. Although Cleveland's infrastructure improvements temporarily center on its treatment plants, the city has had an ongoing distribution system rehabilitation program for 20 years. "Once the plants are upgraded, our capital improvement projects will be weighted more toward distribution systems," Ciaccia says.

Currently, the utility spends about $6 million a year rehabilitating water mains. "We've relined all our large mains," Ciaccia says, "but about 2,000 miles of our 5,000 miles of pipe are still unlined. We've installed a lot of new trunk main because of urban sprawl, but we've spent more money on rehabilitation than replacement because that's more cost-effective."

The Onondaga County, N.Y., Water Authority (OCWA) began projecting capital needs 12 years ago. A public benefit corporation, OCWA, which serves 340,000 people, puts an average of $7 million a year back into its system, according to executive director Mike Hooker. "We've used some of this money for new storage tanks and pump stations," Hooker says, "and we try to spend $2 to $3 million a year replacing water mains. Our mains are generally less than 50 years old, but some are as old as 100."

OCWA manages capital projects with three-year plans, which can change if the capital budget changes. "We've had more rainfall than average the past two years," Hooker says, "so revenues have gone down; 2004 was our fourth wettest summer in more than 100 years, so that ate into our sales quite a bit."

OCWA has coped with Mother Nature's challenges just as it has dealt with its customer base's slow growth — by streamlining operations and acquiring neighboring water systems. The utility has downsized through attrition, outsources noncore functions and has invested heavily in automation.

Today, OCWA has 15 fewer employees than in 1990, though its connections — now at 83,000 — increased by almost 50 percent during that period. "You can't just downsize," Hooker says. "You have to give staff the tools to become more efficient than before, and you have to train them to use those tools."

Concentrating on its core competencies, OCWA turned to outsourcing. "We stopped paving roads, outsourced several accounting functions and hired landscapers to maintain the grounds," Hooker says. "We're running the most efficient operation possible by using the latest software. Our small information technology department uses consultants for support."

Acquiring other water systems has improved OCWA's economies of scale. "We have more people contributing to the bottom line for capital improvements," Hooker says. "On the other hand, some of these systems have generated more capital work for us. But the growth pays for itself."

Streamlined operations have allowed OCWA to reach a debt ratio of 0.07 percent, according to Hooker. "Since 1984, the system has borrowed only $11.5 million," he says. Although rate increases covered the debt, Hooker says the utility went from 1993 to 2001 without a rate hike.

Building New Plants

The water distribution system is not the problem in El Paso, Texas, according to Ed Archuleta, general manager of the community's Water Utilities Public Service Board. "We're keeping up our distribution system, but our issue is growth — meeting demand — and complying with regulations. Because we're in a desert and our service population is growing, we've diversified our mix of supplies."

El Paso depends on surface water from the Rio Grande, and reclaimed water for non-potable uses and groundwater. Diversifying its sources means treating brackish groundwater by building the country's largest inland desalination plant and installing arsenic removal systems to ensure that other groundwater supplies comply with the lower standard that goes into effect in January 2006.

The $35 million Fort Bliss/El Paso Desalination Plant is a cooperative project of the city and the nearby U.S. Army base. Construction is scheduled to begin in July. The 27.5-million-gallon-per-day (mgd) reverse osmosis plant will lower the concentration of total dissolved solids in water from 12 of the city's existing wells, and the treated water will be blended with fresh water from 16 new wells to be drilled on land owned by the base. "Our groundwater supplies are like a sandwich, with layers of brackish and fresh water," Archuleta says. "Cones of depression in the fresh water layers mean we're tapping brackish water for the first time. Modeling showed that Fort Bliss's water would also become brackish eventually, so it made sense to build the plant to help both the city and the base."

The project, including land acquisition, well drilling, engineering, design and construction, is expected to cost $87 million. Archuleta says the army spent $3.3 million for the environmental impact statement and test drilling; the city is paying for the rest. "El Paso sold revenue bonds, which have to be paid for by the ratepayers, to help pay its portion of the desalination plant and the arsenic plants," he says. "We've also received $26 million in funds earmarked by Congress for Border Environment Infrastructure Funds, a program under the North American Free Trade Agreement."

Archuleta says 46 of El Paso's 175 wells will require treatment to comply with the new arsenic standard. "Our wells are 1,000 feet deep on average, so the arsenic comes from deep volcanic formations. We're spending about $50 million on a 30-mgd facility on the west side of the Franklin Mountains, where the volcanic formations are located. On the east side of the mountains, we're building three smaller plants, which will cost about $26 million."

Constructing New Conveyance Facilities

In California, the East Bay Municipal Utilities District (EBMUD), which serves 1.3 million people in Alameda and Contra Costa counties, "has always focused on keeping up with system needs," says director of finance Gary Breaux.

Breaux says $80 million to $100 million a year goes back into EBMUD's system. "Recently, we've been recoating our covered storage reservoirs, and we spend $10 to $15 million a year on distribution system rehabilitation — 8 to 10 miles of pipeline get replaced every year," he says.

The utility's largest capital program involves constructing conveyance facilities for a dry-year supplemental supply, a joint project with nearby Sacramento County. Initiated 30 years ago, the project is finally fully permitted and is in design. The infrastructure to convey the new supply to EBMUD will cost about $415 million, according to Breaux. "The Mokelumne River, 90 miles away, is our main source, and three aqueducts bring the water to our service area," he says. "For the new supply, we'll be taking water from the Sacramento River. We'll build a river intake and a series of pipelines that will eventually connect to our aqueducts. Based on our precipitation history, we expect to use this supplementary supply three out of every 10 years."

Because new customers are estimated to account for 70 percent of demand, according to EBMUD's 15-year-old water supply master plan, connection fees will cover 70 percent of the supplementary supply's cost. Remaining costs will be covered by rate increases to take effect over the next five years.

"We raise rates every year, usually by 3

to 4 percent," Breaux says. "Our board wants the increases to be no higher than inflation and approximately midway between the rates of other providers in the area. The increase will be 3.75 percent for the next two years, then 2.7 percent. We also issue bonds, but we use no more than 65 percent debt to pay for capital programs."

EBMUD also is taking steps to protect residents from the consequences of earthquake damage. In 2007, the utility will complete a 10-year, $225 million seismic improvement program being underwritten in part by a seismic surcharge, which brings in $14 million a year. He adds that customers have been cooperative about the seismic surcharge, viewing it as a way to complete the program more quickly. "We've built a new pipeline and pumping plants to allow us to move water from the east side of the system to the west side, which is more vulnerable to seismic activity," Breaux says. "We're strengthening our covered reservoirs, most of which are aboveground. We've also installed shut-off valves on the transmission mains that cross the fault line so we can divert water from damaged pipelines and use flexible aboveground mains temporarily."

The utility's source water conveyance system currently includes a 7-foot-diameter tunnel that crosses the fault. The seismic improvement program includes a separate bypass tunnel. "The new tunnel actually serves as a vault for a pipeline inside," Breaux says.

In Colorado, where a multi-year drought contributed to devastating forest fires in Denver Water's watershed in back-to-back years, the utility recently constructed two dams to prevent sediment in runoff from scorched, denuded land from entering the city's water supply. "These leaky dams are essentially sedimentation traps," says finance director Dave LaFrance. "They slow the water down and act like big sieves. Water flows on into the reservoir, but the sediment stays upstream."

Like El Paso, Denver recycles some of its limited supplies, using reclaimed wastewater for industrial purposes and to irrigate municipal parks and golf courses. Denver Water's new recycling plant went online in February 2004, and the 31-mile network that distributes the nonpotable supply is still being extended. The plant can produce up to 17,000 acre-feet of water per year, enough to free up potable supplies for almost 40,000 households.

"Denver Water relies heavily on rates, bonding capacity, system development charges and capital reserves to pay for capital projects," LaFrance says. "Our debt issues are primarily revenue bonds, and we also have some general obligation bonds. We use rate hikes to fund distribution system improvements." The utility's potable water distribution system serves just over a million people through 2,600 miles of main.

Winning Support for Rake Hikes

With federal funds becoming almost as rare as a desert rainstorm, communities are turning to their residents to pay for water system repairs and expansion projects. Archuleta offers some advice on securing funding for infrastructure improvements: "Look for potential partners in your region. Be vigilant in seeking state and federal funds. And educate your customers, your board or city council and the media about the value of water service."

LaFrance echoes Archuleta's emphasis on promoting water's value to win support for regular rate increases. "Water is both an amenity and a necessity," LaFrance says. "If utilities priced tap water at its value, it would become a luxury item like bottled water. Cost of service is the generally accepted method for setting water rates, but cost and value are different. In the case of water, its value is greater than its cost."

CHAPTER 18

Delphos, OH, and Other Cities Improve Their Aging Wastewater Systems

Lori Burkhammer

For years, the wastewater treatment plant in Delphos, Ohio, failed to meet federal regulations for effluent limits. The facility was old and could not handle the load from its 7,000 residents and large industry base. Slapped with an enforcement action and fine from the Ohio Environmental Protection Agency (OEPA), city officials were backed into a corner: either upgrade an antiquated system or build a new facility. Both options cost money, and with no federal funding available, residents would have to shoulder the responsibility alone.

For a community with low to moderate income levels, it was a heavy burden to bear. But considering the value of water and wastewater services to public health, the economy and the environment, there was no question about what had to be done. Nearly three years later, the city is ahead of schedule on the completion of a new $32 million wastewater treatment plant funded solely by a 100 percent increase in rates for residential and business users.

In many communities across the United States, failing or overburdened water and wastewater systems are forcing residents and city officials to reevaluate their commitment to funding capital improvement projects for water and wastewater. Without reliable federal funding, communities are rallying to invest in sustainable infrastructure.

A Small Town with Big Actions

When Kim Riddell became superintendent of wastewater for Delphos, she inherited the unenviable task of counteracting decades of non-compliance with the national pollutant discharge elimination system (NPDES). "The non-compliance was a gradual process," Riddell says. "But when I took over in 2002, I don't think there was a month that we weren't in violation in some form."

The main culprit appeared to be the city's combined sewer system, which allowed the release of non-filterable residue from local industries into the city's water system. While those industries, which were predominantly food manufacturers, were not contributing increased flows to the system, they were contributing a mixture of organic and suspended solids well in excess of seven times the population equivalent.

Unfortunately, inaccurate laboratory re-

Originally published as "Paying the Price," *American City & County*, Vol. 121, No. 1, January 2006. Published by Penton Media, Overland Park, KS. Reprinted with permission of the publisher.

sults did not alert the city to the problem. Discrepancies were discovered only after Riddell decided to focus specifically on the lab data. "Previously, the water was sampled the first four days of the quarter. But by the third month I was here, I was sampling every day for two months and saw huge fluctuations," she says. The existing plant could handle 4,983 pounds of carbonaceous biochemical oxygen demand per day. Riddell says she was finding "26,000 pounds on any given day with an average of 9,000 to 10,000 pounds a day."

The City Council decided to satisfy the conditions of OEPA's enforcement action. Needing an operating facility within 32 months, the city decided to build a $32 million membrane bioreactor advanced wastewater treatment facility. It was designed to handle double the flow of the existing plant, exceed the requirements of the NPDES permit and include a new influent pump station to address wet weather issues. Qualified in part by its income ratios, the city received low interest loans from OEPA's Division of Environmental and Financial Assistance. But with no federal grants, the entire amount will have to be repaid by increased user rates.

"We hired a lobbyist to go after federal funding, but were told that there isn't any money," Riddell says. So in 2005, residential rates were increased by 15 percent of that year's current rate over four years. "When it's all said and done, it actually comes out to over a 100 percent increase because it grows every year," she says. Industries will receive the same rate increase with an additional surcharge expected to generate more than $400,000 annually.

To gain the public's support of the project, the city launched an outreach program. Through public meetings and extensive coverage in the newspaper, residents accepted the rate increases. "I have attended several community group meetings to speak about the type of plant we are building, why we have chosen this treatment system, and why we are building it," Riddell says.

Once mired in non-compliance and facing disciplinary action, water has become a priority for Delphos. As it nears the completion of its wastewater facility, the design of a new water treatment facility and 450-million-gallon reservoir is nearly finished. Sourced by nearby Little Auglaize River, the reservoir will replace well water as the city's main water supply.

Delphos is considering selling some of its new asset to help with the enormous cost of improving its water. "The water will be softened and less corrosive," says water superintendent Tim Williams. "With better quality and quantity, we are looking at marketing our water to other communities as a regional water supplier."

With the completion of both the wastewater and water projects by mid–2007, the community will have built approximately $50 million of new infrastructure — much of it funded by local residents. "It's going to be a real stretch for people to afford their water and sewer bills when this is all said and done," Riddell says. But for that small community, it is a price they are willing to pay.

Charlestonians Dig Deep

Before 1970, wastewater treatment in Charleston, S.C., was non-existent. Untreated wastewater was discharged into Charleston Harbor, severely polluting the region's rivers and killing fish. That attracted media attention and prompted legislation requiring municipalities to treat wastewater before discharging it into waterways.

In 1963, state lawmakers passed "The Charleston Harbor pollution law," which ordered municipalities to implement wastewater treatment by 1970. Charleston responded with the construction of the Plum Island treatment plant and a series of deep tunnels — the first of its kind — to intercept sewage discharge before it reached the harbor.

Some 30 years later, the Charleston Commissioners of Public Works (CPW) finds itself in the middle of the largest and most complex capital improvement project in the city's history: replacing the 35-year-old Peninsula tunnel system. Comprised of the Ashley Tunnel, the Cooper Tunnel, the Harbor Tunnel and the West Ashley Tunnel, the project is designed to meet the community's needs for the next 100 years.

Spanning across eight miles and located 130 feet below the city's surface, the tunnels are lined with steel ribs and wooden slats with an internal concrete and steel pipe that carries an average of 10 million gallons of wastewater per day to the treatment plant. Before reaching the tunnels, the wastewater flows through sewer lines and converges at locations around the city where vortices funnel it into a vertical drop pipe that feeds directly into the treatment plant.

Designed to allow air ventilation, the technology used in the vortices and drop pipes results in a chemical reaction that has proved damaging to the tunnels. Unfortunately, at the time of original construction, engineers did not foresee that the mixture of air and wastewater would produce sulfuric acid, a chemical that deteriorates both steel and concrete. If left unchecked, the damage would impair the city's wastewater flows.

"A blockage in the tunnel was the chief concern regarding deterioration of the tunnel system," says CPW's Chief Executive Officer John Cook. "It could cause a wastewater backup and potentially result in sewage overflowing into the streets and people's homes. This was a serious public health and environmental threat and the primary motivation behind replacing the entire system."

While making repairs to the system in 1988, inspections revealed more serious damage, particularly in the Harbor Tunnel where divers discovered collapsed tunnel lining and large holes in the pipe. Supported by the Chamber of Commerce, the Regional Development Authority and other agencies, CPW decided to replace the tunnel system, and in 1998, the City Council approved a $15 million bond issue to pay for it.

After completing the new Harbor Tunnel in 2002, CPW planned to replace the entire system in six phases over 12 years. However, when sections of collapsed tunnel and broken carrier pipe were discovered in the Ashley Tunnel, the project was condensed into four phases and prioritized by extent of deterioration.

Facing an estimated project cost of more than $100 million, including existing debts and money for homeland security improvements, CPW devised a funding plan of low-interest revenue bonds to be repaid over 30 years and $2.5 million in federal funding. However, more than $95 million will come from increased water and sewer rates and water impact fees, which are charged to newly built homes and businesses applying for water and sewer services.

Using the media and public meetings to educate the community, CPW instituted a total of three 5.5 percent rate increases in 2004 and 2006. An additional increase of 0.5 percent to 1 percent was later approved on water and sewer bills with a reduction of $500 to qualified customers for water impact fees.

However, Charleston residents could be facing additional increases. "While we have sought federal funding for major capital projects, we are not waiting to begin staying ahead of both growth-related projects and projects driven by new regulations," Cook says. CPW hopes to convince residents to continue to invest in the city's future.

San Francisco's Seismic Security

Some consider San Francisco's Hetch Hetchy water system to be an engineering marvel that rivals the Golden Gate Bridge. Using gravity, the water system transports 85 percent of the area's supply from a reservoir of Sierra Nevada snowmelt in Yosemite National Park more than 160 miles into the Bay Area. It then connects with more than 1,200 miles of water mains — many approaching 100 years old — to deliver water to the area's 2.4 million residents.

The system, which collects the other 15 percent of water from runoff in the Alameda and Peninsula watersheds, also crosses five active earthquake faults. Based on studies conducted in 2002, the Bay Area Economic Forum found that an earthquake of 7.0 or greater on any one of those faults could cut off Sierra water supplies for up to 60 days and cost more than $29 billion in losses — resulting in a public health and economic disaster.

Although the system has never failed in more than 70 years, the aging system needed major seismic improvements. "Basic maintenance and repairs have been made in subsequent decades," says Susan Leal, general manager of the San Francisco Public Utilities Commission (SFPUC), the system's manager. "But upgrades necessary to keep it in top condition were deferred, in part from a rate freeze that was in effect for years."

The city was facing a major capital improvement project, and its residents, who had been enjoying the lowest water rates in the Bay area, had to decide how much they valued the service. In November 2002, voters approved a $4.3 billion bond measure — the biggest in San Francisco's history — to rebuild the system. The tab will be paid through a series of rate increases for suburban and urban users that will more than triple their current monthly water bills. "Though rates will triple by 2015 to pay for the program, rates will remain at or below other California cities," Leal says. Currently charged $1.71 per unit of water, residents will begin seeing increases of 15 percent for the next two years.

To gain support for increases and help alleviate public opposition, SFPUC launched a citywide education and outreach effort in spring 2005. "We visited more than 40 community organizations, educated the media, opinion and neighborhood leaders, held numerous public meetings and conducted two city-wide mailings about the program," Leal says.

With the support of local leaders, including Mayor Gavin Newsom, the San Francisco Board of Supervisors unanimously adopted the increases with little opposition. In late November 2005, SFPUC's Governing Commission adopted the program, budget and schedule for the 10-year improvement project, which is currently under way.

Similar to Delphos, San Francisco also will simultaneously upgrade its wastewater system. Prompted by age and seismic concerns, the city is pursuing sustainable solutions for upgrading the system, including reducing chemical dependency during treatment, using green technology and environmentally friendly alternatives, full-cost pricing, and anticipating Bay area regulation changes.

"We will look at new alternative ways to improve our wastewater system," Leal says. "But nothing has been decided on because we want the public to have a say in what types of upgrades the project should encompass."

Gaining public acceptance for a billion dollar wastewater project and rate increases is challenging. "There is a general lack of awareness about wastewater issues in the community," Leal says. "People are more in tune with the water issues because of the 2002 bond measure passed to [improve their water supply]."

In early 2006, the utility plans to start a wastewater educational program. "Once people start to think about how much they rely on the wastewater system, they will begin to see [its] importance."

As water and wastewater systems continue to age and demand for water grows, communities will need to replace their infrastructure. Although faced with a looming crisis and economic challenges, local government leaders in Delphos, Charleston and San Francisco demonstrated that when residents are trusted to understand that water is an integral part of nearly everything they value, they will invest in it.

CHAPTER 19

Fort Worth, TX, Removes Levees to Reconnect Waterways to Its Neighborhoods

Richard Sawey

Like so many U.S. cities, Fort Worth, Texas, was transformed between 1940 and 1970.

As residential and retail growth shifted to the suburbs, local industries — meat packing, oil, and gas — began to decline. Sites were abandoned. A levee system that had been built in the early 1900s to prevent flooding was expanded.

While the levees worked, the system threatened to stifle the city's long-term growth by blocking access, both visually and physically, to Trinity River, which had enabled the city's growth since the mid–1800s. A valuable 400-acre tract of land adjacent to downtown Fort Worth lay depressed and under developed.

In 2001, the Tarrant Regional Water District (TRWD) launched the Trinity River Vision Plan (www.trinityrivervision.org) in association with Fort Worth; Tarrant County; the U.S. Army Corps of Engineers; and Streams and Valleys Inc., a local nonprofit organization dedicated to the river's improvement. The resulting master plan for 88 miles of the river and its tributaries includes a flood-control and riverfront-development project designed to spur redevelopment in the central district of Fort Worth.

Funded in large part by federal flood-control and highway grants, the $435 million plan uses a segment of the river and its tributaries to connect the city's discrete neighborhoods and create a multiuse waterfront adjacent to downtown Fort Worth. A portion of the levee system will be removed to create an urban lake, while a new bypass channel will divert flood waters around the lake and provide additional access to the river.

Though its primary purpose is flood control, the plan also is designed to bring residents and visitors closer to the river.

"The goal is to preserve and enhance the Trinity River corridor with greenways, trails, wildlife habitats, and recreation areas," says Jim Oliver, general manager of TRWD. "It will completely reshape how the city relates to the river."

Partnering for Prosperity

To enhance collaboration among project sponsors, the Trinity River Vision Authority (TRVA) was launched last October so repre-

Originally published as "Leaving the Levees Behind," *Public Works*, Vol. 3, No. 6, June 2007. Published by Hanley Wood Business Media, Chicago, IL. Reprinted with permission of the publisher.

sentatives from the TRWD, Fort Worth, Tarrant County, and Streams and Valleys Inc. would work as one agency on funding and implementation.

Accordingly, TRVA is performing overall program management, real estate acquisitions, and environmental remediation of contaminated properties, while Fort Worth coordinates infrastructure improvements for roads, bridges, and utility systems. The Army Corps of Engineers is responsible for the federally authorized project elements that include the flood-protection facilities.

This vertical management structure establishes a high level of accountability that has brought the plan ahead of schedule. In fact, its proposed budget for the year had to be amended to accommodate initiatives that were planned for next year.

"We looked at what made projects across the country a success or a challenge, and horizontal management is typically the way work is performed," says J.D. Granger, the authority's executive director. "That's dangerous because you're always relying on another partner to finish their portion of the project on time.

"Once we became a combined authority, we began operating as a single entity to get this project done."

Infrastructure Resurgence

The plan is being implemented along two parallel paths: one centered on infrastructure improvements and the other on urban design.

The planning effort was divided into eight river segments. Because it encompasses a 3-mile stretch near the confluence of the river's Clear and West forks adjacent to downtown Fort Worth, one segment in particular offered unique opportunities for revitalization.

After studying the area, engineers, waterfront designers, and urban planners came up with the idea of enhancing flood protec-

tion using a creatively designed flood diversion channel. A 2003 feasibility study affirmed the idea; the final design is due next year.

Cambridge, Mass.–based CDM is leading the preliminary design and engineering for the project, which in addition to a 1½-mile bypass channel includes three flood-isolation gates, a dam to maintain a relatively constant normal water surface elevation, and bridges and road improvements to three major thoroughfares. In addition to developing a project database that all parties can access via the Internet, the firm is helping with property acquisition, recreational components, environmental studies, coordinating surveyors and appraisers, and performing floodplain mitigation analysis.

Ecosystem improvements are being planned both upstream and downstream of the channel. Environmental remediation for potentially contaminated sites near the channel and transportation-related improvements are also included in the plan.

The urban-design portion of the project springboards off the channel project to link the Trinity Uptown area to Fort Worth's cultural district and historic stockyards district. Gideon Toal, a local architecture, planning, and urban design firm; Vancouver-based Bing Thom Architects; and CDM worked closely to ensure almost every part of the city will be linked via the river and its tributaries.

The riverfront development will result in a new mixed-use/mixed-income area, essentially doubling the size of downtown Fort Worth. The allure of an urban waterfront was one reason major retailers such as Radio Shack and Pier 1 decided to stay in the city and build new corporate campuses along the river.

Over the next 20 to 30 years, the aging commercial and industrial land adjacent to the river near downtown Fort Worth will be replaced by medium- to high-density residential development, shopping, restaurants, and entertainment venues.

Construction is expected to begin within two years.

Pay to Play

In late 2004, $110 million of federal funding was authorized by Congress for flood control and other purposes under Public Law 108-447, Section 116, making Fort Worth's one of only seven projects that received this form of funding.

In 2005, an additional $12.8 million of transportation-related infrastructure funding was approved under the Safe, Flexible, Efficient, Transportation Equity Act: A Legacy for Users (SAFETEA-LU).

In the end, the federal government will fund approximately half the infrastructure improvement costs. Local project sponsors will fund about 25% and a tax increment financing district the remaining 25%.

CHAPTER 20

Halifax, NS, Improves Harbor Water Quality with Massive Sewage Infrastructure Improvements

Alec Mackie

For decades, officials wrestled with how to treat the 40 million gal per day (mgd) of untreated sewage that flowed into Halifax Harbor in Nova Scotia, Canada. As one of the largest deep-water ports on Canada's east coast, the harbor offers both economic and recreational benefits to the city of Halifax, but pollution problems were starting to overwhelm the ecosystem.

According to Halifax officials, the top problems included:

- Prohibition of shellfish harvesting in the harbor;
- Large areas of contaminated sediment around 40 separate outfalls;
- Poor water quality along the shorelines;
- Widespread bacterial contamination; and
- Poor aesthetics along the Halifax/Dartmouth waterfronts due to particulates, floating trash and odor.

The Halifax Regional Municipality initiated a massive clean-up project in 1997, which included the construction of three wastewater treatment plants, a collection network through three communities, 22 combined sewer overflow chambers and several pump stations.

Environmental & Economic Benefits

In a 2000 survey of city residents, 71% said they were willing to pay $100 to $150 more in order to improve water quality in the harbor, according to a government-funded study conducted by GPI Atlantic. The report also estimated the economic benefits of a clean-up at roughly $1.6 billion over a 60-year period — including allowing shellfish farmers to return to shorelines for harvesting and re-selling. The city also receives economic benefits from increased real estate values, tourism and recreational sports, according to the report, which examined harbor clean-ups across North America, such as the Boston Harbor clean-up in the 1990s.

"In many ways, this is an economic development project as well as an environmen-

Originally published as "Safe Harbor: Massive Clean-up Project to Improve Halifax Harbor's Water Quality," *Storm Water Solutions*, Vol. 4, No. 2, April 2007. Published by Scranton Gillette Communications, Arlington Heights, IL. Reprinted with permission of the publisher.

tal rehabilitation and enhancement project," Halifax officials wrote in the closing of their planning report.

Collection Network

For the massive sewage treatment project, which will serve the cities surrounding Halifax Harbor, contractor Black & McDonald placed an order for 22 Storm Monster overflow screens from JWC Environmental. During heavy rainstorms or overflow events, the 22 Storm Monsters, each weighing more than a ton and some as long as 35 ft, will play a key role in protecting the harbor by screening out municipal and industrial pollutants, discharging them into the downstream sewage flow and preventing them from escaping into the environment.

"The selection of the Storm Monster was a combined effort between ourselves, the general contractor and the design engineers, based on the required performance specification," said Robert Burns, the project team leader for Black & McDonald.

The Storm Monster is a breakthrough technology providing capture efficiency and high flow rates in the extremely demanding sewage overflow application. Rotating stainless-steel panels with ¼-in. (6-mm) perforated openings capture pollutants and solids and move them to a solid-clad cleaning brush that returns them to the sewage flow where they continue on to the treatment plant for processing. Because the Storm Monster allows flow to enter through the top, bottom and front of the screen, it achieves nearly twice the flow rate of a single entry screen.

Burns, who heads Black & McDonald's Harbor Solutions Team, pointed to three key Storm Monster features that influenced his decision:

1) Perforated plate screens offer better captre efficiency than slotted bar screens;
2) Solids are moved downstream without removing, conveying or handling screenings, as a raked bar screen would require; and

3) JWC Environmental has a reputation for handling projects from start to finish.

Installation of the Storm Monsters began in 2005 and continues today.

"We are proud to provide the Storm Monsters for the Halifax Harbor Solutions Project," said Art Melanson, JWC's Nova Scotia representative and director of Engineered & Environmental Products Co. "The overflow screens are a crucial component of the project. Swimming will once again be possible and fun at Point Pleasant Beach, and it's great to make a positive impact on the environment and help improve the lifestyle of the people living here."

The Storm Monster uses a unique "dog-leg" shape for the screening loop. The design places the cleaning mechanism above the highest emergency overflow level, allowing large flow fluctuations without risking brush submergence. This helps ensure screen function is maintained during periods of high blinding and large flows. In addition, two returning panels are partially submerged, allowing additional screening capacity to maximize the hydraulic capacity of the unit. The largest screen can process flow up to 365 mgd.

The panels have moving stainless steel plates that form a continuous seal against fixed ultra-high molecular weight plastics side strips located around submerged areas to prevent unscreened material from passing through the screen and into the overflow. This design helps ensure small trash items such as rags, cigarette butts and latex items are unable to escape into the harbor. Many bar screens with horizontal bars allow this material to slip through, lowering their screening effectiveness.

In a two-year study of wastewater screens conducted in the UK, researchers discovered fine screens capture roughly 75% of material, while bar screens capture only 15 and 40% of the material. The study, conducted by the UK Water Industry Research organization, found that band screens, where material touches only one side of the screening loop, did even better — capturing up to 97 percent of the material.

High-Quality Expectations

In addition to the sewage collection network, the project also involves the construction of three advanced primary treatment plants with UV disinfection systems installed prior to discharge. Each of the three cities surrounding Halifax Harbor — Dartmouth, Herring Cove and Halifax — will receive a sewage treatment plant, and all are scheduled to start operations in 2008.

Each facility has a unique architectural and landscaping design so it will blend in with the surrounding community. The municipality has set aside $1 million for each site in "community integration" funding to build green spaces and recreational pathways around the sites. Many of the pumping stations also were designed to blend in with the neighborhood — including shutters and clapboard siding consistent with the architectural style in the area.

"The city overall is quite excited about the project," said Burns, who is also a 25-year resident of Halifax. "The expectations of the water quality have some in the city talking about applying for international sailing events and the return of recreational activities on the water."

CHAPTER 21

Houston, TX, Improves the Management of Its Stormwater

Amara Rozgus

Stormwater detention (temporary storage) and retention (long-term storage) basins are cropping up across the nation, and there's no end in sight.

Harris County, for instance, is a heavily populated Texas county with 3.8 million people, and its No. 1 natural hazard is flooding. The Harris County Flood Control District has stopped many potential floods in their tracks, however.

"During a rain event on Oct. 16, 2006, about 1500 homes did not flood along White Oak Bayou because of an ongoing project to widen and deepen the bayou and excavate 10 detention basins that combined hold more than 1 billion gallons of stormwater," says Heather Saucier, spokesperson for the district.

"Bayou City" is the nickname for Houston, the major city within Harris County. The county boasts more than 2500 miles of natural bayous and manmade channels that drain into Galveston Bay. Many of these channels were originally lined with concrete in an effort to move stormwater quickly; however, high flood levels often washed over their banks and detention basins became necessary.

The county's flood control district has been using detention basins since the 1980s to reduce flood damage. The 50 regional basins store billions of gallons of stormwater.

The county is relatively flat, gets an average annual rainfall of 45 inches, has impermeable clay soils, and is close to the Gulf of Mexico's tropical storms — all ingredients in the recipe for flooding disasters.

Each year, the Harris County Flood Control District submits an annual five-year capital improvement program. This sliding window advances into the future as each year ends. It encompasses all of the current and estimated capital improvement activities that the district might implement throughout Harris County. The department oversees an operations budget of $102 million each year. The district's $975 million, five-year capital improvement plan just ended; this year's budget is $195 million.

While the price of land is a consideration for the district, it realizes that a basin's effectiveness in reducing flooding for local homes and businesses is the key factor in determining its placement. The district has a planning department that determines the most effective sites for these basins. There are eight basins under construction right now, with several more in the planning stages. Harris County

Originally published as "Are You Holding Water — Correctly?" *Public Works*, Vol. 3, No. 7, July 2007. Published by Hanley Wood Business Media, Chicago, IL. Reprinted with permission of the publisher.

funds these projects with ad valorem property taxes and federal funds through the U.S. Army Corps of Engineers.

Some improvement projects may include channel modifications (modifying of existing streams, bayous, or tributaries), new channel construction, excavation of large stormwater detention basins, or voluntary buyout of homes that have experienced repetitive flooding or are located hopelessly deep in the regulatory floodplain.

Harris County is forward-thinking, too. "There are strict standards in place for private developers and public agencies when they build projects," says Saucier. Developments cannot exacerbate current flooding conditions, and all development is responsible for additional stormwater runoff it creates. As a result, hundreds of smaller detention basins are scattered around the county.

The Green Approach

The best management practice (BMP) trend is moving toward more holistic approaches in lieu of structural holding and filtering components, such as underground storage tanks or filters, says Ian Cooke, executive director of the Neponset River Watershed Association in Canton, Mass. The group works to protect and restore the Neponset River, its tributaries, and the surrounding watershed.

Current BMPs that are growing in popularity include bioretention and "country drainage," or simple ditches by the side of the road. "Public works departments are thinking more holistically, and that construction approach will be cheaper," says Cooke.

Since there is an unaccounted-for rise in the number of devices to hold and treat stormwater before it's released to the drainage system, reducing the amount that municipalities have to spend on these devices will be welcome. "This rise is mostly due to the implementation of National Pollutant Discharge

Elimination System Phase II requirements and other more stringent state and local requirements," says Andy Hadsell, PE, CFM, stormwater group leader for Chas. H. Sells Inc., an engineering firm based in Mooresville, N.C.

While the jury is still out on the best management practice to use since everyone's stormwater problem is different, many stormwater utilities are turning to bioretention as one way to manage stormwater. Bioretention cells or sites are vegetated depressions designed to collect, store, and filter stormwater runoff. These sites can include a mix of hard structures (perforated pipe that sends overflow to a storm drain) topped with soil, plants, and microbes.

Stormwater, as it falls from above or flows from nearby impervious surfaces, slowly percolates through the soil of a bioretention cell, which acts as a filter to remove some suspended solids. Some water is also taken up by the plants. Commonly known as a rain garden, they can add aesthetic beauty to a residential area.

Bioretention areas can provide excellent pollutant removal and recharge for the "first flush" of stormwater runoff. Properly designed cells remove suspended solids, metals, and nutrients (nitrogen and phosphorus), and can infiltrate 1 inch or more of rainfall.

Cooke's nonprofit group, for instance, worked with the Milton, Mass., department of public works to design bioretention cells along the Pine Tree Brook. Bacteria levels — especially coliform — were above the total maximum daily load, or TMDL, levels allowed in the brook, plus Milton wanted to be proactive in cleaning its water.

Milton and the Neponset River Watershed Association partnered to acquire a Section 319 grant through the Clean Water Act to pay for three bioretention cells along the brook. The partnership used the grant to pay $110,000 for the engineering, construction, enhanced wetlands, and other structures for these bioretention cells.

"There's no simple way to measure their

success," says Cooke. No direct inlet or outlet data can be gathered around these cells because there is no outlet pipe, but Reva Levin, Milton's department of public works program manager, says the brook's health is improving.

The O&M Issue

Routine maintenance on bioretention cells can be relatively simple. "Our department of public works is responsible for planting, mowing, and removing invasive species," says Levin. Her team is trying to establish a community agreement in which residents water and weed the sites after the city has put the cell in place.

But the cost and general nature of operations and maintenance of bioretention sites is relatively unknown. Chapel Hill, N.C., is about to open a new public works and transportation facility sited on 90 acres, and there are five bioretention areas onsite.

The town of Chapel Hill has brand new stormwater regulations that require the volume, rate, and quality of stormwater runoff to be controlled. Flooding in low-lying areas of Chapel Hill has historically been a problem, so bioretention cells have been put into place on this new project to help control runoff that might otherwise cause offsite problems. The city also wants to set a good example for private citizens and local businesses by using low-impact development on its own building sites, so it added environmentally friendly options into the overall engineering budget.

The facility also boasts porous asphalt in its parking spots and turf stone in which turf is grown between pervious pavements. These turf stone roads are not major access roads; they're used mostly for fire access. Though the entire site could have achieved Leadership in Energy and Environmental Design certification, they chose not to pursue it.

The bioretention sites are excavated areas filled with sandy loam, with native plants on top to take in some of the stormwater. The trench below has plastic pipes that remove the water not absorbed and filtered by the plants. "We don't know what the future maintenance will hold," says Curtis Brooks, landscape architect with the city's public works department.

In general, bioretention is new, so its long-term requirements and costs haven't been determined. Brooks estimates that in 10 to 20 years he'll have to replace the plants and loam as they become less permeable due to silt buildup. Data are not available to support his estimates, however, and long-term issues have yet to be seen in field trials.

Consultant Hadsell emphasizes that proper initial design and construction can lead to proper operations and maintenance. Many cities that he works with request a yearly check-up of retention, detention, or bioretention sites — smart since problems can be caught early and fixed before they become costly (and a public relations nightmare).

CHAPTER 22

Jacksonville, NC, Reconstructs Its Wetlands and Cleans Its Bay

Carole Moore

When Horace Mann, AICP, built his dream home, he picked a spot on Wilson Bay in the older part of Jacksonville, North Carolina. Mann's lot is a short distance from the city's former wastewater treatment plant, once the source of effluent so foul that it had turned the bay into a virtual septic tank. Mann, the city's first planner and a former assistant city manager, laughs when explaining why he built his house on the edge of an environmental disaster.

The reason is that the city found a way back from the brink. Today, the bay is clean and life for Mann — as well as for numerous birds, fish, and oysters — is just fine.

"It's really exciting to be a part of this rebirth," says Mann.

Every night as he watches the sun dip below the horizon, Mann is even more convinced this is the place he was meant to be.

Sitting on the Dock of the Bay

Court Street snakes through Jacksonville's original downtown, beginning at its intersection with U.S. Hwy. 17 and ending at Shoreline Drive. Well before the city grew to its current population of 79,000, land use

within these 49 square miles was a totally mixed bag. Although zoning has changed things, Court Street still reflects those hodge-podge days: The Onslow County courthouse and its inevitable entourage of law offices anchor one end. Small businesses, vacant buildings, and the former city wastewater treatment plant, as well as a smattering of older homes, are scattered along the street.

Shoreline Drive parallels Wilson Bay, a 108-acre body of water ringed by privately owned piers that jut from the yards of the large, expensive homes owned by Mann's neighbors. Crab pots hang in the water, and here and there someone sits on a dock holding a pole, feet dangling over the brackish bay.

Fishing — or catching crabs — isn't remarkable. Thousands do it every day in this coastal strip of North Carolina. The remarkable thing is that there's anything worth catching, much less eating, in water once so rank with pollution even birds avoided it.

Closing Jacksonville's wastewater treatment plant would have been enough to start the bay's natural healing process. But left to its own devices, nature would take decades to bio-remediate water this degraded. Jack-

Originally published as "The Clean Machine," *Planning*, Vol. 73, No. 3, March 2007. Published by the American Planning Association, Chicago, IL. Reprinted with permission of the publishers.

sonville — and a hungry mollusk — did the job in less than five years.

The Man with the Plan

The Wilson Bay Initiative got its start in 1998, when the old, failing wastewater treatment plant was replaced with a $50 million environmentally sound land application treatment system. Although the city wasn't legally compelled to clean up the bay, city officials felt a moral obligation to do so, rather than wait for nature to take its course. The problem was that no one knew how to proceed.

The bay, a combination of fresh and salt waters, was so dangerous that it was off-limits to recreational use. Pat Donovan-Potts, a water quality specialist with the city's Habitat Protection Division, says the water contained abnormally high nutrients: ammonias, nitrates, phosphates, and fecal coliform.

"You're allowed 200 organisms per 100 mils [milliliters] of water for recreational water, and we had anywhere from 35,000 to 75,000 on a weekly basis," says Donovan-Potts. "When [we] first came to work, we actually had to wear gloves and masks because if that water entered a membrane, we were hugging the porcelain goddess for a day."

The city wasn't the only source of pollution in Wilson Bay. Across the water stands Camp Lejeune, one of the largest Marine Corps bases in the U.S. The Marines once sunk 400 creosote-soaked posts into the floor of the bay, thereby adding to the pollution. Agricultural byproducts from nearby farms, including animal waste and pesticides, also tainted the water. And a nearby subdivision contributed stormwater runoff.

It took half a century, but the once-pristine bay turned toxic. As a result, not only was recreational use impossible, but the few fish that lived in the bay became inedible.

The pollution caused the death of the benthic community, the organisms that lie at the bottom of the bay and constitute its basis for life. "Without a benthic community, you don't have fish, and without fish, there's nothing to draw birds," Donovan-Potts says.

As the bottom layer of food died, each subsequent link in the chain succumbed, until the bay ended up essentially lifeless and depleted of oxygen. Without oxygen, organic matter could not break down, further adding to the water's pollutants.

Enter Jay Levine, a Harvard-educated professor of veterinary science at North Carolina State University. In 1996, Levine and Walter Timm, a Jacksonville resident, had recently returned from a visit to France, where they observed mariculture techniques involving oysters. Timm suggested that the city talk to Levine about applying some of those techniques to Wilson Bay.

Levine studied the problem and offered a different approach: combining the natural filtering abilities of bivalves with aeration in order to speed up the water's self-cleansing process. Levine says he never expected the oysters to do the entire cleanup, just to kick start it. "We hoped to reduce the organic load," says Levine.

Laughter greeted the proposal. The idea of enlisting oysters to correct 50 years of abuse struck many — including scientists — as unrealistic. The oysters were given little chance of survival in the dirty bay. But the city went with the plan, reasoning that the bay was so degraded it was an environmental hazard, anyway. What, city officials asked, did they have to lose?

By this time Mann, the city's former planner, had left to help run a family business, but after running successfully for the city council, he voted to implement the project. Like the rest of the council, he held his breath to see what would happen next.

Eureka!

It worked. Starting in 1998, and using volunteers — mostly teenagers — researchers filled plastic mesh bags with small oysters native to this habitat and placed them near the surface of the water, high enough to benefit from the sun. In the meantime, large aeration units were established to begin adding oxygen to the water.

Donovan-Potts describes the team's reaction several months after the project got under way. "Scientists doubted us in the beginning," she says. "Because of the pollution and the salinity, they thought it was far-fetched that we would be able to keep the oysters alive in Wilson Bay."

But the oysters did more than simply live. They thrived.

"Basically, it's like putting a 17-year-old boy at the Pizza Hut buffet for a year," Donovan-Potts explains. "The oysters grew three times as fast" as they normally would.

As the oysters filtered the detritus and consumed it, the water became cleaner and as it became cleaner, the benthic community reestablished itself. That attracted fish, which in turn attracted birds. Soon even sea otters splashed in the bay.

But city officials knew the project couldn't begin and end with fixing the bay. "While initially the city's only goal was to improve water quality, the success drove residents to question why we shouldn't also improve habitat," says Glenn Hargett, a project manager with the city manager's office.

Wetlands were reconstructed, resupplying lost habitat to many species that had previously abandoned the area. An environmental engineer oversaw construction of rain gardens and swales in the neighborhoods bordering the bay. Then the city extended the project to the New River, which feeds into the bay, and to its tributaries.

City officials also decided this type of environmental disaster should never be repeated. To educate residents, the city established an institute called Sturgeon City, which functions as an environmental educational center for the area's youth, who also monitor the bay and keep track of the wildlife, salinity conditions, and the dissolved oxygen level.

A New Day in the Neighborhood

"I caught a two-and-a-half-pound trout in my backyard yesterday," says Horace Mann. He leans back in his seat with a grin and confides that a friend beat his catch by landing a six-pounder. He's a big fan of the Wilson Bay Initiative and sits on the Sturgeon City board of directors. Without the initiative, Mann says, the revitalization of downtown Jacksonville would never have gotten this far.

"I wouldn't have built over a sewage hole or gone out back to catch supper," he says.

City officials say the bay and river have experienced a rebirth both environmentally and in popularity. The city has constructed new waterside parks from which residents watch fishing and pleasure boats while strolling along the banks. The Wilson Bay Initiative has also been a boon to downtown revitalization, with new businesses opening up and developers building high-end houses, which in turn increase the tax base.

"We're seeing projects that were not envisioned when the downtown master plan was created," says the city's planning administrator, Rhonda Parker. "Sturgeon City and the habitat restoration efforts changed that. People want to be near clean water; people want to be near success."

Mann points out that most cities must worry about urban sprawl, but Jacksonville's growth has been redirected inward. "Before it was totally outward, but now it's core growth," he says.

He says the project has helped increase public interest and thus public investment in the old downtown area. "It draws people back to where we have water, sewer, firefighters, and the like already in place," says Mann.

The city has also learned a lot from its past mistakes. Instead of allowing waterside development that might reintroduce pollution, officials allow a very limited amount of impervious surface in new housing projects. Mann cannot build more on his property —

something the majority of the city's property owners take for granted.

"I can't add a storage building, but I knew that before, and besides, living here is worth it," he says.

The Flip Side

Directly across from Mann's property, on the banks of the New River, sits the Georgetown Community, a traditionally lower middle class, African American neighborhood. Georgetown has seen a recent influx of wealthy people buying and building on riverfront lots. A recent county tax revaluation resulted in a five- or six-fold increase in property values on or near the water. The result has both a positive and negative effect on the city, Mann says.

"We cleaned up the river and made it more desirable," he says. But even though the tax base has benefited from the Wilson Bay Initiative, those who have traditionally lived near the water in inexpensive homes now find themselves strapped to pay their property taxes and stay in their own neighborhoods.

The councilman says the city shouldn't be in the business of displacing people from their homes. "We need to do a better job of meshing the new and the old," he says. "From a planning point of view, we need to mediate better."

The city has benefited both from the extra value generated by property along the water and the added quality of life a clean bay brings. Some $1.7 million in startup funds for remediation of Wilson Bay came primarily from grants. Those grants — from the Clean Water Management Fund, EPA brownfield funding, and others — kept Jacksonville's investment in the initial project down to only $313,365.

The city continues to fund the remediation project, which costs about $250,000 annually, from funds generated by a stormwater fee added to residents' water bills. A second remediation project on Chaney Creek, a small tributary of the New River, has received about $162,000 from the National Oceanographic and Atmospheric Administration, while Jacksonville's costs are about $63,000.

And now, the Wilson Bay Initiative may have found a surprising new source of funding.

Fish Farm

When Wade Watanabe, a research professor and coordinator of the University of North Carolina at Wilmington's Center for Marine Science Aquaculture Program, toured the Sturgeon City facilities on the recommendation of a colleague, he found an opportunity: The drying beds and other parts of the facility would be ideal for an aquaculture project.

Harry Daniels and Tom Losordo, both professors at North Carolina State University, helped Watanabe design the project, which was scheduled for completion this winter.

Basically, the project will consist of a pilot-scale recirculating system for marine finfish. The project will use the same size tanks as a full-scale operation, but fewer of them. The system, which is land-based, allows for the recycling and reuse of water by removing waste and supplying the fish with oxygen.

"These systems grow fish under high densities and are therefore compact and do not require large amounts of land," says Watanabe.

Waste generated by the fish will be used to produce microalgae, which will be fed to oysters that will then be stocked into Wilson Bay. Watanabe says this particular circle of life fits nicely into Sturgeon City's goals of environmentally friendly economic development.

Southern flounder and black sea bass will be bred in captivity and raised until they can be marketed. "These technologies will also help to conserve the wild populations, which are being depleted through overfishing and habitat degradation," Watanabe says.

Shawn Longfellow, who, as part of his MBA project, will manage the program under contract with the university, says local fishermen needn't worry about competition from the aquaculture program. "We'll be serving the off-season market," Longfellow explains. Plans are to live-haul the fish to market, and Longfellow says if everything goes as planned, the new program will generate both income and jobs, not only for the city of Jacksonville, but for others interested in aquaculture.

As for the fish: Longfellow promises they will taste divine. "They will be pellet-fed," he says. "No one will be feeding them other fish that aren't fit for human consumption."

Often Duplicated, Never Equaled

Although bivalves such as oysters have been used elsewhere to help clean water, Jacksonville cleaned the water and restored the wetlands in a fraction of the time nature would have taken to repair the damage; in addition, the city is on the cutting edge of environmental education.

"We now have life where we only used to have death," Mann says. "I've not seen anyone else turn a sewer treatment plant into an environmental education center. It's a crazy success story."

Not too long ago, Wilson Bay was abandoned — a place where fishermen never dropped a hook and birds never visited. Today, the sky above Wilson Bay swirls with hundreds of pairs of beating wings as seabirds swoop and dive over the water, looking for the tell-tale silver flashes of fish swimming beneath the surface. Restored to life through this unique project, the bay was repopulated, and the habitats of keystone species such as eagles and ospreys reestablished.

Fishing and pleasure boats dot the horizon as turtles and frogs cling to grass and logs in the surrounding wetlands. Crab and fish have staged comebacks in the bay and on dinner tables. The bay's chain of life has been rebuilt.

CHAPTER 23

Kansas City, KS, Restores Its Urban Habitat and Improves Water Quality

Laurie Brown

Development patterns within the 3000 square mile Kansas City metropolitan area are greatly impacting the existence and function of natural systems. This article will focus on how communities throughout the Kansas City region are stepping up to the challenge of understanding, protecting, and incorporating natural resources into development and stormwater management. By including natural resources within the development process with the same weight as infrastructure planning, communities will be better able to reach a balance between the economic, social, and environmental aspects of growth management. Stream inventories like the Kansas City Stream Asset Inventory Phase I, used in conjunction with other regional initiatives (Kansas City Metropolitan Natural Resources Inventory and the Kansas City Region Green Infrastructure), will provide planners with the tools and strategies critical to successfully manage stormwater, prevent flooding, and provide healthy communities in the future.

Impacts of Urbanization

Watersheds in urban areas commonly suffer changes in their hydrology due to development. These changes include: decreased water quality; increased water quantity whereby flows reach higher stages more quickly; total runoff is increased; dry-season base flows are reduced; channel instability; channel migration; loss of connections among landscape features; and loss of native vegetation and wildlife habitat. As a result, small changes in topography can lead to dramatic changes in habitat features, while changes in hydrology can negatively impact plant and wildlife species that are dependent upon the critical timing and duration of flooding. Hydrologic changes (changes in natural pulsations of water by dams, drainage, channelization or other influences) can result in species composition shifts within plant and wildlife communities as: bottomland species are replaced by upland species; large wide ranging species are lost; genetic integrity is lost when habitats are too small and isolated to support viable populations; populations of interior species that can only reproduce in large tracts are lost; and as numbers of predators, competitors, and parasite species tolerant of disturbed environments increase. Historical data can be useful in correlating changes in stream geometry with land use changes and watershed protection efforts.

Originally published as "Restoration of Urban Habitats: Tools for Designing with Nature," *Land and Water*, Vol. 48, No. 3, May/June 2006. Published by Land and Water, Inc., www.landandwater.com, Fort Dodge, IA. Reprinted with permission of the publisher.

For the same level of urbanization, streams with intact riparian woodlands have been found to have higher biotic diversity than those that do not. Stream degradation and channel instability due to more frequent bankfull flooding, higher peak discharge rates, lower dry-weather stream flows, and loss of instream (pools & riffles) and streambank habitat structures, can occur at levels of imperviousness as low as 10%. At levels of imperviousness of 25% or more, few if any streams can support diverse aquatic insect communities due to increased turbidity, toxicity, salinity, and decreased dissolved O_2 (Wenger, 1999).

KC Community Initiative

An integrative, three-tiered approach (Inventory, Prioritization, and Protection) has been developed for conducting stream asset inventories and deriving planning tools and strategies necessary to achieve successful long-term growth and stability within the Kansas City community. The goals of this approach are:

- Improving stormwater management and water quality while preventing flooding;
- Integrating and prioritizing economic, environmental, and social resources;
- Increasing base knowledge of existing resources;
- Making ecologically sound land use decisions; and
- Decreasing infrastructure costs and maintenance.

All of the steps within this three-tiered system are critical to providing planners and other decision makers with the necessary strategies and tools to integrate the natural environment and the human environment in a healthy and balanced manner. By implementing short-term and long-term guidelines for resource protection, the biological health and function of streams, rivers and other natural re-

sources will be maintained and improved throughout the region.

KC Inventory Process

The Line Creek Watershed north of the Missouri River and Stadium/Park East Planning Area south of the river were the two areas selected for this study. Initial selection was based upon location; past, present, and proposed development patterns; and stormwater issues. As part of the Inventory process, the project team verified and expanded in-house information provided by City staff. Current aerial photographs were used to determine the optimal number and location of field sample sites. Sample sites were chosen based on a variety of positive and negative land use conditions. Criteria used in selecting sample sites includes:

- Geography — physical location;
- Geology and topography — soils, steepness, length, and shape of slopes;
- Hydrology — water sources and drainage patterns;
- Land cover — vegetation;
- Land use — rural/urban, undeveloped/ developed, older/newer development; and
- Project budget.

The rapid stream assessment methodology used for this project has progressed through a development and testing process initiated with the City of Lenexa's Stream Assessment and Natural Resource Inventory Project (December 2001). Methodology for future stream asset inventories will further refine data collection by integrating GPS units. Preliminary field reconnaissance consists of the following characterizations:

- Streambank and streambed characterization is used to determine the physical stability of the stream channel;
- Erosion characterization including overland runoff, water turbulence, tree fall distur-

bance, natural debris, stream channel constriction, toe erosion, streambank slippage, and agricultural use;

- Stream flow rate;
- Identification of vegetation types, diversity, and condition are important factors in determining the condition of the riparian corridor and its ability to protect the stream;
- Prominent aquatic invertebrates (damsel fly larvae, dragonfly larvae, snails, crayfish, etc.) present are identified to the family level and grouped into a general water quality category;
- Site photographs; and
- General observations of stream conditions.

Field data collected is downloaded into an Excel spreadsheet for scoring and analysis. The stream characterization factors described above are given numeric scores based on USDA scoring methods. The score values are then weighted using the professional knowledge and judgment of field biologists involved in this project. The numeric score then provides the basis for classifying the stream segments into one of the following types.

Type 1— Generally described as the highest quality naturally occurring stream with little negative impact. Erosion and sedimentation is low, water quality indicators are positive and the surrounding riparian zone is a healthy, mature, succession woodland or other high-quality environment.

Type 2 — This type of high quality stream may have some down or side-cutting; however, bank and bed composition (bedrock) assist in keeping the impact low. Water quality is generally good and the riparian zone is largely intact, although vegetation may be altered from that of a typical native plant association. Stream segments are classified by type as to their overall quality.

Type 3 — The riparian corridor is still restorable although deterioration is much more noticeable. While some remnant plant associations may be present, overall vegetative

canopy cover is comprised of immature tree species. The potential for restoration exists although erosion and sedimentation can be greater than desirable.

Type 4 — Impacts are greater on this low quality stream type with significant indicators of bank erosion and sedimentation present. The adjoining riparian corridor may be intact but vegetation is not representative of a native plant association.

Type 5 — The channel in this type is the most changed and of the lowest quality. The riparian corridor is impaired to the point of providing little protection or benefit, and erosion and sedimentation indicators are significant. Water quality is questionable with noticeable phosphate and nitrate loading (large algae blooms).

KC Inventory Results

Although many of the conditions and impacts noted during the field survey were common to both study areas, the streams within these two study areas are in distinctly different phases of their evolutionary cycle. One note of particular interest is that neither study area contains any stream reaches of highest (Type 1) or lowest (Type 5) quality. Streams within the Line Creek Watershed exhibit a greater diversity of conditions within adjoining stream reaches; however, many are showing evidence of damaging influences from increasing development within the watershed. The majority of streams within the Stadium/Park East Planning Area are in moderate to good condition, appearing to be reaching a level of stability associated with the absence of new development. Development within this area reached its peak many years ago, and left undisturbed, the streams are returning to a level of relative equilibrium.

Studies show that a disproportionate amount of damage is done to stream quality during the relatively short period of active site development. Field observations indicate the existence of turbidity and sediment plumes attributable to development within the watershed. Cumulative downstream impacts of sediments and other pollutants are a significant contributor to water quality degradation in the study area. Unless proper erosion and sediment control practices are enforced as development occurs within the watershed, these cumulative impacts will increase the negative impacts on water quality and aquatic systems.

KC Inventory Recommendations

Recommendations for the two study areas reflect major differences in existing resources, development age, structure and type, and the potential for implementation of "greener" solutions in future developments. Development potential within the Stadium/Park East area is primarily limited to vacant lots, while there is substantial open space within the Line Creek Watershed that has potential for development. Pressure to develop the remaining open space is placing a considerable burden on City staff to make quick decisions without enough base information regarding resources present to assist them with these decisions. Recommendations for this watershed focus on protecting the high quality stream reaches within Line Creek through vegetated buffers, parkways and open space, cluster development, relocating the proposed Community Mixed Use Center, and realigning a few proposed streets and intersections.

City Planning staff plays a pivotal role in protecting the city's natural resources in that they are the "first line of defense" in making land use recommendations and then reviewing development proposals on a site-by-site basis. The information contained here will guide the preservation thought process so that the most effort is spent protecting the most valuable assets. This information should be shared with the development community as early as possible in the design process so the private sector becomes a partner in preservation with the City.

City decisions impact stream stability and water quality in three primary ways; land use planning/regulation, site development regulations, and design standards for public infrastructure. Recommended resource protection strategies relate to each of these areas with the primary goal of allowing development while retaining the existing, working natural systems. This goal can be achieved through protecting and retaining high quality natural resources, using natural systems such as vegetation to return stormwater to the soil rather than continuing to rely on structural storm drainage solutions, and managing precipitation as close to where it falls as is physically and economically possible. Improving stormwater management is often seen as a site issue rather than a larger scale planning issue. When the objective is to protect and retain high quality natural resources, however, the process begins with conservation-sensitive land use planning. There is a direct relationship between land use intensity and resource degradation.

KC Regional Initiatives

The Mid-America Regional Council (MARC) through sponsorship of the Metropolitan Kansas City Natural Resource Inventory Project, aims to implement the first of a multiple phase, collaborative, community-based initiative to document, map, and ultimately conserve natural resources within the Kansas City metropolitan region. The development of a comprehensive inventory and assessment of natural resources is a critical first step toward solid environmental planning at the local level, and a systems-based framework for watershed management, resource conservation, and restoration at the regional level. Cities, counties, agencies, and developers will be able to reference local and regional resource conditions. The project will provide an inventory of critical ecosystems and valuable natural resources throughout the region in order to meet 5 key goals:

- Provide a current assessment of the state of ecological resources within the bi-state region as an initial step toward broader watershed management and ecosystem protection in the future;
- Compile a consistent set of baseline information in a usable GIS format to provide base information to local governments that can be used in the local planning process;
- Support identification and implementation of high priority MetroGreen trail segments around the region. MetroGreen is a proposed 1000-mile regional greenway system centered largely along the region's stream networks that has been strongly endorsed by the region's elected and civic leadership;
- Offer multiple opportunities to educate targeted audiences about the value of sound environmental planning; and
- Create a regional framework for an interconnected, landscape scale conservation and restoration plan.

This plan will form a key component of all local and regional planning efforts related to such factors as land use, economic development, transportation, water resources and air quality. Over the long term, beyond the scope of this grant, project goals would expand to create a regional framework for an interconnected, landscape scale conservation and restoration.

The Kansas City Region Green Infrastructure Project is another regional initiative sponsored by MARC. The vision of this initiative is to create and implement cost-effective green planning and design. Increasingly, communities have begun to reevaluate the ways in which they develop. They simply cannot resort to conventional approaches and expect different results. Communities have long understood the need for infrastructure, like water and sewer lines, power lines and roadways. With strong support for "MetroGreen" in the Kansas City region, communities now recognize the value of open and green spaces. Many communities increasingly appreciate the importance of "green infrastructure"—a planned, managed, interconnected network of natural areas like waterways, wetlands and forests; conservation lands like greenways and parks; and adjacent working lands like farms, ranches and corporate lands. The primary goals of this project are to improve stormwater management through the use of natural systems while creating successful partnerships across political boundaries. Promising designs and management strategies are being demonstrated on selected sites within the metropolitan region through large-scale municipal and county level projects and smaller scale educational demonstration projects.

Summary

Development patterns are altering the habitats of both wildlife and people. Urban development does not just present issues for our past; it also prompts issues within our present and our future. Conservation of our natural resources takes all of us learning and working together to create a greener, healthier future for our communities. Knowledge gained from conducting the stream inventory and integrating regional initiatives includes:

- The necessity of providing decision makers with tools and strategies for protecting natural resources;
- The importance of these tools to integrating planning and development of the human and natural environment;
- Stream Assessment methodology must be user friendly, easy to understand and implement, and reasonable to enforce;
- Development of a comprehensive inventory of natural resources within the region is a critical first step toward environmental planning at the local level;
- The regional conservation plan is a key component to all local and regional efforts; and

- Community involvement and education are the foundations of successful planning and implementation.

The Stream Asset Inventory project was funded through the City of Kansas City Planning and Development Department, using the consultant team of Patti Banks Associates (prime), Applied Ecological Services, Inc., Taliaferro & Browne, and Tetra Tech EMI, Inc. (subs).

CHAPTER 24

Las Vegas, NV, Master Plan Focuses on Regional Flood Control, Neighborhood Drainage, and Sanitary Sewers

Amara Rozgus

Charlie Kajkowski is not a gambling man. A 34-year veteran of Las Vegas Public Works, the recently promoted director doesn't play around when it comes to planning for the growth of the city's infrastructure.

A professional engineer by training, Kajkowski has one major theory on how to keep Las Vegas a "future city": build everything big. "We've never built anything too big" for today's population of 600,000 he says.

Reports suggest that Nevada will have the fastest-growing population in the nation over the next 20 years. About 1 million people already live in the Las Vegas Valley, which includes Las Vegas. His predecessors didn't think the valley would get this huge, but Kajkowski knows better.

"You can never build anything too big — roads, sewers, anything," he says. "History has taught us this."

For example, when constructing a 3-mile sewer interceptor in the late 1990s, Kajkowski (then city engineer) and his team knew they had only one chance to roll the dice. They built the interceptor based on anticipated rather than actual need for the cities of Las Vegas and North Las Vegas.

Although projections showed an estimated flow need of 80 mgd, the city designed and built the interceptor to a capacity of 90 mgd at 90% full to accommodate growth in the northwest portion of the valley.

Instead of specifying 66-inch pipe for a portion of the project, the city opted for 72-inch pipe. Most of the project costs were associated with trenching, dewatering, bedding, and backfill, which the city would have to pay no matter what size pipe was placed. So upsizing the pipe capacity to handle larger future flows was incremental.

"The decision to build this infrastructure project with more capacity than normal projections turned out to be extremely beneficial and cost-efficient for the cities," says Kajkowski. And that's why he keeps doing it.

The Bigger Picture

The city's master plan is the key element to making sure Las Vegas is ready for what-

Originally published as "Smart Water," *Public Works*, Vol. 3, No. 6, June 2007. Published by Hanley Wood Business Media, Chicago, IL. Reprinted with permission of the publisher.

ever the next generation brings. It focuses on four areas: streets and highways (adopted in 1981), regional flood control (1986), neighborhood drainage (1994), and sanitary sewers (1994).

These plans are fluid and are updated regularly, some every five years, others on an as-needed basis as the city expands. The engineering planning division of public works is dedicated solely to implementing the plan. Although they track day-to-day engineering tasks, planning engineers focus on the big picture.

The 30 people in this division know what, when, and where infrastructure is needed to support new growth. They conduct surveys of the city's infrastructure and handle land acquisition. The city occasionally acquires land from the U.S. Bureau of Land Management, which will help the city expand physically as the population grows.

Technology is key to remaining dynamic. Dennis Moyer, land development project manager, uses Rancho Cordova, Calif.–based Hansen Information Technologies enterprise software to track building trends through permit requests. The Internet-based enterprise software has cut the approval process for the 2700 permits in its system at any given time from as long as a year down to 20 business days.

Las Vegas has a 20-year capital improvement plan. This year, the city has $272 million set aside for capital improvement. A chunk of that (about $62 million) is earmarked for flood control and sanitary sewer projects. Private funds (via public-private partnerships) total $40 million, and $168 million is set aside for other projects, including streets and roads.

Public-private partnerships play a special role in filling the city's infrastructure needs. For instance, the Fremont East Entertainment District Improvements project, which started in January, is a partnership between the city, which initiated the plan, and local business owners to spruce up this section of downtown.

It includes three blocks of streetscape between Las Vegas Boulevard and Eighth Street.

Neon-lighted gateways, neon elements placed in new median islands, decorative signage, expanded sidewalks, landscaping, lighting, banners, and bronze medallions embedded in the sidewalks all are the public works department's responsibility. The $5.5 million redevelopment project is slated for completion in August.

Staying Hydrated

"Our two biggest challenges are transportation infrastructure and water resources," says Jorge Cervantes, deputy director/city engineer in Las Vegas. "We solve it by using high-tech equipment."

Las Vegas grows by 4000 to 6000 residents each month, so public works is hit squarely in the face every day with two challenges: an increase in cars on the roads and water demand.

The city can't simply spin the roulette wheel on its water supply, and hope for the best. This is where the Southern Nevada Water Authority comes into play.

Formed in 1991 by the Las Vegas Valley Water District, Las Vegas, North Las Vegas, Henderson, the Big Bend Water District, Boulder City, and the Clark County Water Reclamation District, the authority addresses the region's water issues by securing water resources and designing conservation programs for member agencies, which pay to connect into the system.

"It's growth paying for growth," says Kay Brothers, the authority's deputy general manager of engineering/operations.

The authority pulls 300,000 acre-feet of water from Lake Mead, a man-made lake about 25 miles from Las Vegas that was created when Hoover Dam was built on the Colorado River, and is responsible for directing its flow through more than 160 miles of distribution pipe. That amount has not changed with the area's population boom, nor has the authority gone over its allotment, determined in 1922 and monitored by the U.S. Bureau of Reclamation.

For every gallon of treated wastewater that a member sends back to Lake Mead, the authority gets to pull another gallon out and give it back to that community. Last year, this return flow credit process provided the authority with an additional 220,000 acre-feet of water.

But It's Still Not Enough

In April, the state's Division of Water Resources approved the authority's request to develop a maximum of 60,000 acre-feet of water from the Spring Valley ground-water basin annually to reduce members' reliance on Lake Mead. Members won't be able to use this new water source until 2014; 40,000 acre-feet will be pulled the first 10 years, and another 20,000 acre-feet will be added to the total in stages.

The authority's 50-year projections show that conservation is going to be the key to ensuring that the Valley has enough water to sustain its growth and tourism (about 39 million people visited Las Vegas last year).

The relationship between Las Vegas and the Southern Nevada Water Authority is quite simple: The authority gives the city's water purveyors a certain amount of water to meet water demands, offers guidelines on how to use and re-use it, and offers both residents and businesses tips and rebates so water is used wisely. Then it steps back and watches.

Through the return flow credit process, last year Las Vegas used about 520,000 acre-feet of water. In addition, the city's wastewater agencies treat and send back to Lake Mead all of the water that's used indoors, stretching every drop. Many hotels and casinos treat water on their property and re-use it to fill canals, water plants, or maintain equipment that requires water.

Anyone who has ever been to Las Vegas knows it's an eye-popping, over-indulging, and sensory-overload place. Water plays a big role in everything from hotel fountain displays to the ice cubes clinking in gamblers' drinks to keeping the golf courses green.

Kajkowski follows this goal of conservation, and he doesn't worry about the next generation running out of water.

"It's all about vision," he says. "We're in the middle of a desert, but with more efficient use of water and energy, I'm confident Las Vegas will survive well into the future."

CHAPTER 25

Los Angeles, CA, Inner-City Renewal Plan Focuses on Restoring the "Lost" River

Hilary Kaplan

On a Sunday afternoon, venerable Bilboa Park smells exactly as it should — like charred hot dogs. From atop bicycles and in strollers, beneath kites or behind dogs, English, Spanish, Hebrew, Farsi, and Russian voices exchange the news of the day in Los Angeles's San Fernando Valley. Couples picnic on the grass with deli takeout, alongside extended family barbecues and inflatable castles full of bouncing nine-year-olds. There are even a few weddings beside the park's centerpiece, Lake Balboa. The newlyweds don't seem to mind the paddle boaters, or fly fishermen, or children chasing ducks and geese around the lake. The man-made, curvaceous body of reclaimed water, with its decorative cascade and flower-trimmed gazebos, captivates everyone in the Valley's heat.

Twenty miles east, City Councilmember Ed Reyes is walking precincts in his working-class, largely Latino district just north of downtown LA. Neither the rain nor the pitbull at his heels deters him from describing the area's future. "Open space and development of natural settings [are] important in creating relief for all the kids and all the families in these corridors," he insists. "We're rivaling Manhattan in terms of density." But there are precious few parks. A trained urban planner, Reyes sees the neglected Los Angeles River, which runs south through his district and then into downtown, as a logical place to begin renewing the city center. William Mulholland, the early 20th century Los Angeles water czar who reengineered an entire state's water supply to allow the building of a city in the desert, once called the river "a beautiful, limpid little stream." Today, partly thanks to Mulholland, the river lies straitjacketed into a concrete channel. Nobody would think about getting married here.

"If we use our natural habitats wisely and we strategically locate them in areas that need this kind of investment, then you're gonna have a magnet to create multiple uses in one site — like live-work space," commercial investment, and desperately craved recreational space, Reyes believes. Reyes wants to create a new equivalent of Balboa Park in his neighborhood, with the river at the heart of the enterprise. He repeats his rallying cry, the one that gets quoted in all the papers: "We've been

Originally published as "Los Angeles' Lost River," *The Next American City*, Vol. 1, No. 12, June 2003. Published by The Next American City Inc., Philadelphia, PA. Reprinted with permission of the publisher.

treating the river as the city's backyard. It's time that we make it our front yard."

Performance Act Spawns Vision for River

Nearby, ex-beat poet and avant-garde art historian Lewis Macadams recounts how this chapter in the struggle to revitalize the river began 17 years ago as a performance art series. Part One involved cutting through a wire fence with two friends, "going down to the river and asking if we could speak for it in the human realm. We didn't hear it say no." Thus was born the Friends of the Los Angeles River (FoLAR), Macadams's non-profit environmental advocacy "artwork." In 1989, Macadams spoke for the river by saying things like "Over our dead bodies!" when the chair of the State Assembly Transportation Committee proposed to turn the riverbed into a freeway. Now that the state and local governments finally are catching up with FoLAR's restorative vision, Macadams's Loraxian voice sounds just like the politician's: "Once people come down to the river and it becomes part of their life, then it becomes part of the city.... It's a way of making the river the front yard." But for Macadams, a front yard is wilder than the neat patches of green grass that stand before L.A. homes. Suggest to most folks that you want to open up green space along the river, and they might think about sweeps of meadow and playing fields along the banks, with playgrounds cooled by the river breeze. The river of Macadams's dreams is open space for "not just the two-leggeds but the four-leggeds and the flying ones and the swimming ones."

"I got into this to takes out concrete," says Macadams, but he has yet to see the jackhammers. Nevertheless, he is optimistic, not urgent. "I can't afford to think in those terms," he says of the time gone by and the concrete that hasn't budged. He focuses forward while savoring the victories so far, like FoLAR's office in the 5-year-old Los Angeles River Center adjacent to the intersection of the I-5 and Highway 110.

The 5/10 interchange that FoLAR's office overlooks is not just freeway, after all. It is L.A.'s original front yard. Here at the confluence of the L.A. River and the Arroyo Seco, El Pueblo de Los Angeles was settled in 1781. The ocean and the mountains that today are the city's defining natural icons were several days' horseback ride away then.

From River to "Flood Control Channel"

For 120 years, the freshwater mecca served as L.A.'s hub and main water source, so people more or less paid attention to the river's health. But they were also sucking it dry. By 1900, the water demands of an exploding population were about to exceed the river's supply. In 1913, Mulholland's Los Angeles-Owens River Aqueduct began delivering all the water the metropolis needed from hundreds of miles away, and the L.A. River became most useful as a dumping ground.

The river continued its seasonal flooding amid the pollution. Little more than a creek most the year, the river swelled in winter with runoff from the San Gabriel Mountains, and refused to follow a fixed course through its increasingly-developed basin. In 1930, parkland innovator Frederick Law Olmstead Jr., along with Harlan Bartholomew, proposed a chain of riverside greenways for the dual purposes of flood control and recreation. Developers, hungry for property in the basin, quashed the public space plan before it was widely known.

Within eight years, two floods killed 87 people, damaged property, and provided a perfect excuse for a flood-control project palatable to real estate interests. The U.S. Army Corps of Engineers embarked on a 30-year paving projects to reign in the unruly river, conveniently freeing land in the former flood plain for private construction. The project "was a holocaust" for wildlife, notes

Macadams. Five native fish species are now extinct; the remaining two are precariously close. Five cramped soft-bottomed areas (totaling 11 miles) provide crucial habitat for 400 species of birds displaced from the overdeveloped city. The other 41 miles of the river are concrete-lined, an inaccessible eyesore slicing through the neighborhoods of Los Angeles and Long Beach.

The Army Corps' paving job removed the river from the public's sight and imagination. The severe concrete encasement disguised a natural resource as a public works project. The country renamed the river to reflect its new purpose, christening it "Flood Control Channel" on maps and documents. The enormous, mostly dry channel is a convenient catch-all for household, agricultural, and street runoff, storm drain contents, illegal toxic dumping, graffiti, and those ubiquitous shopping carts and plastic bags. In a heavy storm, the equivalent of a year's water supply for the City of L.A. can wash these toxins straight down the channel into Long Beach Harbor.

Restoration for People or Restoration for Birds?

Ed Reyes tells a story about the river's problems and promise: "As a kid my friends and I, when we thought it was too dangerous to hang out at the local park because of the gang situation, we would maneuver our way to the rail tracks, unbeknownst to our parents, and find ourselves in the river. We had a little pond area that was surrounded by trees and shrubbery. Only after a few smelly weeks of coming home did we realize what was really going on there, and we realized it was very dangerous [because of the pollution]. But it just goes to show that it has great potential as a recreational facility."

But Macadams cautions that recreation is not the only demand that a revitalized river needs to serve. "It's not like I'm not in favor of parks," says Macadams. "I have kids too and

I know what the park situation is now. It's egregious. But more than 95%—I would venture to say more like 98%—of the wetlands in Los Angeles County have been destroyed. That's a screaming need to restore riparian habitat." An ecologically restored river might be able to coexist with the recreation areas that neighborhoods want, but it will require some crossover compromise between these parallel visions of a new L.A. River—some give and take between people and nature.

Last fall, Reyes convened four other councilmembers into the Ad Hoc Committee on the Los Angeles River. They are the City Council's answer to front yard detail. The committee is pursuing $2.7 million in federal funding to sketch out ideas to rezone and remake the 30 miles of river within the City of Los Angeles.

A coalition is already at work on the river's first major transformation. The abandoned Chinatown Cornfield rail yard is in the process of becoming Cornfield State Park. These 32 acres exemplify an urban ecological dream: historical open space (the land really was planted with corn at an earlier time) rescued from misuse and returned to the public and the earth. The Cornfield Advisory Committee (CAC), an ethnically diverse group of representatives from neighborhood, environmental, and religious organizations, has shepherded the park since a FoLAR-backed lawsuit enabled the state to purchase the riverside land.

The Cornfield illuminates the challenges that face the Los Angeles River. If a relatively small project with dedicated land and dollars, and many dedicated stewards, takes so long, other, more grandiose and less well-backed ideas will have even greater problems taking hold. State and city budget deficits call funding sources into question. Likewise, there is no guarantee of federal funding, points out Joe Linton, FoLAR board member and Ad Hoc Committee staffer. River-friendly progress ebbs and flows with administrations.

With Reyes at the helm, the Ad Hoc

Committee is looking at the whole river system. Reyes thinks in green design terms, like "adaptive reuse" (converting existing buildings for new purposes) and "polishing the water" (employing riparian flora and microorganisms to create a self-cleaning river). But Reyes acknowledges that committee members have local priorities. In a downtown scrambling to revive itself, he speaks of creating a public recreational lake by setting inflatable rubber dams in the river that can be deflated quickly in floods. His colleagues want to create rivulets off the main channel, to bring scenic waterways to neighborhoods where the river currently doesn't run. Because individual neighborhoods have individual needs, and more than 30 governmental agencies have jurisdiction over the river, the best way to effect change at the river might be segment by segment.

The risk of a segmented approach is that flashy, user-friendly recreational projects might impress people and win support without really doing anything to heal the river. "Very few people are interested in riparian restoration.... It's turned out to be the most difficult thing. I think we have not accomplished it at all," reflects Macadams. But a recent studio project by Harvard landscape architecture students shows that habitat restoration downtown can be viable, creative, and appealing to the masses. Their designs portray bike paths through bird habitat, and beaches along flooding basins. Before L.A. can host a river that supports neighborhood children and native fish, someone must turn these student sketches into a real place. Taylor Yard, sixty acres just north of the Cornfield, is Macadams's choice. In place of the empty rail yards and the channel's concrete trapezoidal walls, he envisions space for floodwaters to gather and sustain wetlands. There, people will engage with a piece of L.A.'s natural heritage, while the watershed begins to restore itself.

For all of Macadams's organizational efforts, he believes the secret to a revived Los Angeles River is simple: "Add water and that's about it." Time and nature will do the rest. Ed Reyes takes the "Field of Dreams" approach: he hopes to lay the groundwork for river revitalization projects downtown that will encourage community and commercial investment. In any event, the emerging coalition's strength derives from the fact that it cares enough to take on projects that may not come to fruition under its current leadership. Its members are willing to work in service of a long-term vision that could turn Los Angeles' concrete desert around. Enough people see now what Macadams has known all along: despite decades of abuse and ignorance, in the heart of L.A., "the river's there."

CHAPTER 26

Miami, FL, Shapes Its Future by Restoring and Preserving Its River

Herb Hiller

For its first 100 years, Miami was Florida's poster child for sprawl. A bare trading post on Biscayne Bay in 1896, when the railroad arrived, Miami passed through the twentieth century fanning landward in all directions, filling coastal edge, farmlands, and glades with subdivisions.

As urbanization spread, Miami's downtown languished. The explosive growth that followed World War II added more than 1.7 million new people to the suburbs but a scant 130,000 to the city. Only in the last few years has a drive been mounted to attract people back to the city to live. And, ironically, that drive almost stalled when archaeological traces of Miami's first inhabitants, the Tequestas, were discovered at a downtown construction site at the mouth of the Miami River.

Almost three centuries after the Tequestas disappeared, evidence of these early peoples was unearthed at the Miami Circle, an artifact believed to be 2,000 years old. Carved into the limestone bedrock, the mysterious stone circle, 38 feet in diameter, bears witness to a prehistoric culture that once thrived here. The stone circle has some striking features. First, the cardinal directions appear to be intentionally marked. A set of holes defines a

line that runs east-west, with a carving of a human eye at the eastern terminus. Other directions are marked with unusual cuts in the stone or rocks placed in holes.

Until the unexpected discovery last year of the Miami Circle, Miami's pre–Columbian ancestors were believed to be primarily hunters and fishers. Spanish records from the middle of the sixteenth century reveal that the Tequestas controlled a territory centered around the Miami River where it empties into Biscayne Bay. They lived chiefly from the sea, judging by the shell mounds that once rose along the coast but were ravaged by early twentieth-century development. Based on findings at the circle, however, archaeologists now believe the Tequestas were traders, too. The site has turned up axes of basalt, a material not naturally found within 600 miles of the Tequesta village.

The circle's exact purpose isn't known and may never be. The Tequestas themselves remain mysterious. "The material heritage of the Tequesta and other native people of southeast Florida has been almost totally erased from the landscape," says Jerald T. Milanich, an authority on Florida Indians. But scholars speculate from axial points and animal

Originally published as "The Miami Circle," *Land and People*, Vol. 12, No. 2, Fall 2000. Published by The Trust for Public Land, San Francisco, CA. Reprinted with permission of the publisher.

remains — including a five-foot shark — that the circle might have been a ceremonial platform or an astronomical calendar. Enthusiastic observers suggest comparisons with Stonehenge and other grand artifacts of lost civilizations.

A more conservative guess, based on post holes and related evidence, is that the circle may simply outline a thatched structure — archaeologists suggest a council house or chief's residence. "We knew this was something significant," says Bob Carr, the lead county archaeologist at the time of the discovery and now head of the Miami-based Archaeological and Historical Conservancy. "There was a culturally created circle here. But what was it?"

In the Path of Redevelopment

The land at the mouth of the Miami River had once belonged to the pioneering Brickell family, who established a trading post there in the 1870s. Until recently, the Brickell Apartments, built in the 1950s, occupied the site but were demolished to make way for twin residential towers. Because the building site lay in a zone of archaeological significance, a city ordinance triggered the dig. Soon the searchers began uncovering odd holes in the rock filled with the black dirt called midden. Larger basins began showing up, distinctly different from the holes. The position of the basins suggested an arc. A backhoe used to remove rubble from the surface proved the scientists' hunch correct, and soon the circle lay exposed. Carbon dating showed that the artifact was about 2,000 years old.

Archaeologists had been given only four to six weeks to excavate the site. Now they pressed for an extension. "It wasn't until we cleaned out the circle that we began to realize that perhaps this was of greater importance than we thought — not just locally, but perhaps to the whole country," says Carr.

For archaeologist John Ricisak, Carr's successor with the county, elation was tempered by knowledge the discovery was probably doomed. "It's a gateway to Miami, to the region. Yet there was no doubt in anybody's mind that this site and everything on it was going to be destroyed." Eight months of legal motions between the county and the developer followed. Public sentiment weighed in on the side of saving the site. At the Brickell Bridge, which spans the river in the heart of downtown, a statue of a Tequesta archer — his arrow aimed at the sun — became a de facto shrine. In an emotional protest against a century of developer rule in Miami, people decorated the statue and the gate enclosing the site with lace and incense, pictures of Jesus and the Blessed Virgin, fans, shawls, Cuban and Rastafarian flags, Indian turbans, a hibachi for burnt offerings, and an 1886 photograph of Geronimo with a group of renegade Apaches.

Letters poured in from schoolchildren to Governor Jeb Bush and to local mayors. Pedestrians crossing the Brickell Bridge at the site volunteered at the dig. Native Americans prayerfully danced at the site to invoke protection from "redundant development." When a stonemason refused to dismantle the artifact and walked off the job, the story made the front page of *The Miami Herald* and rallied the public anew. *The Herald*, which once had endorsed the idea of dismantling and relocating the circle, now came down on the side of preserving the ruin in situ.

When the county began talking about taking the property by eminent domain, the developer floated a buyout price of $50 million. Nobody was ready to spend that kind of money.

Miami-Dade County Mayor Alex Penelas, however, wanted to save the site. "Deep down everyone understood why the circle was important," Penelas says. "The link to Miami's past, our trading history, our ancestral heritage — all argued for the site's preservation." With Penelas spearheading negotiations, the developer finally agreed to sell the property for $26.7 million. The county came up with $3 million from the Safe Neighborhood Parks Act bond, and, quicker than usual, the state put up $15 million more. As days, then hours, ticked toward the deadline for settling up with the developer, a breakthrough occurred. TPL bridged the gap with an $8.7 million loan.

Focusing on the River

Almost a year after the site was discovered, archaeological excavation has resumed and discussion has turned to how the Miami Circle might best be both preserved and showcased. Many ideas are in play. Florida Senator Bob Graham has proposed that the site be linked to Biscayne National Park, 25 miles south of the city, via a water taxi. Miami-Dade County Mayor Alex Penelas wants to establish a museum that teaches about the city's history in long-distance trade. There is also talk of housing a privately owned pre–Columbian art collection there.

These proposals all draw attention to the river itself, which, after decades of neglect, is newly valued as a resource for attracting people back to downtown. A chief priority is getting the Miami River — whose name is said to mean "sweet water" — cleaned up. The U.S. Army Corps of Engineers has committed some 80 percent of the funds needed to dredge the river, and local sources are coming up with the balance.

Yet even before dredging and clean-up begin, people-friendly businesses are coming back to the river. Residents and tourists have popularized new restaurants. In nearby East Little Havana they've discovered a compound of historic houses that preservation leader Sallye Jude snatched from condemnation and restored as the Miami River Inn, popular for meetings and overnight stays. "The river is the heart of this 1910 neighborhood," says Jude,

who serves on TPL's National Advisory Council. "By preserving Miami's past, we felt we could help shape its future. The Miami River is key to that vision." Meanwhile, investors who successfully backed the renaissance along Brickell Avenue and in Coconut Grove and South Beach have assembled parcels for more than a thousand apartments, restaurants, shops, and nightclubs along the river.

"Developers have been extremely enthusiastic about connecting their projects to the circle and to the envisioned Miami River Greenway," says Brenda Marshall, senior project manager in TPL's Miami office. The Trust for Public Land is spearheading a master plan for the greenway, which Marshall foresees will provide neighborhoods with access to parks along a renewed Miami River, while encouraging existing small businesses and new investment. Downtown, the greenway will connect with an existing section of the city's riverwalk, begun years ago on the river's north bank. There are several places from which residents and visitors can watch tugs and freighters navigate the channel from Biscayne Bay.

With funds from the Safe Neighborhood Parks Act, a $200 million referendum championed by TPL and approved by Miami-Dade County voters in 1996, parks along the proposed greenway are getting a needed boost. Lummus Park, built in 1909 and one of the city's oldest, has reopened to the public after being closed for want of maintenance and security. TPL has assisted the city in acquiring Spring Garden Point Park in the historic Spring Garden district, the first new park on the river in nearly 20 years.

At the start of the greenway and at the center of Miami's renewal will be the Miami Circle, now preserved, where Miami began and will begin again.

CHAPTER 27

Moscow, ID, Restores Nature to Improve Its Rivers and Their Wetlands

Amanda Cronin

Improving Our Home Watershed: Paradise Creek

In 1989 Paradise Creek was described as Water Quality limited stream by the Idaho Department of Environmental Quality (IDEQ). The designated beneficial uses protected under Idaho Water Quality Standards are cold water biota, secondary contact recreation and agricultural water supply. Since 1990, Palouse-Clearwater Environmental Institute (PCEI) has directed projects to survey discharge pipes, remeander channel segments, restore floodplains, revegetate riparian areas, stabilize streambanks, construct wetlands and educate our community about the Paradise Creek Watershed.

Paradise Creek is located in the Palouse Basin. The Palouse River is a tributary to the Snake River, the largest tributary to the Columbia River in the Pacific Northwest. Originating from Moscow Mountain (elev. 4,983 ft.), in Latah County, Idaho, Paradise Creek flows southwest for 20 miles, through Moscow, Idaho (elev. 2,520 ft.), ultimately entering the South Fork of the Palouse River in Pullman, Washington. Average annual precipitation is 24 inches in Moscow, mostly occurring as snow or rain in the winter months. Paradise Creek drains 34 square miles, and is comprised of 55 stream segments, of which 49 flow through agricultural fields. Wetlands associated with riparian areas along Paradise Creek are in poor condition due to past and present management activities such as draining and tiling. In late winter and early spring, melting snowpack and rain fall onto frozen soils causing peak runoff and flood events, with the largest event approximately 1,000 cfs. During periods of low flow, in the summer, effluent from the Moscow Wastewater Treatment Plant (MWWTP) contributes more than 90% of the flow in Paradise Creek downstream of Moscow.

Cropland is the most prevalent land use (approximately 73%) in the Paradise Creek Watershed, but provides the least diverse plant community type. The lack of multi-story riparian vegetation is probably the most limiting factor to restoring a diversity of wildlife species and available habitat in the watershed. Over 240 species of wildlife are seen in our watershed, including elk, moose, mink, bobcat and cougar, with the greatest diversity

Originally published as "Restoring Paradise in Moscow, Idaho," *Land and Water*, Vol. 47, No. 2, June 2003. Published by Land and Water, Inc., www.landandwater.com, Fort Dodge, IA. Reprinted with permission of the publisher.

found in birds. Over 160 species have been observed, including bald eagles, warblers, long-eared owls, peregrine falcons, and Rufous and Calliope hummingbirds. Historically, Paradise Creek supported cold water fisheries. Currently, the creek only supports limited pollution tolerant fish species: Redside Shiner, Speckled Dace, Northern Squawfish, Columbian Largescale Sucker and Longnose Sucker.

Today, Paradise Creek is a simplified ecosystem impacted by habitat destruction, excessive sediment, nutrients, high temperatures, altered flow, pathogens and ammonia, which combined, have significantly decreased its biological integrity and impaired its beneficial uses. Negative impacts on the stream continue to increase along with growth in the urban areas of Moscow and Pullman, so that it is becoming even more difficult for the creek to repair itself.

In 1994, PCEI received "Phase One" of the "Paradise Creek Watershed Restoration" grant from the IDEQ and Environmental Protection Agency under section 319 of the Clean Water Act. This was to restore the floodplain and streambanks at a site owned by the Moscow School District, and to develop an erosion control ordinance for the City of Moscow. Currently, we are in the process of completing "Phase 7," of Paradise Creek watershed restoration, also supported by IDEQ, which calls for the implementation of nonpoint source controls to achieve Total Maximum Daily Load (TMDL) allocations, as outlined in the TMDL Implementation Plan, written by the Paradise Creek Watershed Advisory Group in 1999. The project includes: animal waste prevention and treatment wetlands, revegetation of riparian areas in the urban and agricultural environment, streambank stabilization and agricultural land restoration in association with other local agencies and community partners.

East Mountain View Road Restoration Project

This chapter will focus on our most recent urban restoration project on Paradise Creek located in the City of Moscow. The main restoration objectives for this channelized reach of Paradise Creek were: to reduce the amount of sediment entering the creek from urban runoff and to alleviate erosion occurring along streambanks, the creation of a functional floodplain, and the reestablishment of native vegetation along the channel banks and in the floodplain to create a riparian corridor. The project was planned to be constructed in 2001 but was delayed until summer 2002 as a result of increased modeling needs. Revegetation efforts began immediately following construction in the fall of 2002 and will continue in 2003. Monitoring and maintenance of the site will continue for up to ten years, primarily by community volunteers, AmeriCorps members and University students and professors. Future plans for the site include an educational observation deck and boardwalk and a path through the site for the public.

Prior to restoration, the 860 ft reach of stream channel had near vertical, eroding streambanks that were straightened and incised due to dredging activities. The banks were generally steep averaging between 1H:1V and 2H:1V. Streambanks were either exposed soil or covered with reed canary grass and other invasive weeds. Except for a few non-native willows, the site was completely devoid of riparian species to shade the creek. The reach flows from the east to the west at the site and the project boundaries were defined as a city road and bridge to the west, a public charter school upstream to the east, an apartment complex with a parking lot to the south and a house and horse pasture to the north.

Working with the City of Moscow and TerraGraphics Environmental Engineering, PCEI designed a restoration plan to increase the flood storage capacity of this reach by lowering the floodplain by two feet and constructing two major meanders, a narrow low flow channel, and associated wetlands. The constructed channel was intended to mimic natural conditions as much as possible. The lowflow channel was designed with a 3 foot bottom width and a depth of 1.5 feet. In addition, a revegetation plan was devised using exclusively native woody and herbaceous species of the Palouse Basin. Approximately two and a half acres of floodplain were created. The goals of this project were ecological as well as societal. PCEI aimed to reduce listed non-point source pollutants (sediment, bacteria, temperature, and nutrients) in Paradise Creek by decreasing sediment delivery through the installation of shallow wetlands. We also planned to reduce instream erosion by stabilizing severely eroded streambanks and to improve aquatic and riparian habitat by vegetating with native plants. This was fundamentally a community based restoration project, designed to raise citizen awareness about water resources and increase stewardship within our community, as well as provide a recreational, educational and aesthetic benefit.

Channel Stabilization

A variety of bioengineering techniques were used for bank stabilization. Bank revetments were placed in scour susceptible zones along outer bend banks. Extensive revetments were required because of the flashy flow regime of this stream and because of downstream sediment concerns. Bank revetments will also ensure the stability of the channel over time, which was particularly important with the urban setting. At the upstream end of the project, a log crib revetment was utilized for enhanced bank stability as well as to simulate an overhanging bank for shade and habitat. A buried log crib revetment was installed to stabilize the path of the previous channel. The buried log crib was placed in the newly constructed bank to direct the flow of the water in

the new channel. A soil wrap was also placed in front of the log crib. Soil wraps consist of wrapping soil like a burrito using biodegradable fabric made of woven coir yarn. These have an added benefit of being able to be planted into. On the outside of both meander bends, 4 to 5 foot diameter rootwads were installed. On the downstream meander bend, coir logs were used in conjunction with the rootwads to stabilize the toe of the slope. The coir logs can also be planted with native herbaceous vegetation.

The top of the stream channel bank was rounded off to make a smooth transition to the floodplain surface. All outside bank slopes were subsequently seeded with a native riparian grass mix and lined with 100% biodegradable geotextile fabric made of woven coir yarn. Erosion control fabric was installed over the top of the slope crown onto the level edge of the floodplain surface. A low density straw erosion control blanket (ECB) was used in lower energy areas and a high density coir fiber ECB was used in higher energy areas. The organic fiber geotextiles, coir logs, and ECB's will retain structural integrity for multiple growing seasons allowing time for the establishment of dense native herbaceous ground cover on all bank surfaces.

A portion of the excavated soil was used to fill in the existing channel, the remainder of the excavated soil (5,000 cu. yards) was moved off site and used by the City of Moscow and the local university.

Wetland Creation

Two newly constructed wetland areas were also created for a total of 5,260 sq. feet of wetlands. Designs called for two shallow oxbow wetlands but when it came to construction, one of the wetlands was expanded to include two, for a total of three wetlands. These wetland areas are approximately 1–1.5 feet in depth and have a 5:1 slope on each side. An existing wetland at the site was extended to enhance its habitat. In November of 2002, habitat structures constructed by AmeriCorps volunteers were installed in both wetland areas. The habitat structures were built with salvaged logs approximately six inches in diameter and six to ten feet long and bundled together. They were anchored using wooden stakes and boulders and then filled with wood chips to simulate decaying logs. Four structures were installed in all, two vertical and two horizontal.

Revegetation

Our native revegetation strategy included grass seed, woody and herbaceous stock. Of particular emphasis was the Quaking Aspen — Dougles Hawthorn riparian plant community, which was historically found along streams and wetlands in the Palouse Basin and is now endangered. Planting commenced immediately after construction. We began by harrowing the floodplain area and seeding an upland seed mix of: ⅓ Idaho Fescue, ⅓ Mountain Brome and ⅓ Secar Bluebunch Wheatgrass at a density of approximately one lb per 1000 square foot. The wetland depressions and lower streambanks were seeded with a native wetland mix of: ¼ Bluejoint Reedgrass, ¼ American Sloughgrass, ¼ Tufted Hairgrass and ¼ Fowl Mannagrass at the same density. In addition to native seeding we also experimented with seeding of sterile winter wheat in attempt to gain vegetative cover more quickly.

Planting of over 1,500 woody trees and shrubs began with the second annual Paradise Creek Watershed Festival which included 10 classes of fourth graders from Moscow schools and University of Idaho volunteers. Under the supervision of PCEI staff, the bulk of the planting was completed during the following weeks by volunteers. The following woody species were integrated into the design: Quaking Aspen (*Populous tremuloides*), Dougles Hawthorn (*Crataegus douglassi*), Rocky Mt. Maple (*Acer glabrum*), Thinleaf Alder (*Alnus incana*), Red Osier Dogwood (*Cornus stolonifera*), Serviceberry (*Amelanchier alnifolia*), Syringa (*Philadelphus lewisii*), Chokecherry (*Prunus virginiana*), Nootka Rose (*Rosa nutkana*), Douglas Spirea (*Spirea douglasii*), Common Snowberry (*Symphoricarpos albus*) and Ponderosa Pine (*Pinus ponderosa*). Our budget allowed us to focus the planting on larger nursery stock; the majority of woody plants were one, two or five gallon sizes. As is the procedure at all our restoration sites, all woody plants (with the exception of conifers) are protected from rodent damage and browse by 18 inch blue plastic tree protectors, secured in place by bamboo stakes. Ponderosa pines on site had shorter 6 inch tubes around their base.

Herbaceous plants included: Water Sedge (*Carex aquatilis*), Creeping Spikerush (*Elocharis palustris*), Baltic Rush (*Juncus balticus*), Common Rush (*Juncus effuses*), Daggerleaf Rush (*Juncus ensifolius*), and Small-fruited bulrush (*Scirpus mircocarpus*). A total of 1,140 herbaceous plants were planted in 10 cubic inch sizes. Plugs were inserted in the coir logs using a dibble. In the areas without coir logs, herbaceous plants were placed along the stream banks, keeping in mind the ecology of each species. In addition to the nursery plugs, PCEI staff, interns and volunteers transplanted seventy Blue Flag Iris bulbs (*Iris missiouriensis*). These bulbs were dug up and stored in pots during the Summer 2002 construction season.

Planting at this restoration site will continue into Spring 2003. The bulk of this will be native willow cuttings planted near the top of all streambanks and around the wetlands, especially focusing on potentially unstable areas. Eventually willows, Red Osier dogwood and other species will provide intertwining root networks for long-term bank stabilization in these areas. Willow cutting will be planted using a hydraulic stinger, which consists of a 5 foot 1 inch diameter pipe that is connected to a water pump, and used by inserting it into the ground to make a hole for each cutting. Cuttings are planted so that ⅓ of the plant is above ground and ⅔ below ground.

Community Partners

Hundreds of volunteers from the Moscow community made this project possible and will continue their stewardship and enjoyment of the site for years to come. A total $143,500 of in kind match has been generated to date. IDEQ nonpoint source grant funds expended on the project total $132,000. The amount of match for this project far exceeds the 40% requirement. Partners and local match include: TerraGraphics Environmental Engineering, AmeriCorps*NCCC, City of Moscow, Washington State University and University of Idaho students, Moscow Elementary School Students, Synthetic Industries, and community volunteers.

Lessons Learned

As is the case with restoration project designs, our actual construction in the field did not completely mirror the design on paper. A few modifications were made based on site conditions at the time of construction. These included enlarging one of the planned wetland areas to include two shallow depressions. During construction of the last log crib revetment, the design was a bit more flexible compared to the upstream structures and was built based on availability of materials. Also during construction, coir logs were added between rootwads on the downstream meander bend.

In December of 2002, we observed some small rills forming near the top of the outside, upstream meander bend. The rills were forming as a result of standing water in the floodplain and probably exacerbated by impervious surfaces adjacent to the project. We were concerned about the erosion undermining the stability of the rootwad revetment and erosion control fabric below. So, on the morning of our first snow we rented a mini excavator, dug out the problem area, and placed cobble and boulder sized rocks in the depression. Moscow has been experiencing a mild winter with lower than average snowfall and we expect this trouble section to remain stable.

Our first high water event occurred after 3 inches of rain over two days at the end of January 2003. The creek swelled to the top of the new channel and flowed overland in much of the floodplain. After the water subsided, all revetments and plants remained intact.

Overall we are pleased with the success of this restoration project and we are especially appreciative of the community support it has enjoyed. As is the nature of land rehabilitation, the primary determining factor is time in achieving habitat and stabilization goals. We are eager to watch this project grow and become a sustainable natural system within the City of Moscow. The extent to which the stated objectives were met will be evaluated through further monitoring efforts by PCEI, the University of Idaho and additional project partners. Use of the term restoration is debatable, since we are not truly restoring this piece of ground to a former more pristine state. Rather, we are attempting to restore the functions of the creek by providing a functioning floodplain and associated wetlands, a diverse meandering stream channel, and native Palouse Basin habitat in a setting that has much public benefit.

CHAPTER 28

New Orleans, LA, and Other Cities Restore Inner-City Parks and Their Waterways

Jim Miara

Before Hurricane Katrina blasted through in August 2005, New Orleans's City Park was a recreational paradise, the city's outdoor heart and soul. Annually more than 11 million people visited its grounds, playing golf, tennis, soccer, and baseball; strolling through its grove of mature live oaks (some of them 600 years old); visiting the New Orleans Museum of Art; attending weddings and other celebrations; boating; picnicking; or pursuing myriad other activities the park accommodated.

Established in 1854, when a 100-acre parcel near the center of New Orleans was willed to the city by its former owner, City Park expanded over time to more than 1,300 acres, making it one of the largest urban parks in the country. Katrina left 90 percent of the park covered with floodwater and its infrastructure in shambles. But a year and half later, City Park is again beginning to hum with activity as New Orleanians find refuge and respite there. The story of its valiant struggle to recover from the storm testifies to both the resilience of a city and the healing role that parks can play in a time of extraordinary psychological stress.

No city in the country today is more in need of the physical and psychological benefits that parks can offer than still-recovering New Orleans. Much of the city remains in ruins and less than half of New Orleans's pre–Katrina population of 485,000 has returned.

Many who did stay or return are still suffering. According to a June 2006 report in the *New York Times*, "New Orleans is experiencing what appears to be a near epidemic of depression and post-traumatic stress disorders, one that mental health experts say is of an intensity rarely seen in this country."

"These are classic post-trauma symptoms," Susan Howell, a political scientist at the University of New Orleans, told the *Times*. Howell, who conducted a survey on how people are coping with everyday life, said, "People can't sleep, they're irritable, feeling that everything's an effort."

People Helping Their Park

The evidence that city parks contribute to improved physical and mental health of

Originally published as "Parks for the New New Orleans," *Land & People*, Vol. 19, No. 1, Spring 2007. Published by The Trust for Public Land, San Francisco, CA. Reprinted with permission of the publisher.

residents continues to mount — beyond the expectations of even the most enthusiastic park advocates. Under normal conditions, parks — even small oases of grass and trees amid the concrete and asphalt of the metropolis — allow city dwellers to commune with nature, interact with neighbors in a serene environment, exercise or lounge, and return home refreshed. In New Orleans, where once vibrant neighborhoods remain piles of rubble, where crime is rising and uncertainty reigns, the need for a place of serenity is magnified beyond calculation. In this environment, City Park has become a refuge, a reminder of happier times, and a harbinger of the city's return to life.

The road back was a long and difficult one, though. With a few minor exceptions, every facility, every maintenance building, and every piece of maintenance equipment was severely damaged or destroyed. The park's pre–Katrina staff of 240 was reduced to 23, and Bob Becker, CEO of City Park, was left in charge to pick up the pieces, literally. "We got back the first week after the storm and there was tremendous damage," recalls Becker, a deep-rooted New Orleans resident.

"All our equipment was destroyed, and we couldn't even get back into our office until the first week of October. But people were anxious to get back in the park. There weren't a lot of other diversions. Movies and even private health clubs were closed. So people wanted to use the park, and they were willing to help to get it going." The first to turn out were tennis players. Falling tree limbs had shattered fences in the tennis area and remained lying athwart them like triumphant wrestlers. The courts and surrounding facilities also were wrecked.

The volunteers began by cleaning up the tennis house, then removing limbs and debris from the fences and courts. The fences were repaired and their windscreens hung. The courts were swept, the nets replaced, and by mid–October — less than two months after the storm and with much of the city still paralyzed — people were playing tennis at City Park.

The golf courses were a little more problematic to revive, but the same need for recreation inspired the city's golfing community. "The golf courses were flooded, and we didn't even have lawn mowers," says Becker. "So when the waters receded, we decided to get the driving range open — give people a chance to get out their frustrations whacking a golf ball and at the same time generate some revenue for the park."

With his skeleton staff and an infusion of volunteers, Becker managed to clean up the driving range, though there was still no fresh water for irrigation and no electricity to power lights. Adding to the difficulty, the ballpickup machine was destroyed and the supply of balls was severely depleted. Nevertheless, Becker says, when the driving range opened in late February, "the turnout was tremendous. When we ran out of balls, we'd blow a whistle and golfers would go out and retrieve them. We only had a few balls, so there was a lot of whistle-blowing."

Sports enthusiasts weren't the only ones who needed their park. One day last spring Becker received a call from a woman asking if the park's Storyland facility was available to rent. Storyland is a playground adorned with 26 exhibits from children's fairy tales, and for generations it has been a traditional venue for birthday parties. The woman wanted to celebrate her young daughter's birthday there, in the same place she had celebrated hers as a child. Storyland was still closed but, according to Becker, the woman pleaded: "I'm not having a birthday for my daughter in a gutted house. I want it in a nice setting." Two weeks later — just in time for the birthday celebration — Storyland reopened. The pattern continues. "Once we get something back open, it is used," says Becker. "Well used."

To date, 6,500 volunteers have invested more than 34,000 hours in bringing City Park back after Hurricane Katrina. Observers feel that City Park's slow rise from the ruins is an important symbol for beleaguered New Orleanians. John Beckman served as an urban planning consultant to the Philadelphia-based planning firm of Wallace Roberts & Todd, which oversaw the Bring New Orleans Back Commission, charged by Mayor Ray Nagin to plan for the city's recovery. "Volunteers are coming in, and so is outside capital," Beckman says of City Park. "It gives people the feeling that, yes, there's movement. Yes, things will be better." Restoring the park also is a goal on which all New Orleans residents can agree, says Ed Marshall, who serves on TPL's New Orleans Advisory Board. "City Park is this wonderful piece of earth where political differences, ethnic background, and economic status cease to matter. It has been for years New Orleans's common denominator and our most treasured landscape."

Hope for a Better Park System

Hurricane Katrina was unquestionably a disaster for the city of New Orleans. But the rebuilding process presents unprecedented opportunities to create a model city with a new park system as a unifying element. "New Orleans has large parks — City Park, Audubon Park — that are centrally located, but it doesn't have many smaller parks in neighborhoods," notes Larry Schmidt, director of TPL's New Orleans office. "This is a chance to build a park system that links the city together. In the midst of this colossal rebuilding effort, we can't forget the value of parks." Major cities across the country have learned the value of parks and are in various stages of retrofitting green space into the urban fabric. Both Atlanta and Boston are replacing decrepit infrastructure with new green space, parks, and trails.

In Chicago, Mayor Richard Daley recently announced his intention to make the Second City the first city in green space. Chicago boasts impressive parks near downtown and along the shore of Lake Michigan, the newest being highly regarded Millennium Park, opened in 2004. Now the greening effort is moving into underserved neighborhoods. Chicago is replacing asphalt schoolyards with grass, adding gardens in high-rise buildings, and insisting that developers planning projects along the Chicago River include a public promenade along the river's banks. Renewed enthusiasm for urban green spaces is fueled by both aesthetic and practical considerations, urban planners explain. Green cities are more visually appealing, to be sure, but statistics show they are also safer and effectively increase the value of surrounding properties, which means more tax revenue.

"New Orleans has a great opportunity to create a model city where people go and say, 'Wow, they did it right,'" says Ron Sims, executive of King County, Washington, and a strong advocate of park development in his Puget Sound county. "Parks are an essential part of the infrastructure. Good neighborhoods have them and bad ones don't. A great people doesn't rebuild past mistakes. New Orleans officials have to have vision, a vision that promises people a better future. And nothing enhances the value of the urban experience more than a walkable city with trails and parks."

Alex Garvin, a principal with the New York City–based planning firm Alex Garvin & Associates, makes the case for how parks enhance property values in his book *The American City, What Works and What Doesn't.* But he also emphasizes the health and utilitarian benefits of parks, especially in New Orleans.

"New Orleans is an unusual city, and rebuilding has to pay attention to historical conditions. But parks in flood-prone areas can be useful," explains Garvin. "Boulder, Colorado, has a park that floods every spring. It is designed to absorb water. When the water recedes, the park goes back to being picnic areas and ballfields." He cites another example: "Louisville's waterfront park is designed to absorb overflow from the Ohio River. New Orleans can apply the same concepts."

The Case for More and Better Parks

In the aftermath of Hurricane Katrina, Mayor Ray Nagin established the Bring New Orleans Back (BNOB) Commission to create a framework for reconstruction. Chaired by Joseph Canizaro, a local developer and past president of the Urban Land Institute, the commission was composed of approximately 200 members — experts in a variety of fields, from geologists and engineers to The Trust for Public Land's Larry Schmidt, who cochaired the land use subcommittee.

The commission's goal was to create a comprehensive master plan for rebuilding, concentrating on safety issues but also emphasizing aesthetic elements, particularly parks and open space interwoven throughout the city. One recommendation envisioned new parks in floodprone areas that would combine both aesthetic and utilitarian functions. In these low-lying areas, parks would incorporate cleverly landscaped canals or reservoirs capable of handling stormwater runoff.

Yet to many New Orleans residents, creating parks seemed a low priority in the midst of all the damage and chaos, where so many problems cried out for immediate attention. Even Bob Becker, manager of City Park, sympathized with his neighbors' reaction. "If you are in a devastated neighborhood, the condition of the local park is the last thing you think of," he acknowledges. "Government has to make decisions about what is important, and you take levees before parks."

But the commission, as it was charged to do, adopted a long-range view. Its mission was to create a master plan that went beyond repairing neighborhoods to restoring a world-class city. And a hallmark of all such cities is parks and open spaces. "With the discussion so far focusing on infrastructure," the commissioners wrote in the "Parks and Open Space" section of the report, "we might remember to ask a question: If the city is not also a beautiful and inspiring place, why would anyone want to live there?"

The report noted that while New Orleans boasts the large, nationally renowned Audubon Park and City Park, open space in most of the city's neighborhoods was nonexistent or inadequate. During the rebuilding, the report recommended, open space should be added and neighborhood connectivity achieved by thoughtful use of the city's "neutral grounds," wide roadway medians that could be used by pedestrians and cyclists and for public transportation. The report also recommended incorporating canal rights-of-way into the park system.

The report outlined potential sites for new parks in various districts and identified specific areas within which property could be acquired and parks created — which specific properties might be acquired would be determined with ongoing citizen involvement.

The key issue, commission consultant Beckman says, is, "How many people will return?" The commission anticipates a phased resettlement. "We will talk to people, involve them in the process, as they return," Beckman says. By midsummer of 2006, news reports indicated that houses, even severely damaged houses, in virtually every neighborhood were selling for higher than expected prices. According to the reports, many of the buyers were developers and investors, an encouraging sign of confidence in the city's future. "Many neighborhoods have already gone ahead and tried to plan," said Beckman. "There is an awareness that parks are important in the redevelopment of New Orleans."

Waterfront Park

The BNOB Commission enthusiastically endorsed ongoing efforts to increase access to the Mississippi River. New Orleans is a working port, and for centuries public access to the river's banks has been blocked by loading docks and warehouses. Many of these in the downtown area are no longer in use, however, and over recent decades the city replaced such derelict structures with the Moon Walk, Woldenberg Park, and the Riverwalk, creating a pleasant open space along the river from Canal Street to Esplanade Avenue.

Since 1999, when TPL opened its New Orleans office, Larry Schmidt has made considerable progress developing plans to extend recreational space even farther along the riverfront. A new park along the riverfront proposed by TPL will be close to a mile in length and about 150 yards to 200 yards wide, and will include bicycle and walking paths, benches, a museum, a restaurant, and a concert venue. In April 2003 the Port of New Orleans signed a memorandum of understanding with TPL, assigning the organization the task of designing the park and then finding sources to fund its construction and maintenance.

The BNOB Commission embraced the TPL plan and, in fact, recommended broadening its scope, suggesting that the riverfront walkway be extended all the way from the Industrial Canal to Jefferson Parish.

"New Orleans has been handed a unique and rare opportunity to utilize parks as a catalyst for rebuilding our city," said developer Joseph Canizaro, who also serves on TPL's New Orleans Advisory Council, of which he was founding chair. "We need to utilize every incentive that can be offered to stimulate our economic recovery. It has been proven time and time again, across the nation, that parks and open space do exactly that."

The riverfront park has already stimulated significant investment activity. Samuel & Company, a major Miami-based developer, is far along in negotiations with Entergy, the New Orleans electric power company, to purchase an abandoned power plant next to the proposed park. "I'm sure we'll get it done," said company principal Michael Samuel. "This project will be a mixed-use city within the city. It's going to take a rundown area and make it beautiful."

Samuel, who has undertaken similar projects in Miami and Baltimore, said the renovated building will include residential units and retail and office space. It will also include a major music venue. He estimated the cost of renovating the power plant and building a bridge connector to the waterfront park at around $500 million.

Rebuilding Communities

Schmidt says that TPL will be actively engaged in the rebuilding process. "We will continue to emphasize the opportunity New Orleans has to create beautiful and valuable open space, but we will do it while working with neighborhood planning groups," he explains. "If the community wants a park, we will help them design it. We will help with the design of neutral space along roadways. We will help with the restoration of City Park, replanting trees, or building community gardens. We want to be an intellectual resource and help with land acquisition."

A recent $3.2 million grant from the Rockefeller Foundation will facilitate the rebuilding planning process begun by the BNOB, notes John Beckman. As people return — or choose not to return — determining the location of new parks will become easier. "The networking of neighborhoods through parks provides many benefits, especially a connectedness that does not exist right now," Beckman explained. "As the experience in City Park shows, at a very basic level, people understand the importance of open space."

CHAPTER 29

Philadelphia, PA, and Other Cities Clean Contaminated Sites to Restore Their Aging Riverfront Areas

Roshi Pelaseyed

Hundreds of municipalities in the U.S. were developed along waterways to facilitate industrial development and transport of goods. The location helped these communities prosper, but also left them scarred with hundreds of abandoned, contaminated sites. Federal legislation and state efforts have helped many to reverse this trend and reuse these waterfront areas. The list of famous locales that have undertaken riverfront brownfield redevelopment includes Brooklyn, Pittsburgh, Richmond, Virginia, Memphis, Cincinnati, Reno, Nevada, and more recently Los Angeles. Numerous smaller municipalities also have used creative financing and federal and state resources to reinvigorate their waterfronts.

The Philadelphia Metropolitan Region provides a case study of the latest trends in brownfield redevelopment. Brownfields, as defined by the U.S. Environmental Protection Agency are "abandoned, idled, or under-used industrial and commercial facilities where expansion or redevelopment is complicated by real or perceived environmental contamination." This broad definition encompasses any contaminated property from a local dry cleaner to a massive industrial site.

The biggest hurdle in bringing these properties to better and higher uses is the perceived risk of contamination and the fear of liability for clean-up. Yet, redevelopment of these sites makes economic sense in the face of the nationwide efforts to stop sprawl and to make use of existing infrastructure, for in-place infrastructure reduces the cost of redevelopment. In recent years, the EPA has helped communities overcome these barriers to redevelopment by providing financial assistance through grants and revolving loan funds and by publicizing brownfield redevelopment efforts.

As the fourth largest metropolitan region, the Philadelphia Metropolitan area is home to more than 6 million people and numerous brownfield sites. According to the 2000 U.S. Census, it was the slowest growing large metropolitan area in the '90s. The city has lost most of its population to its suburbs, where a 3 percent population growth has led to a 33 percent increase in development of greenfields. According to the Metropolitan Philadelphia

Originally published as "Riverfront Brownfield Redevelopment," *The Commissioner*, Winter 2003. Published by American Planning Association, Chicago, IL. Reprinted with permission of the publisher.

Policy Center, a nonprofit policy research organization, approximately one-fourth of the nation's population and consumer buying power lives within one day's drive of the area.

The region is also home to hundreds of abandoned industrial sites, the legacy left by industries. To turn this around, the region is taking advantage of the available financial tools to convert these brownfields into ratables, such as luxury waterfront townhouses to multipurpose community centers. It is no surprise that President George W. Bush chose Conshocken, a community just on the border of Philadelphia on the Schuylkill River, to announce his new brownfields legislation last February: the Small Business Liability Relief and Brownfields Revitalization Act will double available funds for brownfield redevelopment for fiscal year 2003 to $200 million.

The City on the Delaware

Philadelphia, despite its historic significance and its strong prominence in the health-care and pharmaceuticals industries, has struggled to become competitive with most metropolises around the nation. Although the city is home to two rivers, the Schuylkill and the Delaware, most of the city's redevelopment efforts ignored that potential, leaving the riverfront areas to trash, crumbling factories, and other unwanted uses. But times have changed. In November 2001, the city unveiled plans to create an American Venice in the tradition of great European cities.

The city soon unveiled plans for redevelopment of two riverfront areas. The City Planning Commission has developed a plan for an 11-mile expanse along the Delaware River to convert this underutilized area into residential and recreational uses, allowing the public greater access to the water.

The proposal includes an incremental clean-up strategy, including phytoremediation. This is remediation technique using plants to remove or stabilize contaminants

thereby transforming the blighted landscape into flowering fields. Other innovative techniques that will be used in this area include use of porous pavements on roadways, wetland/vegetated swales along the roads, green infiltration trenching along street, bike trails and parking areas for water quality improvement that will reduce the need for wastewater treatment infrastructure. The cost of clean-up for the area is estimated to be at least $250 million.

The visions for the North Delaware Riverfront include:

- A trail and a linear river park.
- A river road with public access to the river.
- Thousands of new residential and commercial units.

This will require zoning changes and incentives to entice suburban developers. The plans have already captured the EPA's attention. In March 2002, the EPA announced its intention to provide technical assistance and guidance through its regional Smart Growth Agreement with the City of Philadelphia. The city has committed funding from its neighborhood economic stimulus fund to bring to fruition.

In addition to these plans, the Schuylkill River Development Council also has outlined similar plans for the western part of the city. The goal is to create a river trail that connects the existing popular Kelly Drive path to Center City, Philadelphia's downtown district, to encourage further development.

"Two Cities, One Exciting Waterfront"

Nearly a dozen New Jersey towns share the Delaware River with Philadelphia, affording spectacular views of Philadelphia's skyline. Camden, once a bustling industrial port, is home to RCA and Campbell Soup Company. Camden is the poorest municipality in New Jersey, and among the poorest in the nation, with an annual unemployment rate of 12 percent and a median household income of $23,421. In its heyday, the Camden riverfront, known as Cooper's Ferry, served as a tourist destination. The area boasted hotels, taverns, pleasure gardens, and residences. With the economic shift from manufacturing to service and river transport giving way to other alternative modes of transportation, Camden slid into decline.

Camden's salvation came in 1984 with the establishment of the Cooper's Ferry Development Association by the city, the Campbell Soup Company, RCA, other private companies, and government and civic leaders. Since then, the waterfront has been transformed into an entertainment mecca with the infusion of millions of public dollars. Just seven years after the State of New Jersey's announcement of $52 million funding for its development, the New Jersey State Aquarium opened in 1992. It is now one of the five most visited attractions in the region. The addition of a four-acre $9 million horticultural playland, the Children's Garden, made this destination even more attractive. Other new attractions on Camden waterfront include the Tweeter Center — a $56 million indoor-outdoor entertainment facility that can seat up to 25,000 people, and a minor league baseball stadium, Campbell Fields.

While Cooper's Ferry has made the plans for the rebirth of Camden's waterfront, the Delaware River Port Authority of Pennsylvania and New Jersey, a regional transportation and economic development agency, and owner and operator of four of the river bridges, has financed most of the developments. It has invested more than $200 million in waterfront projects on both sides of the river. Just last summer, it provided $2.5 million for the completion of the pier and visitors center for USS *New Jersey* battleship, one of the latest tourist attractions in Camden. Another high-priced investment is the $32 million tram to link Philadelphia's Penn's Landing to the Camden waterfront.

As Camden has made steady progress in redeveloping this side of the waterfront, plans on the other side have been at a virtual standstill. Philadelphia's plan for Penn's Landing is a family entertainment center to house, among others, the Please Touch Children's Museum. Since 1997, the city has relied on the promise of one developer to create this magnet. Yet not a single brick has been laid due to continued delays in starting construction. The city is attempting to get construction started by March 1, 2003.

Despite the setbacks with the planned developments in Philadelphia, plans for capitalizing on the tourism potential of the area are in full gear. The Delaware River Port Authority, the agency that has created many of the existing tourist attractions along the river, recently announced the development of a new nonprofit agency to coordinate all tourism marketing efforts.

A Public-Private Partnership

The Borough of Paulsboro also has tackled brownfield redevelopment. This 2.1-square–mile borough of 6,535 residents ranks 20 on the list of 100 most stressed municipalities in New Jersey with 21 percent of the population living below poverty level in 1990.

The borough maintained a relatively small industrial base, with BP and Essex Chemical as two of its major industries. Paulsboro suffered an economic blow when these two entities ceased operation due to stricter environmental regulations. The closing of the Mobil plant in a neighboring town has further eroded employment. Lack of developable land is another impediment to Paulsboro's economic growth as most land use is residential.

The 150-acre BP property, the largest available land for industrial/commercial development, is located directly across the Delaware River from the Philadelphia International Airport. The property, better known as tank farm, served as an oil storage and distribution center. Several years ago, BP, in an effort to dispose of unused properties around the nation, started investigating the possibility of alternative uses for the property. The company retained an engineering firm to conduct a market feasibility study to determine the highest and best use for the property. At the same time, BP initiated discussion with Essex Chemical about the adjacent property that was used as a gypsum landfill. Essex was receptive to BP's suggestion for redevelopment of the area and pledged its willingness to follow suit with BP plans.

From the start, BP approached the borough about its plans. Because of the location of the site, one of the initial thoughts was to develop the site as a niche port. It was also important to make adequate provisions for public access to the waterfront. The recommended site development plan includes:

• **Waterfront Port Development**, including a 900-foot wharf structure that can accommodate mid-sea ocean-going vessels up to 800 feet in length. The wharf has upland storage of 30 to 40 acres. The location of the borough and an analysis of river traffic indicate the site could be partially developed as a port facility. Paulsboro is among the four South Jersey municipalities under consideration for the Port Inland Distribution Network.
• **Industrial/Commercial Development** at the south end of the project site, adjacent to existing industrial uses (five-acre parcels, to be used individually or combined).
• **River Gateway**, a commercial/retail development with public access to the riverfront.
• **Open Space** provision consists of a green buffer to separate the industrial uses from the surrounding neighborhood and creation of a neighborhood park.

One of the most innovative components of this project is the building of a solar plant on the Essex-owned former gypsum landfill.

The plant, the largest thin-film solar plant in the Northeast, will generate power for the operation of the on-site environmental remediation equipment. While the original plan called for the location of the plant on a more pristine portion of the site, known as the employee ballfield, to increase the development potential of the site, it was decided to move the plant to the landfill, which meant an additional $250,000 for its construction.

The most challenging part of the project is creating access to the site. To reach the riverfront from Interstate 295, the north-south highway which connects the town to the Northeast U.S. market, traffic has to go through a residential neighborhood. To connect the site directly to I-295, an overpass would be needed. This part of the project has proven to be challenging. In addition to the $25 million price tag, the project has to make the list of the transportation improvement plan created by the regional metropolitan planning agency. The borough was able to secure funding from the same agency for initial studies. The construction of the overpass and the site's development are still several years away.

The Feds to the Rescue

One of the brownfield tools the federal government has made available to localities is the grant program. The EPA Brownfield Pilot grants provide $200,000 to municipalities and counties to conduct an inventory of the brownfield areas and investigate the extent of contamination in order to determine a remediation plan and future end uses. More than 300 localities have used these grants. In the Delaware Valley, all suburban counties in Pennsylvania have been awarded an EPA Pilot grant to identify potential brownfield sites for development. On the other side of the river, the Township of Pennsauken in Camden County received a pilot grant. The township has 700 acres of vacant and underused property along its seven miles of riverfront on the Delaware River

Since 1980, Pennsauken Township has undertaken an aggressive economic redevelopment strategy that targets the riverfront. First, it designated the entire area as a waterfront management area under New Jersey environmental guidelines that limit certain types of development and preserve open space. Then it acquired 230 acres of tidal marshland.

The township has identified several properties suitable for redevelopment. Among them is Petty's Island, a 450-acre island in the Delaware River between Camden and Philadelphia. Once an oil storage and distribution facility, the island presently hosts only a container cargo shipping operation. Another major site is a 137-acre inactive landfill used for construction debris and home to a warehouse. The area also includes 17 acres of scattered smaller sites. The township has used the EPA grant to investigate the contamination level at the sites to ensure their suitability for future development.

Pennsauken hopes that, with the completion of the pilot project, it can embark on an aggressive marketing effort to redevelop its waterfront. With two fiber-optic lines serving the area, and the completion of a light rail line by New Jersey Transit, Pennsauken's waterfront should be an attractive magnet for development for commercial, entertainment, and recreational uses. As in Paulsboro, site access remains a challenging issue that must be addressed along with cleanup and acquisition.

Pennsauken has faced some resistance from the site owners. For example, site visits for the EPA grant project has been refused by one owner. In the meantime, the township officials learned about possible negotiations between the land owner and the operator of a cogeneration plant to locate a plant on the site; this development would be inconsistent with the township's current plan. More recently, as the township was preparing to embark on the last steps of the acquisition process of another site, the site owner decided to resume operation of the site as an oil storage and distribution facility.

Other Waterfront Dreams

A number of other Delaware River municipalities have plans. Gloucester City, New Jersey's 12th poorest municipality, is another recipient of an EPA Pilot grant; it has been planning for waterfront revitalization for 25 years. With the help from state grants, the city improved its waterfront park with various active and passive recreational opportunities. Future plans include development of brownfields on the southwestern edge of the city.

In the summer of 2002, Gloucester County, where Paulsboro is located, rolled out its brownfields program at Riverwinds, a 1,200-acre multi-use facility erected on a former brownfield site in West Deptford. Using New Jersey's 1992 Local Redevelopment and Housing Law, the county developed a countywide redevelopment plan to reuse old industrial sites and blighted areas, targeting some 14 municipalities. Burlington and Salem counties, New Jersey, as well as Chester and Bucks counties, Pennsylvania, also have expressed interest in riverfront redevelopment. Further south, Wilmington, Delaware, has been rebuilding the waterfront and redeveloping on its brownfield sites.

Developing housing, shopping centers, office complexes and recreational facilities on once-contaminated land is no longer viewed as undesirable. In densely populated areas, it may be the truly feasible option for development. Despite myriad financial incentives and tools, brownfield development has not yet received complete acceptance as a planning strategy.

CHAPTER 30

St. Augustine, FL, Creates New Wetland Areas to Offset Urban Growth Patterns

B.J. Bukata, Debra Segal,
Toney Cubbedge, and Rich Turnbull

As with many municipalities, St. Johns County (SJC), on Florida's Atlantic coast, is experiencing unprecedented growth. This growth creates greater stress on existing infrastructure and such service areas as potable water, sewer, and roads and results in a heightened need to expand that infrastructure. Florida has more than 11 million acres of wetlands, encompassing approximately 30 percent of the state. As a result, infrastructure expansion inevitably results in unavoidable wetland impacts.

Wetlands in Florida are regulated by both the State of Florida (Water Management Districts of Florida Department of Environmental Protection) and the U.S. Army Corps of Engineers. These agencies prefer wetland mitigation to occur on-site when feasible. If on-site mitigation is not feasible, off-site mitigation can be proposed at an alternative site if it occurs within the same hydrologic basin or mitigation bank credits can be purchased from a bank that services the watershed where the impacts are to occur. The prices of private mitigation bank credits vary greatly, from less than $30,000/

credit in northwest Florida where demand is low to over $100,000/credit in Central or South Florida where credits are at a premium.

Most municipal infrastructure improvement or expansion projects require activities such as expanding or constructing new facilities, widening or extending roads, or retrofitting stormwater systems. Many of these projects are typically linear and conducted within or next to County right of way (R/W). As a result, mitigating wetland impacts on-site within an often narrow R/W is rarely feasible due to minimal land area and conflicting land uses. The municipality is thus required to look for suitable off-site areas to perform mitigation or must purchase mitigation bank credits. This scenario has created difficulties for municipalities as they expand their infrastructure.

St. John's County's Approach

SJC has planned several large transportation projects such as construction of new

Originally published as "Balancing County Expansion with Wetland Mitigation," *Land and Water*, Vol. 50, No. 6, November/December 2006. Published by Land and Water, Inc., www.landandwater.com, Fort Dodge, IA. Reprinted with permission of the publisher.

roads, 4-laning existing roads, and upgrading intersections. Realizing that these projects would likely have wetland impacts, SJC purchased two tracts of land totaling over 700 acres in the eastern portion of the County to use as a regional off-site mitigation area (ROMA). The proposed ROMA, called the *Turnbull Regional Mitigation Area* (TRMA), will restore hydrologic patterns along Turnbull Creek and its associated wetlands, improve wetland and upland communities, create additional wetland habitat, create valuable wildlife habitat in previously disturbed areas, and enhance on-site wetland and upland community structure which has been altered by years of silviculture. Additionally, the site will provide opportunities for environmental education and limited public resource-based recreation. The County will implement the mitigation activities in advance of any proposed wetland impacts associated with County capital improvement projects.

Evaluating the Turnbull Creek Property

The TRMA project site consists of two non-adjoining parcels in St. Augustine, St. Johns County, Florida. The parcels are within the St. Johns River Water Management District's (SJRWMD) Basin 5 (Six-Mile and Julington Creek Nested Basin) and are next to an approximately 382-acre County-owned parcel that has been placed in a conservation easement for previous wetland impacts associated with a nearby residential development.

The TRMA includes wetland and upland communities and has been managed for timber production since the early 1990s. Past land practices included clear-cutting uplands and wetlands, planting dense stands of slash pine, constructing logging roads without culverts, and ditching to drain wetland areas. These activities have resulted in widespread soil disturbance and dehydration of large acreages of wetlands, decreasing the ecological function of these areas and reducing habitat quality for wildlife.

Turnbull Creek traverses the northern parcel along the eastern and southeastern boundaries and is an important tributary and headwater stream of Six-Mile Creek, which discharges into the St. Johns River approximately 4 miles downstream. Ditches currently convey water quickly to Turnbull Creek and stages in these ditches are very flashy. Thus, the project area provides important headwater protection as well as water quality improvement and flood attenuation

An environmental assessment of TRMA was conducted by Jones Edmunds and Turnbull Environmental, Inc. (TEI) during July and August 2005. During this assessment the approximate limits and quality of jurisdictional wetland and upland habitats were mapped using handheld global positioning systems (GPS) with accuracy of 3 to 5 meters. All onsite roads, ditches, culverts, berms and other infrastructure were located and assessed to determine their effect on adjacent habitats, paying particular attention to wetlands. These features were compiled into a Geographic Information System (GIS). Jones Edmunds also conducted vegetative community assessments. From these inspections a list of proposed wetland and upland creation, restoration, and enhancement mitigation sites was generated that would restore historic water flow-ways and associated vegetative communities. Each site was characterized by identifying various ecological parameters such as vegetative community, hydrologic properties, degree of disturbance, and in some cases soil properties.

The Proposed Mitigation Plan

Eleven specific mitigation projects were identified at the TRMA site. These projects entail creating 7.6 acres of wetlands in two disturbed borrow areas, removing roads and backfilling adjacent roadside ditches, breaking berms, thinning or removing pines, removing exotic species, and implementing a controlled-burn program. Removing road beds, ditches, and berms will re-create the historic sheetflow in adjacent wetlands as well as other low-lying areas and increase wetland and upland soil water retention. Thinning pines in uplands and implementing a controlled-burn program will enhance the uplands by increasing plant diversity and promoting an uneven-aged stand with older growth.

The length and width of roads, ditches, or berms to be removed/backfilled were estimated using 2004 aerial photography and field measurements. The acreage of these features was then calculated to determine the area of uplands and wetlands that would be restored and the number of plants to be installed. All of these areas will be replanted with native upland and wetland plant species found in more undisturbed areas of the site.

Adjacent reference wetlands were used to identify desirable wetland design elevations for the proposed creation areas. Ground elevations that signify low, high, and target elevations based on the vegetative community were staked and surveyed. The seasonal high water table elevation was also determined in several locations using hydric soil indicators. These elevations were then reviewed to determine the design target elevation range for the created wetlands. Detailed planting plans were also generated.

Hydrologic and Hydraulic Model

A hydrologic and hydraulic (H&H) model was developed for the TRMA to investigate any potential hydrologic changes that could occur upstream or downstream of the mitigation area due to the implementation of the proposed mitigation projects. This model allowed the potential risk of off-site flooding that could occur from the proposed mitigation activities to be assessed.

The model schematic was created using ESRI's ArcGIS 9.1 and geographic informa-

tion system (GIS)-based tools developed by Jones Edmunds. Once the model was parameterized in ArcGIS, it was imported into Interconnected Channel and Pond Routing software package (ICPR) (v 3.02, Service Pack 6b). The ICPR model output for the 25-year 24-hour storm event indicates that the proposed peak discharges at boundary or off-site nodes are expected to decrease or remain the same compared to the existing peak discharges. This is partially because there is minimal topographic change, a typically high groundwater table, and very little internal water storage at the site. Based on the results detailed above, the proposed restoration activities at the TRMA should not result in negative hydrologic effects such as flooding to property owners upstream or downstream of the project site.

Public Use of the Property

When complete, the TRMA will provide limited public use opportunities, such as hiking, bird watching, picnicking, horseback riding, and environmental education. In cooperation with the St. Johns River Water Management District, the SJC School Board has established a Legacy Program at several schools. The Legacy Program is an environmental education program developed for middle and high school students, but also offers opportunities for developing skills in such areas as landscape architecture, carpentry, and recreation management. The TRMA will be incorporated into the Legacy Program to help with some of the management needs at TRMA, while serving as an outdoor classroom for students.

With St. Johns County's unprecedented growth, wetland impacts will be inevitable as new County infrastructure is constructed to keep up with this growth. SJC's proactive approach in purchasing the TRMA will benefit the County in several of the following ways:

- Increasing the publicly-owned lands in the County for environmental education and passive recreation.
- Providing a cost-saving method for supplying wetland mitigation credits (rather than paying a private mitigation bank).
- Ensuring that the ecological benefits that are provided by the mitigation activities occur to County owned lands.

- Improving the ecological quality of regionally significant land as well as downstream receiving waters such as the St. Johns River.
- Solving the wetland mitigation needs upfront so future wetland permitting of upcoming capital improvement projects can be expedited.

CHAPTER 31

St. George, ME, May Acquire Property to Ensure Public Access to Its Shoreline

Peter Ralston

On Horse Point in Port Clyde, a third-generation lobsterman sold his house and wharf to a Washington, D.C., couple for a second home. Another Horse Point house is on the market for $1 million, and the lobsterman's shack on the lot is advertised as a "studio."

Such conversions, typical on the Maine coast, are not a new phenomenon, and as real estate sells for higher and higher prices, the landscape, seascape and character of the coast is changing. High-end real estate conversions are shrinking and squeezing access for commercial fishermen. Some have formed co-ops or pooled money to buy and share a pier. Some just hang on.

Are "people from away" really the problem here? At a meeting last year on a proposed land bank for the town of St. George (Port Clyde is part of St. George), the man who bought the Horse Point house and wharf stood up and admitted he was the kind of guy locals were complaining about.

John McIlwain drew some sympathetic laughter for his candor, and then he made a plea for protecting public access to the sea for the fishermen and for everyone. A senior fellow at Washington's Urban Land Institute, an agency that encourages responsible development to meet people's needs, he said the coast from Maine to Florida is being snatched up by affluent baby boomers, and paying $1 million for a waterfront home in Maine is cheap compared to prices on Cape Cod.

McIlwain and his wife, Wende, bought their property from Alton Jupper, whose grandfather built the house in the 1880s. "We're very lucky; we were the ones who could afford to buy it," said McIlwain, adding that they bought the place in 1997, before prices went sky-high. Shortly after they bought it L.L. Bean heiress Linda Bean said she had thought of buying it for a guesthouse.

For now, Port Clyde, one of Maine's busiest fishing ports, has adequate access to boats and wharves through a co-op and several commercial piers. But if owners sell or if the co-op disbands, what then? Perhaps, suggested McIlwain, St. George could buy some waterfront and lease it to lobstermen and other fishermen. Lobstering remains strong in the Midcoast, and Mellwain — supported by marine biologists — believes low fish stocks for

Originally published as "Hanging On," *Holding Ground: The Best of Island Journal — 1984 to 2004,* Island Institute, 2004. Published by the Island Institute, Rockland, ME. Reprinted with permission of the publisher.

other species will eventually rebound, bringing back Maine's depleted fishing fleet as they do.

Alton Hupper, widowed and living away from the sea in Warren, said he fished 50 years but never made enough to retire until he sold his Horse Point home. "It got so you couldn't afford it," he said. For years taxes on the place he grew up in were manageable. "But you can't own anything on the shore now. The tourists have got it all," he said. "There are more and more people, and there's less and less land."

McIlwain called fishermen "a very independent group of people, deeply devoted to their perception of private property rights. But they're coming to recognize the value of cooperation, that they're all in it together." The St. George land bank, which would make use of a real estate transfer tax to raise money to acquire public access, would require legislative approval before it could be set up. It's a concept that has been successful in Nantucket and Martha's Vineyard, among other places.

St. George harbormaster David Schmanska said he has heard real estate brokers recommend that whatever value the town puts on your property, triple it, and make that your price. Sometimes buyers bid up the sale even higher than the asking price. "The price of real estate has gone bonkers," Schmanska said.

The town's demographics reflect the real estate boom; 60 percent of St. George is now owned by seasonal residents. In winter, "you can drive around and see how many driveways are unplowed," Schmanska said. There are few starter homes left, and the town has no public fish pier. But fishing is still the heart of the community, he believes. A committee is studying various options for access. "The granite quarries are gone. This town is here because of the fishery."

St. George isn't the only place considering how to save working waterfront. Since it came together in 2003 with a dozen people, the Working Waterfront Coalition has expanded to 100 members ranging from state officials to the Maine Lobstermen's Association, Fishermen's Wives, Maine Aquaculture Association and the Island Institute. The coalition is looking at several ways to help fisherman preserve access, said the Island Institute's Rob Snyder.

One way is to expand the state's "circuit-breaker," which makes property taxes more affordable to lower-income residents. Another idea is for the state to develop a "current use" policy, whereby shorefront properties used for commercial fishing would be given a tax break comparable to those for working forests and farms.

Another option, one stirring some excitement, is creation of a $20 million state fund that would be used to help fishermen bridge the gap between asking prices for shore property and wharves, and their collective ability to pay. Such a fund would come from a bond needing legislative as well as popular approval through a referendum.

"The market pressures on the shorefront are real, and are only going to get worse," and David Etnier, former legislator, former fisherman and currently deputy commissioner of the Department of Marine Resources. "The state can only do so much. Maine is a home-rule state," he cautioned. But he said tax breaks plus a working waterfront access fund could be part of the solution. Etnier himself lives on the water in Harpswell in a house his artist father built in 1948. Ten percent of Harpswell's population has a clamming, lobstering or groundfishing license.

In Cundy's Harbor — part of Harpswell — several fishermen are working to purchase Holbrook's Wharf from its Cape Cod owners, and local fishermen have a state planning grant. They're working with The Trust for Public Land, a national conservation agency. Land conservation can dovetail with fishing, as when the York Land Trust worked with local fishermen to preserve one of the last waterfront access points in York, raising $450,000 to match the fishermen's $300,000. The Island Institute's Snyder points to York as an example of a coordinated effort to preserve working waterfront even where the financial challenge is daunting.

Jim Connors, a waterfront coalition member and senior planner with the state's Coastal Program, called the real estate boom "a tidal wave coming at us." He believes a combination of local zoning, state funding and help from conservation groups can save at least some access points. In downeast Jonesboro, the Great Auk Land Trust worked with a property owner and town officials to establish a permanent right-of-way to the Chandler River, a traditional clamming and worm digging area. The walking-only access wouldn't have been created without a willing landowner.

Connors believes the coalition should focus on the fishing industry. Some water-dependent businesses, such as marinas and yacht yards, seem quite capable of competing economically, and Connors sees no need for subsidy there.

Jonathan Wood of Edgecomb bought a 200-year-old house despite neighbors' warning that worm diggers walked right past it to get their boats, and parked their vehicles on the lawn. Because of that, the selling price was discounted — or, as Wood put it, "affordable." Rather than kick diggers off his Cross Piont land, Wood called a meeting and agreed to create a permanent, deeded right-of-way along one edge of his property. He built a six-car lot and diggers pay him a free to park there. A designer of underwater research and aquaculture equipment, Wood said, "The guys who make a living off the water really should have first crack at it. These guys were digging worms before any summer houses were built — if you make a deal that works for everybody, they police it. The only downside is, I don't have complete and utter privacy. But these are good guys; I know them. They work hard for a living," Wood said.

In East Boothbay, fisherman lost a bid to buy the last remaining wharf and a small parcel of land in sheltered, deepwater Little River. The price was $1.2 million. Rachel Tibbetts, sternperson with her lobstering husband,

Gary, said their group raised $825,000 with help from Boothbay Region Land Trust, but a New Jersey couple bought the property first. The new owners want to buy and ship lobsters, but have not offered the use of their wharf to local fishermen.

"It's happening too fast," said Rachel Tibbetts. She has watched as houses are built on nearly every possible waterfront lot in her town. "How beautiful it was," she said.

In Southport, fishermen were able to convince 96-year-old Eliot Winslow, patriarch of a tugboat business, to sell Robinson's Wharf to them instead of selling to a wealthy Californian. Fishermen now run a market and restaurant at the pier. On the Sheepscott River, a former Westport Island boatyard was purchased a few years ago by 16 lobstermen who needed access. They formed North End Coop, helped by Coastal Enterprises Incorporated, an economic development agency with a $300,000 waterfront loan fund. Point East, the business organization that bought the site of the former Maine Yankee nuclear power plant in Wiscasset, has promised Ferry Landing to local fishermen.

Eliza Bailey of Thomaston, former head of the Georges River Land Trust and a former real estate broker, understands the pressures on the coast. She believes many vacation home buyers are seeking refuge from crowds, traffic and the stress of their jobs. She also sees dwindling opportunities for fishermen, and she favors balanced growth. "It won't happen by itself," she said. "The state needs to take a look at what really is a precious resource."

Last year the Maine legislature failed to renew funding for the popular Land for Maine's Future program, which ran out of money. This year, Maine governor John E. Baldacci has proposed borrowing $50 million to revive the program, which has protected coastal and inland properties from development and guaranteed public access. Land for Maine's Future has saved some working farms, but has so far not been involved in preserving working waterfront.

In Waldoboro, where clamming is a $1 million business, generations of local people have dug the mudflats of the Medomak River. Yet even here, upriver from Muscongus Bay, the shorefront is changing. An investment banker purchased an entire point of land and built a $4 million vacation house, boathouse and pier. Today the estate on Havener Point lies across a cove from Gross Neck, where some of the town's lowest-income fishing families live, back from the waterfront: the old and the new, cheek by jowl. As the town's second-largest taxpayer, its owner is topped only by Osram Sylvania, a plant expected to move overseas in the fall of 2005.

New residents are turning the lobster coast into the gold coast. Can the old ways be preserved? It will take a lot of teamwork to make that happen.

CHAPTER 32

Salt Lake City, UT, and Other Cities Benefit from Public and Private Wetlands Preservation and Mitigation Programs

Michael M. Brodsky

Salt Lake City's stunning snow-capped mountains are the first sight greeting air passengers as they approach the city's international airport. As the descent begins, however, passengers are often startled by the somewhat surreal landscape that lies below. A swirling, muted palette of blues, browns, white, and gray is created by the 1,500-square-mile Great Salt Lake, the 30,000 acres of salt flats stretching to the south and west, and more than 400,000 acres of wetlands ringing the lake on its eastern and northern shores — all encircled by the towering Wasatch and Oquirrh mountain ranges.

This abstract landscape is an important ecosystem — a treasure designated as a site of hemispheric importance by the Western Hemisphere Shorebird Reserve Network council. More than 250 species of shorebirds and waterfowl use Great Salt Lake and its surrounding wetlands as a breeding ground and wintering place. During peak migration periods, 5 million birds rely on the lake and wetlands for feeding, sanctuary, breeding, or migratory stopovers.

In addition to the lake, with its favorable location and blend of fresh and hypersaline water highly attractive to waterfowl, Utah boasts two other points of distinction: it is the second driest state in the country after Nevada — only 1 percent of Utah's land is wetland — and it is one of the nation's most urbanized states.

Most of Utah's urbanization is adjacent to this wetland ecosystem along a 100-mile-long corridor known as the Wasatch Front, where 80 percent of Utah's 2.5 million residents live. Along this corridor, three primary population areas — Salt Lake City, Provo, and Ogden — for decades have been separated by miles of open space and farmland, dotted with small rural and suburban communities.

Today, however, Utah's robust economy, strong economic development programs, and international exposure during the 2002 Olympic Winter Games have spurred unprecedented population growth, predicted to hit 3.5 million by 2020, primarily along the Wasatch Front corridor. New and expanding communities are burgeoning at an incredible pace, filling in these open places to create a corridor that is decidedly more urban than

Originally published as "Utah Banks on Wetlands," *Urban Land*, Vol. 65, No. 4, April 2006. Published by the Urban Land Institute, Washington, DC. Reprinted with permission of the publisher.

rural. And as the corridor continues to fill, development is moving east up the foothills and west toward the lake, getting ever closer to protected wetland areas and their uplands.

It is no wonder, then, that many agencies, organizations and individuals are passionate about preserving Utah's precious — and scarce — wetlands.

The value of Utah's wetlands is widely recognized by federal, state, and county agencies. Additionally, commercial and nonprofit organizations work independently and as partners to preserve these wetlands through a variety of means.

At the forefront of this effort is the U.S. Army Corps of Engineers, Sacramento District. The corps is charged with wetlands restoration and protection as defined by the Clean Water Act and the comprehensive National Wetlands Mitigation Action Plan, issued by the Bush Administration in late 2002. One corps goal, that there be no net loss of wetlands, is pursued through the management of a permit program that closely governs the actions of developers and builders seeking permission for activities affecting such lands. All projects with the potential to affect wetlands must first seek to avoid, then minimize, and finally provide compensation for any impacts on waters of the United States, including wetlands.

Since the corps started tracking wetland impacts in Utah in the early 1990s, it has issued permits affecting 6,321 acres, including wetlands, says Shawn Zinszer, chief of the corps's Intermountain Regulatory Section. More than 9,600 acres of compensatory mitigation has been proposed and accepted as compensation for these impacts, primarily in the form of wetlands creation, restoration, enhancement, and preservation.

A Living, Breathing Ecosystem

Like many wetland areas, the shoreline of Great Salt Lake experiences the fluctuations associated with seasonal and climate changes. Unlike most, however, these wetlands range from fresh to hypersaline water, and because of the shallowness of the lake — 13 feet deep on average — and the gentle grade of its shores, a relatively small rise in the water level can inundate hundreds of thousands of acres of upland shoreline.

Great Salt Lake's average water level is 4,200 feet above sea level, at which it is 75 miles long and 30 miles wide with 335 miles of shoreline — equivalent to the distance between Salt Lake City and Yellowstone National Park in Wyoming. It occupies 1,680 square miles, or 1 million acres, and contains 15.4 acre-feet, or 5 trillion gallons, of water. At the lake's record high of 4,212 feet in 1987, the surface area nearly doubled, expanding to 2,500 square miles and covering with water a majority of the surrounding recreational, industrial, wildlife management, and transportation facilities.

While flood control is a long-recognized value of wetlands, the dramatic fluctuation of the lake level is a natural process that both destroys old habitat and creates the conditions for new vegetation to take hold — thus preserving the mosaic of habitat types that support so many different kinds of bird species. Upland habitat that escapes inundation provides a critical buffer feeding and living space for migratory birds when the lake level is high.

"The lake is a living system that needs room to breathe and, therefore, requires protection from development impacts along its shorelines," explains Lynn de Freitas, executive director at FRIENDS of Great Salt Lake, a volunteer, nonprofit organization working to protect the lake's ecosystem. Over the past 100 years, the lake level has varied as much as 26 feet in elevation. "With the potential for such dramatic fluctuations over time, planners should regard this as a matter of fact," she says. "The periodic flooding — a term that is used when structures and developments are located within the floodplain — while inconvenient to those who have chosen to develop close to the lake, provides the benefits of nutrient dispersal and plant revitalization that is part of the dynamic of wetlands."

Chris Montague, director of conservation programs for the Nature Conservancy, agrees. "Preserving the shorelines and wetlands of Great Salt Lake is critical to protecting a natural resource important well beyond Utah's borders," he says. "This is not just a backyard saline lake. It is a world-class jewel that sustains wildlife visiting from across our hemisphere and improves our quality of life in ways we rarely recognize or appreciate.

"Many people think of Great Salt Lake as a dead sea. On the contrary, the lake and its 400,000 acres of wetlands support innumerable plants, invertebrates, mammals, and birds; provide needed flood control; help clean the water of contaminants; and provide hunting and birding recreation for our citizens."

Great Salt Lake's reputation for bird-watching and recreational activities generates more than $500 million from wildlife enthusiasts visiting the lake. Duck hunting alone, according to a 2001 survey by the U.S. Fish and Wildlife Service, annually accounts for more than $13.3 million in trip and equipment purchases, $21.2 million in total economic output, 240 jobs, and a job income of $6.3 million, which, in turn, generates $1.2 million in state tax revenue and $1.6 million in federal tax revenue.

The ecological and economic sustainability of Great Salt Lake creates a challenge because the lake not only generates billions of dollars for the Utah economy, but also is an extremely fragile and complex system. All agree that a concerted effort needs to be made to protect the lake for future generations, while at the same time accommodating anticipated residential and commercial development along the Wasatch Front corridor.

Public Sector Preservation Efforts

Many public endeavors are striving to protect Utah's wetlands. Nonprofit conservation organizations joining this effort include the Nature Conservancy, National Audubon Society, FRIENDS of Great Salt Lake, and Ducks Unlimited, one of numerous duck clubs. Federal agencies lending their support include the Utah Reclamation Mitigation and Conservation Commission, and the federal Bear River Migratory Bird Refuge. State agencies include the Governor's Office of Planning and Budget, and the Utah Department of Natural Resources, including its divisions of Wildlife Resources, and Forestry, Fire, and State Lands.

The federal Utah Reclamation Mitigation and Conservation Commission was established specifically to support the acquisition of vital wetland properties; support the restoration, enhancement, and rehabilitation of state and federally managed wetlands adjacent to Great Salt Lake; restore and manage commission-acquired properties; and develop and implement wetlands strategies in support of the conservation plans developed by Davis and Box Elder counties, which border Great Salt Lake. The commission also partners with nonprofit agencies such as the Nature Conservancy and the National Audubon Society in their efforts to protect, preserve, and mitigate damage to these wetlands.

The Nature Conservancy established an office in Salt Lake City in 1986 and has purchased wetlands or established conservation easements using public and private funds. Over the past 20 years, in partnership with the federal mitigation commission and other major partners, the conservancy created the Great Salt Lake Shorelands Preserve, an undiked natural landscape consisting of 11 contiguous shoreline miles and more than 4,000 acres of salt- and freshwater marshes, ponds, pools, sloughs, and mudflats located between the Farmington Bay Waterfowl Management Area and the Antelope Island State Park Causeway. Home to an award-winning visitor center, the preserve's rich feeding ground for tens of thousands of migrating birds has been the site of some of the largest gatherings of wildlife ever observed on Great Salt Lake. In total, the Nature Conservancy has helped to preserve more than 10,000 acres of wetlands around the lake.

The National Audubon Society, also in partnership with the mitigation commission, has been working in a broad area called the South Shore Ecological Reserve, comprising 8,000 acres on the southern and eastern shores of Great Salt Lake. Much of this area has already been acquired by entities that need to mitigate wetland impacts and want to develop an area reserved for wetlands and avian wildlife, particularly shorebirds. The National Audubon Society Gillmor Sanctuary covering 1,416 acres is located in this area. The organization also owns part of and manages the Lee Creek Natural Area, which covers 305 acres.

FRIENDS of Great Salt Lake uses advocacy and education as tools to encourage sustainability and smart growth principles for development along the Wasatch Front. The group works collaboratively with public and private partnerships in the watershed to promote accountability, lake management strategies, and development of policies that are consistent with good stewardship practices.

Ducks Unlimited, likewise, serves as a steward for wetlands preservation. Since it started conservation work in Utah in 1987, organization programs have benefited 38,320 acres through easements, fee title acquisitions, and restoration/enhancement of wetlands at a total expense of just over $6 million. In addition, the organization has provided technical assistance affecting 35,000 acres of Utah land.

Private Sector Mitigation Programs

Private mitigation and mitigation banking are also viable methods of wetland protection used by Utah development companies. All private sector mitigation programs work in conjunction with the U.S. Army Corps of Engineers' regulatory and permitting programs, after the corps ensures that developers have first sought to avoid and minimize activities that affect wetlands. Impacts must be compensated for through the restoration and/or preservation of existing wetlands, or the creation of new wetlands.

While several large Utah corporations, including Kennecott Utah Copper and the Salt Lake Airport Authority, have created wetland mitigation areas, one company, Diversified Habitats, manages the only private wetland bank operating in Utah — and one of the few found in the United States.

Diversified Habitats works in conjunction with the Army Corps of Engineers and other public agencies to develop wetland mitigation sites that can be used as part of an exchange by a developer whose project will damage or destroy an existing wetland. Diversified Habitats is given credits by the corps as high-quality wetlands are created or enhanced. Developers can then buy these credits to pay for the new wetlands, which essentially replace those affected by their own projects and thereby constitute no net loss of wetland areas. Diversified Habitats has developed four wetland mitigation sites and sells credits from these sites to developers. Once a wetlands area is established and approved by the corps, which generally takes at least five years, Diversified Habitats donates the land to a conservation organization.

A recent example of this process is the company's presentation to the Nature Conservancy of 104 acres of high-quality wetlands, accompanied by a $37,000 gift to fund an endowment dedicated to managing the land. Diversified bought the acreage — half farmland and half low-quality wetlands — in 1996. The corps and the Nature Conservancy helped the company select the parcel, located adjacent to the conservancy's Great Salt Lake Shorelands Preserve, for the sole purpose of carrying out the donation. If the Nature Conservancy were to buy this land today, it would cost about $300,000.

Diversified Habitats also has an active

mitigation bank site known as Bailey's Meadow that incorporates more than 123 acres, says company cofounder Jim Paraskeva. This site will be donated to a conservation organization once the monitoring process has been completed to the satisfaction of the corps. "Our goal at Diversified Habitats is to solve wetland mitigation problems for developers while improving wetland habitats along the Wasatch Front," he says. "We are continually striving to strike a balance that allows the filling of low-quality wetlands while increasing the availability of high-quality wetlands."

Wetland mitigation is also conducted for private mitigation needs by several major Utah corporations, notably Kennecott Utah Copper. In 1996, Kennecott purchased land adjacent to Great Salt Lake, where it created the Inland Sea Shorebird Reserve (ISSR) to offset the loss of wetlands affected by expansion of its tailings impoundment, where it disposes of waste rock created in its operations. By cleaning the reserve site of garbage created by years of illegal dumping; obtaining, directing, and damming water sources to sustain the wetland communities; and fencing off the site, Kennecott was able to transform the area into an important component in Great Salt Lake ecosystem. The ISSR attracts about 100,000 migratory shorebirds and waterfowl each year, and provides habitat for many other wildlife species. In 1998, Kennecott expanded the 2,500-acre ISSR to 3,670 acres and created one of the largest wetland mitigation banks in the United States. In 1999, the ISSR was designated the Outstanding Environmental and Engineering Geologic Project by the Association of Engineering Geologists and has been used as a model of successful wetland mitigation in the Salt Lake valley.

The Salt Lake City Department of Airports manages a 450-acre wetlands mitigation site that it created in 1992 upon receiving a corps permit for construction of a new west runway at the Salt Lake City International Airport. The Department of Airports had to replace 338 acres of wetlands that were affected either directly or indirectly by addition of the runway, says Tim Gwynette, manager of environmental programs for the airport. This upland region, 10,000 feet west of the new runway, has new wetlands that include open water, marsh, playa, and wet meadows fed by water from the North Point Canal Company, in which the airport owns water rights. For the past 13 years, the Department of Airports has monitored, maintained, and managed this wetland, and will continue to do so in the future.

The growing communities along the Wasatch Front are addressing their need for urban expansion, as well as their responsibility for a hemispherically important ecosystem. As they do so, Utah's broad coalition of public and private entities will continue to deliberate and make decisions that dramatically affect the future of the state's wetlands and of generations of residents to come.

CHAPTER 33

San Francisco, CA, Enhances Its Water Quality by Using Stormwater Pollution Prevention Plans

Gary J. Goodemote

After several years of planning, the public works project is finally approved. The rush begins to get permits in place and procure the necessary support to move the project along. The team makes a final check of the drawings and is ready to break ground. Then at the project kick-off meeting, someone mentions stormwater pollution prevention. Suddenly, the room gets very quiet.

Thus begins the scramble to submit proper notification, a Notice of Intent (NOI), and prepare the legally required Stormwater Pollution Prevention Plan (SWPPP) for the jobsite. Lack of an SWPPP, failure to adhere to its various components, or failure to update it as construction site conditions change can mean the difference between a project proceeding on schedule and one requiring the extra time and attention of water-quality officials. It can mean the difference between a project on budget, and one facing expensive delays or even citations and fines.

In most states, stormwater regulations for construction sites were first implemented in the late 1990s to control polluted runoff from construction sites disturbing five or more acres of soil. In 2003, stormwater regulations for these jobsites underwent several key changes in most states. Most notable was the reduction in size of construction sites for which an SWPPP was required — from five or more acres down to one or more. Linear construction sites that disturb one or more acres of soil were also included. Additionally, a local water-quality board may choose to regulate a project disturbing less than an acre if there is reason to believe that the project may pose a threat to water quality.

"It is unusual to require SWPPPs on projects that are less than an acre, unless the project is near a particularly sensitive resource," said Keith Lichten, an environmental engineer with the San Francisco Bay Regional Water Quality Control Board. California has nine such boards charged with developing and enforcing water-quality objectives and implementation plans within their local areas.

"However, most of the municipalities in this area have their own municipal NPDES

Originally published as "Keeping It Real: Updating Your Stormwater Pollution Prevention Plan," *Public Works*, Vol. 1, No. 7, July 2005. Published by Hanley Wood Business Media, Chicago, IL. Reprinted with permission of the publisher.

(National Pollutant Discharge Elimination System) stormwater permits with us," said Lichten. "Under those permits, the municipalities conduct a series of activities, including public education, industrial and commercial inspections, and regulation of new development and redevelopment projects. They control discharges into storm drains and regulate grading in construction sites. They may require an SWPPP-like document for smaller sites, often as part of a grading permit approval."

Once the determination is made that a site is subject to stormwater regulations, several requirements must be met. These include preparing and submitting an NOI, preparing and implementing an SWPPP, conducting site observations and audits to verify that the SWPPP is being properly implemented, and, in some instances, sampling stormwater discharge. Often one firm creates the plan and paperwork, while another is responsible for implementing the plan.

The general contractor or construction management firm will often contract with a civil engineering firm or an environmental consulting firm to create an SWPPP. The consultant must develop the SWPPP based upon proposed construction drawings, a preliminary construction schedule taking into account weather patterns, a preliminary list of contractors that will be onsite, and other factors. The SWPPP is created during the permitting process and before the final site plan is completed. Once the SWPPP is complete, its implementation becomes the responsibility of the lead construction contractor.

Updating the SWPPP

Some construction contractors believe that once they have obtained an SWPPP and have experience with such plans, they are automatically in full compliance with the stormwater regulations. But if onsite inspections by the local water-quality board or department of environmental quality deem the

SWPPPs inadequate, the construction contractors quickly turn to their SWPPP consultants for help. Typically, the review indicates that while the SWPPP contained the required regulatory elements, it had not been updated as the site conditions changed.

"One of our most challenging goals is to help people keep their SWPPPs up-to-date," said Lichten. "The SWPPP is a living document that must take into account construction site conditions, and not just be sitting on the shelf. We frequently find that folks are adept at best management practices (BMPs), but their plan may not be telling them what to do."

Some of the common changes on a construction site that often are not updated in the SWPPP include:

- Location of the equipment or material storage areas. This includes keeping an updated list of hazardous materials stored onsite and their locations.
- Key site personnel. During long projects it is very common that contractors or key personnel leave the job. As new personnel or contractors are added to the site, the SWPPP should be updated to reflect the changes.
- New or different BMPs. SWPPPs are created before construction begins, often for an undeveloped piece of land. The person responsible for preparing the SWPPP makes assumptions on the types and locations of the BMPs based upon pre-construction drawings. During construction, however, the site conditions may change, rendering a particular BMP useless or in the wrong location. As a result, the BMP is moved to the correct location. The SWPPP also needs to be modified to explain why the BMP was moved or installed differently. Another scenario is that site conditions are not significantly different from the pre-construction drawings, but the BMPs are not effective. Making changes to or adding additional BMPs is an excellent practice, but the

SWPPP must then be modified to explain why a particular BMP was modified.

- Construction schedule. Changes in the schedule should also be noted in the SWPPP. This is especially true when the changes have to do with site grading or stabilization. For example, one of the BMPs that may have been identified in the SWPPP is to grade only during the dry season. The schedule slips a bit, and suddenly dryseason grading is being conducted during a wet time. If so, additional BMPs may be needed to protect from erosion problems on the site or to further reduce tracking of soils offsite.

California's unusually early and wet winter of 2004–2005 provided plenty of examples. One company in the San Francisco Bay Area, embarking on a major project to redevelop a quarry, had filed a thorough SWPPP. But the SWPPP anticipated that the project would be much further along in its grading when the rains came.

"When the rainy season hit they had a lot more exposed dirt and were still grading in areas that should have been stabilized," said Lichten. "They lost a lot of dirt down into the creek below. We worked with the company, and they responded, but it was more expensive than if they had addressed the changing situation and updated their SWPPP. They should have thought more in advance about what might happen if the grading went slower than anticipated. They should have stockpiled needed materials onsite. They should have opened up a smaller area, which would have enabled them to stabilize the site more easily."

The company was not fined, mostly because of its quick and extensive response when the citation was issued, he said.

Making Changes

Unexpected wet weather can affect a project in a number of ways and it is the responsibility of managers to consider them all, said Bonnie Slavin, a construction manager with Kleinfelder Inc. in Sacramento, Calif. "As project managers, it's important we look at the big picture and how weather affects all aspects of the project. That must always include the SWPPP."

With each change to a construction site, the SWPPP also must be changed. But this does not mean that the SWPPP must be sent back to the contractor who created it. The person responsible for implementation of the SWPPP should make the change (using a pen is sufficient) and document that the SWPPP has been changed using the "Amendment Form" included with the SWPPP.

On a yearly basis, the construction contractor should have changes that were made in pen converted to electronic format. This is especially true for projects that will not be completed for several years. In making changes, a consultant can help provide a more in-depth understanding of regulatory requirements and can ensure that the SWPPP meets any regulatory changes.

Updating an SWPPP gives regulators a better understanding of how a construction manager is trying to meet stormwater requirements. Regulators are more apt to work with a manager they believe is making the effort to stay in compliance.

"In general, fines are a last resort," said Lichten. "Our hope is to work with companies. If someone is being proactive and trying to update their SWPPP, and trying to do the right thing, we may understand that they have been affected by this one big storm that they were unable to handle.

"On the other hand, we would feel differently if we go out to a site, look over the SWPPP and find that they have not updated it, do not have proper controls in place, and the project manager and superintendent don't know what we are even talking about. These are flags to us. The more flags we see, the greater attention we are going to pay to that site and the greater chance we may enforce, including considering fines," he said.

What most construction site managers don't realize is that there is more at stake than their own project. "Construction sites can have real impacts on habitats and species that are threatened," said Lichten. "We also have learned that the way we manage construction sites can have a real impact on taxpayers. Addressing problems created by sediment and erosion can be very expensive for taxpayers.

Preventing these problems from ever occurring can result in substantial savings of public funds."

The main message here is to update regularly. An SWPPP should be considered a living document that evolves as a construction project evolves. Consider this: How often do "pre-construction drawings" end up as "as-built drawings"? Almost never. The same is true of SWPPPs. Even the best SWPPPs are only accurate until construction begins.

CHAPTER 34

Santa Barbara, CA, Protects Its Coastline While There's Still Time

Gordy Slack

For thirty miles west from Santa Barbara, the Amtrak line hugs the coast, passing an extraordinary stretch of oceanfront where the Santa Ynez Mountains meet the sea. The ocean and beach here look as they did hundreds, or even thousands, of years ago. Even from the train, the birdwatching is remarkable: kestrels, white-tailed kites, red-tailed hawks, and pelicans ply the sea breeze. Shorebirds crowd the water's shimmering edge and swirl in coordinated blinking clouds over the water. Dolphins arc out of the ocean below. A whale puffs a misty exhalation a few hundred yards offshore.

The Gaviota Coast, as it is known (the name means "seagull" in Spanish), defies powerful trends. Geologically, the coast follows the Santa Ynez Mountains on their east-west course, defying the north-south direction of most California coastal ranges. Biologically, many southern species reach their northern limit here, and many northern ones find their southern limit; and where they overlap, hybrids and unusual groupings of species form, defying biological norms.

But the Gaviota Coast's most atypical feature may be its resistance to the development that has overwhelmed so much of southern California's Pacific edge. The 180-mile stretch from San Diego to Santa Barbara is crowded with urban and suburban development. The frantic building activity only begins to wane a few miles west of Santa Barbara, and then, miraculously, the coast opens up; for miles and miles it is spectacularly intact. The Gaviota Coast encompasses 50 percent of the remaining rural coastline in southern California. While a small fraction of the land is protected in California state parks, most of it has been held in large, private cattle ranches.

And what a coast it is! Elevated mesas fall away in steep cliffs to spectacular stretches of remote beach. Near the eastern, or Santa Barbara, end of this east-west coast, lies Ellwood Mesa, where unusual vernal pool wetlands shelter rare plants and animals. Concentric rings of wildflowers encircle the pools as the water evaporates through the spring. Eucalyptus groves on Ellwood Mesa harbor the largest unprotected wintering site in California for monarch butterflies, which migrate hundreds or even thousands of miles from breeding grounds in California's Sierra Nevada or the prairies of Canada. Some years as many as 60,000 butterflies gather in the trees, hanging

Originally published as "Saving the Seagull Coast," *Land & People*, Vol. 16, No. 1, Spring 2004. Published by The Trust for Public Land, San Francisco, CA. Reprinted with permission of the publisher.

in bunches like giant clusters of fruit. As morning sunshine warms them, a cluster will burst into a colorful cloud as the butterflies scatter in search of water and food.

For conservationists, the presence of such a biologically rich, spectacular, and undeveloped coast so close to a growing population center presents an irresistible opportunity, but also a fleeting one. Within an easy commute of Santa Barbara, the coast is a prime development target, and several large development companies have purchased ranches there in recent years.

In 1999, recognizing the urgent need to protect the coast, local community groups launched an effort to promote a feasibility study for a national seashore. The study concluded that while the Gaviota Coast was worthy of national seashore designation, and while protecting the coast should be a top conservation priority, acquiring the land would be prohibitively expensive.

Meanwhile, residents of Santa Barbara County are doing what coastal residents across the country do when their best-loved coasts are endangered. They are getting organized, envisioning conservation possibilities, holding meetings, raising funds, writing and e-mailing their legislators, seeking help from national nonprofits such as The Trust for Public Land, and protecting the coastlines that they can protect, one property at a time.

Working together over the last few years, residents, governments, community groups, and TPL have protected one major property along the Gaviota Coast. The acquisition of 2,500-acre El Capitan Ranch will create an unbroken swath of public land from the existing El Capitan Beach State Park inland to the two-million-acre Los Padres National Forest. Protecting the ranch had been a dream of state park officials and local conservationists for 25 years. Within days of the announcement that $500,000 was needed to complete the transaction, the late Pierre Claeyssens, a well-known local philanthropist, offered a $250,000 challenge grant to jump-start the campaign. Over

---

Fast Facts: OUR CROWDED COASTS

Approximately 3,600 people move to the nation's coasts each day.

Coastal counties make up less than a fifth of the lower 48 states' acreage, yet they are home to more than half of all Americans.

In many coastal areas, sprawl development consumes land at a rate of five or more times the rate of population growth.

Population along America's coasts will likely increase by another 20 percent by 2015.

Source: *America's Living Oceans*, a 2003 Pew Foundation report.

---

the next seven weeks, nearly 300 Santa Barbara area residents made donations, closing the funding gap to complete the project.

Even before the El Capitan transaction was completed, TPL announced to the community that Ellwood Mesa itself—home to the wintering monarchs—was available, if funding could be found for its purchase. Abutting both an existing housing development and the campus of the University of California, Santa Barbara, in the city of Goleta, Ellwood Mesa is sometimes referred to as the "Gateway to the Gaviota Coast." One plan, since scratched, proposed building 500 houses here. More recently, a plan to build 150 homes—some right up against the butterfly grove—was nearly implemented. Protests and legal challenges stalled it in the permit process.

Even though much of the mesa is privately owned, hundreds of joggers and hikers travel its trails daily. At the height of the butterfly season, hundreds more visitors come to see the butterflies, says Christine Lange, a local activist and founding member of Friends of the Ellwood Coast, a community group organized to work for the land's protection. The butterflies deserve a lot of credit for the land's imminent preservation, Lange says. "Without them it would have been a lot harder to get the commitment and attention we needed to keep this effort going for the past fifteen years."

The complicated deal TPL negotiated among the landowner, the City of Goleta, and a coalition of environmental groups would protect 137 acres on Ellwood Mesa and create, when added to existing protected land, two miles of contiguous public open space along the coast. In exchange, the landowner would receive cash and 36 nearby acres on which to build housing for the community. The developed area would not threaten important habitat, the butterflies, or Ellwood's vernal pools; nor would it block the bluffs or restrict access to the mesa.

To complete the transaction, however, TPL and the community needed to raise more than $20 million in government grants and private funds. Children in butterfly costumes kicked off the fundraising campaign, and donations large and small began pouring in. School groups sold cookies, and one class assembled and raffled off a quilt decorated with butterflies to support the project. A "jog-a-thon" was held to raise funds, and an artists' group sold paintings of the Ellwood property.

Singer-songwriter Jackson Browne recorded radio spots urging people to give to save Ellwood Mesa, and well-known protector of oceans Jean-Michel Cousteau encouraged people to "give, and give generously." A local couple urged guests at their wedding to make donations to support Ellwood in lieu of a gift. Local philanthropists gave generously, including Peter and Stephanie Sperling, who pledged $5 million, and Wendy P. McCaw, who pledged $1 million. In all, individuals contributed nearly $8 million over eight months.

This local generosity, combined with an

Federal Funding for the Coast

In 2002, TPL worked with Congress to create the Federal Coastal and Estuarine Land Conservation Program (CELP), which offers pass-through grants to state and local governments for land acquisition in the coastal zone. In its initial two years, the program has granted $53 million and helped protect 35 properties, including TPL projects in East Sandusky Bay, Puget Sound, and along the California coast. Administered by the National Oceanic and Atmospheric Administration (NOAA), CELP was created by conservation-minded senators Ernest Hollings (D–SC) and Judd Gregg (R–NH), and representatives Frank Wolfe (R–VA) and Jose Serrano (D–NY). The FY 2004 appropriation—expected to be more than $1 million—will help protect an additional 33 coastal properties.

infusion of public funds from California's Proposition 40, has made it likely that Ellwood Mesa will become public property within months.

Ellwood will be a major victory, but the job of conservation will continue to intensify on the Gaviota Coast, says TPL Project Manager Debra Geiler, who is already strategizing with governments, environmentalists, and landowners on ways to extend protection to more of this extraordinary coast. "When we see a stretch of undeveloped coast like this, we tend to assume that it must already be protected, that it will remain wild and beautiful forever," says Geiler. "That's not necessarily so. Development pressure is already strong here, and it's building. In five or ten years it may be too late. Our window of opportunity is now."

CHAPTER 35

Santa Fe, NM, Works with Citizen Groups to Restore a River and Its Corridor

William Poole

From time to time, Land & People tells the story of a conservation effort through the voices of participants and community members. The characters in this story come from the historic community of Agua Fria, on the outskirts of Santa Fe, where TPL recently helped enlarge the San Ysidro River Park as part of a larger effort to acquire open space along the Santa Fe River.

Maria Albina's Granddaughter

Melinda Romero Pike remembers when the new parkland was a verdant meadow along the Santa Fe River. Slender, vivacious, and elegant, with a coiffed cap of snowy hair, Pike does not willingly confess her age. It is enough to know that this memory comes from before the 1930s, when the one-room Agua Fria School stood across the street from the meadow, and the teacher would take Pike and the other students to play in it.

"A big meadow was there," she says, "and years ago when I was a child — like five or six — there was some gentleman who had herds of goats. And he had long white whiskers to here. And that man would come with his goats and he would graze them there, but they didn't make a dent in it. It was just like you'd planted a lawn, but it was natural."

Pike traces her family line in Agua Fria back to the early 17th century, and her adobe home down the street from the San Ysidro River Park is named Casa Maria Albina after her grandmother, who lived here. The village priest once boarded in this home. Her great-grandfather donated the land for the local church, built in 1835 and named for San Ysidro, the patron saint of farmers. And during the Depression what is now Pike's living room served as a community store.

Even for a part of the country that measures its age in centuries, Agua Fria is venerable, thanks in large part to the Santa Fe River and flat fertile ground it once watered. (Agua fria means "cool water" in Spanish.) Pueblo ruins dating from before the conquistadores have been discovered along the river. And at least some current Hispanic residents trace their lineage back to officers in the Spanish army who were rewarded for their service with rich agricultural lands. The main road along

Originally published as "A Once and Future River," *Land & People*, Vol. 18, No. 1, Spring 2006. Published by The Trust for Public Land, San Francisco, CA. Reprinted with permission of the publisher.

the river, Agua Fria Street, is part of a prehistoric trail system that in colonial times became known El Camino Real. The route ran from Mexico to the colonial capital of Santa Fe, only five miles upriver from Agua Fria.

In her comfortable kitchen, Pike unrolls an undated map that shows the town at its productive peak. The map shows slivers of land as little as 50 or 100 feet wide where they intersect the river but stretching back from there up to several miles — giving everyone access to water as the land was divided within families over generations. Other water for planting came from acequias, irrigation ditches off the river, and from springs and shallow wells.

Map details suggest the fecundity of Agua Fria in the decades before World War II. Plots of land are labeled as alfalfa, row crops, corn, orchard, and plowed ground. Along the meandering stream ran a bosque — a riverside forest of cottonwoods and willows, Pike recalls. "On the high side of the bank my brother would lasso the tree branch and we would swing, and down below we would climb the trees."

Then, pretty much overnight, Agua Fria all but dried up. The cause of this calamity was the damming of the river to slake the thirst of a growing Santa Fe. Instead of running in all but the driest weeks of summer, in most years the river ran only in the wettest winter weeks. With the water gone, gravel miners quarried the river's banks to make concrete for the growing city. The water table dropped so that wells had to be dug deeper and deeper. The bosque and other vegetation dried up, and without the vegetation to slow it, the river, when it did flow, ran like an express train, straightening the channel, undercutting the banks.

"There was no river left," Pike says. "It was the memory of a river." Today there is very little agriculture in Agua Fria. Horses graze in dusty pastures, and houses look out on weedy fields or drooping barbed-wire fences. Along Agua Fria Street, many homes are compact

and modestly prosperous. Farther back from the road, house trailers march along old family plots where crops were once planted and acequias once ran. There is no store, and the closest thing to a community center is the elementary school. It is a place that some might consider "underutilized," a series of cul-de-sac subdivisions waiting to happen — an option most residents definitely do not embrace.

As for the former meadow across from where the old school had stood, it has dried to gravelly desert, enlivened by the shrubby yellow bloom of rabbitbrush and purple asters. Despite this, the land's protection as part of a larger effort to preserve open space, build new parks, and create a trail system along the river has been widely celebrated in Agua Fria and greater Santa Fe. Some folks simply welcome the recreational values the project would bring. But for Melinda Romero Pike and others it symbolizes the possible recovery of a community from the insults that began with the damming, the possible revival of a river nearly given up for dead, and the chance to make the river a focus for community life once again.

The Social Worker

"Like everyone else, I wasn't aware that it was a river at all," confesses Nichoe Lichen, volunteer director of the El Camino Real River Connection (CRRC), an alliance of nonprofits and government agencies working to protect open space and create trails along the river. A social worker by profession, Lichen exudes the sincerity and warmth you would expect from a woman who helps connect babies with adoptive parents. She also possesses a hair-trigger sense of humor and erupts into genial laughter when reminded of her own unlikely evolution, in only a few years, from someone who does not know a river exists to one of its major champions.

This story line begins in 2000, when Lichen and her friend Ann Lacy began raising funds for a successful effort to conserve a highly visible property at the entrance to Santa Fe. With funds left over from that project, they began to ask residents on the poorer south side of Santa Fe, including Agua Fria, what land they would like to see conserved. They did this, she says, because she is a social worker by nature, not just by profession.

"We knew that the kids didn't have parks or anything," Lichen says. "And we told residents that if they could recommend a place to us, we could get something going and give it as a gift to that side of town. They said, 'Well, we'd really like for you to save the river, and by the way, did you know that this was also the route of the Camino Real?'"

Thus began the latest of several efforts over the last decade to think about the Santa Fe River's relationship to its fast-developing region, and about how to maximize its potential for recreation, environmental restoration, historical interpretation, and community-building. Early in the process, The Trust for Public Land's Santa Fe office hired an intern named Karyn Stockdale to talk to landowners along the river and look at how parcels might be protected. Today Stockdale — whose physical trademark is her thick shock of kinky, sand-colored hair — is a TPL project manager and has completed three projects in support of the park-and-trail program. "There's going to be a myth about her along the river some day," Lichen says, "that wild-haired woman who saved the river."

Another nonprofit partner in the project is the Santa Fe Watershed Association, which has focused on community organizing and on planting vegetation and restoring the river's banks after years of erosion and mining. The association took the lead in meeting with Agua Fria residents.

Key to the project's success so far, Lichen says, is its deep commitment to community participation. "We weren't saying, we have a plan or this is what we're going to do. Nothing happened in that village that wasn't led and determined by the village. In the past outsiders have come in and said, 'Boy, have we got a plan for you.' We spent a lot of time meeting with the community and letting them know that nothing was going to happen unless they took the lead on it."

The Community Activists

Ramon Romero left Agua Fria as a young man in 1970 and didn't return for almost 15 years. He wanted to repair heavy machinery in Montana, until his father told him, "I don't know what you're doing the way in the heck over there, but you got all this property here, and if you don't come back I'm going to sell it."

Today Romero, a tough, bearded, spark-plug of a man with warm brown eyes and a ready smile, fixes diesel trucks in a cavernous and spotless shop behind his mother's house on Agua Fria Street. (On the shop's walls hang antique tools, cowboy gear, and other reminders of Agua Fria's past.) As chair of the Agua Fria Village Association, he meditates a lot on the community's past glories, the decline that began when the river was shut off in the 1940s, and a future he believes could be better.

The big question for almost anyone who cares about Agua Fria is whether it can resist the rising tide of development from Santa Fe. To many residents, this feels like the final assault that could obliterate in only a few decades a community that took four centuries to build.

A few years back Agua Fria secured an official state designation as a Traditional Historic Community, which prevents its lands from being annexed by the city without a vote of residents. In addition, the narrow slivers of family land make it hard for developers to assemble large parcels for a shopping mall or housing development. But despite these impediments, development is eating away at the edges of town. Romero, who built his own home on his family's strip of land in the 1980s, is going to move soon because a big-box home-improvement store is arriving next door. As one family leaves, this puts pressure on the family next door to sell, and pretty soon a developer is able to put a parcel together, and the nature of the place begins to change.

To Romero and others, the conservation work along the river could create a communal focus, prevent development of the conserved parcels, and empower residents to tackle other civic tasks, such as forging a united response to development threats.

"Our goal would be to preserve traditional density, ruralness, and open space and keep the young people in the village, where the properties have been passed down from generation to generation the last four hundred years, which is the custom and the tradition," Romero says. "This land along the river is all going to be open space and is going to get renovated and fixed up. Once people can enjoy the river as they used to in the past, it might encourage them to stay."

But not everyone in Agua Fria is as optimistic. Some residents believe the tide of change, while undesirable, is inevitable. Among them is Tamara Lichtenstein, who with her husband, artist Michael Bergt, and their eight-year-old daughter, Siena, lives in a cozy, art-filled home just down the road from Ramon Romero. When they moved there in 1991, the boarded-up fixer-upper was what they could afford in Santa Fe.

Almost before renovations were complete, Lichtenstein had thrown herself into community affairs, and for more than a decade she has been fighting with the county and city to give the community control over its own growth. Some battles have been won: in part because of her work, Agua Fria Street remains a narrow, local street where it runs through the village. (One plan would have seen it widened.) And stop signs have been installed to calm traffic and protect children.

But on the big battle to keep land use traditional, she is more pessimistic. "For a long time, developers looked at those long narrow strips and realized that if they want to do things their way they're going to have to convince a large number of people to put their pieces together," she says. "But that's what they started doing. And they're not just from Santa Fe, they're from out of state, or international. The high-density development that's coming in, that's money from all over. And it's highly unlikely that most people who will be living there are from here."

In this scenario, the importance of the river conservation work has to do with children — in particular, the children who will live in those densely packed new neighborhoods, Lichtenstein says.

"Because there are going to be kids growing up here, going to overcrowded schools — living in the trailers and the high-density developments. If they didn't have this land along the river, what else would they have? If you think about some of the most damaged and challenged neighborhoods TPL has dealt with in L.A., that's kind of like what you're going to be seeing here down the road. But in this instance you're able to be proactive instead of coming along later and saying, 'Oh Gosh, I wish there was something we could do for these kids but there's no open space left.'"

The 91-Year-Old Weightlifter

Across the dry riverbed from the new piece of San Ysidro River Park, on a warm September afternoon, Roy Stephenson and Karyn Stockdale hunt for ripe pears in his small family orchard. "The ones on the tree are probably too hard, and a lot of the ones on the ground are mushy, but if you find a firm one, they are delicious," he says, holding up a sample for Stockdale's inspection.

Stephenson's family owned the land that will become the park addition, but their dedication to the project transcends that transaction. Over the last six decades they have deeply inhabited this land and offered it up for the common good. Their hillside orchard of apple, pear, and cherry trees is a mouth-watering landmark in Agua Fria. Rising high and green above a sere landscape, it is easily visible across the river from Agua Fria Street, and every summer by tradition families pick ripe cherries for free.

Roy's father, John Stephenson, is a wiry man of 91 and the American record holder in his weight class in Olympic-style weightlifting for men over 75. John spent his career working for the U.S. Forest Service and moved out from Santa Fe in the late 1940s, building a modest home in the orchard. Despite being relative newcomers to Agua Fria — they arrived centuries later than most neighboring families — the Stephensons have felt accepted here, and their open-handed good nature hasn't hurt.

Between the orchard and the river are about 4 acres of plowed ground, irrigated from a deep well. Since the mid–1980s this land has been known as the Community Farm, all its produce going to residents in need, homeless shelters, food banks, and other charities. A local nonprofit administers the farm, and volunteers come from across the region — across the country, in fact — to work it.

For this and other volunteer work, John Stephenson was honored as one of the first President Bush's "thousand points of light." His son, Roy — sandy-haired and affable — works for the New Mexico Public Regulation Commission and serves on the board of the Santa Fe Watershed Association. Both men were aware of the conservation effort along the river and assumed that sooner or later they would sell some of their land for the park-and-trail system.

Some of the money they received — far less than the land would have brought for development — will be plowed into the Community Farm, which they envision will someday be an important stop for walkers and cyclists along the river trail.

"I view what could be here as a kind of continuum," Roy says. "There'll be the streetscape along Agua Fria Street, and the park and the river — we might get some cottonwoods back. We've talked about shaping

an oxbow in the river and doing some planting. That would transition into a brush corridor for wildlife, and then you'd have the farm. People could come out from Santa Fe on bicycles. People could have their own little plot at the farm and contribute 10 to 20 percent of what's grown to the community."

But could the river ever come back? Stephenson is adamant that it can. If new plantings can slow down the water in winter so more of it is absorbed, if more water can percolate down through protected landscapes instead of rushing off parking lots and roofs, if water can be captured and channeled to the river — then the damage done over the last five decades can be ameliorated, if not completely reversed. "The goal of the Santa Fe Watershed Association is to have water in the river. That's the mission statement," Stephenson says.

The River Blessing

In the winter of 2005, nature made its own valiant attempt to revive the Santa Fe River. Rain and snow came early and often, and the river ran through May. "The most beautiful sight your eyes could behold after seeing that barren, dry riverbed," recalls Melinda Romero Pike.

With the river doing its part, Karyn Stockdale and Nichoe Lichen sat down with folks from the County's Open Space Program and the Watershed Association to plan a special dedication of the new river park addition. For generations before the water dried up, farmers would conduct river blessings, giving it their respect and recognizing its bounty. Following that tradition, on May 15, 2005 — San Ysidro's feast day — a small parade left the Agua Fria church bearing the saint's image and walked to the riverfront park.

Nichoe Lichen would later call it: "My favorite experience in Santa Fe in 30 years." Deacon Mike Siegle gave the blessing. Flowers were tossed into the current. Ramon Romero spoke, as did Roy Stephenson, Melinda

Romero Pike, Karyn Stockdale, State Senator Nancy Rodriguez, and County Commissioner Virginia Vigil. Afterward, neighbors who had not seen one another in years sat around and talked and ate tamales — drawn together by a river that had been the heart of their community for a dozen generations and was now being rediscovered, preserved for some as yet undetermined but vital future.

At the event, Melinda Romero Pike read in Spanish a poem entitled "Nocturno" ("Night") by the Argentine poet Conrado Nalé Roxlo (1898–1971). Months later, in her kitchen at Casa Maria Albina, she consents to translate for a visitor, her voice touched with both longing and memory:

> The bosque sleeps and dreams;
> the river does not sleep, it sings.
> In between the green shadows
> the rapid water flows,
> leaving on the dark edges
> bundles of white foam.
> With eyes filled with stars,
> in the bottom of a boat
> I go with great emotion
> by the music of the water.
> And I take the river in my lips.
> And I take the bosque in my soul.

Project Snapshot

TPL Office: New Mexico State Office, Santa Fe

Project goals: To create parks and trails along the Santa Fe River, roughtly following the route of the old Camino Real. To provide recreation and a focus for community unity while interpreting the region's Native American, Hispanic, and postcolonial history.

Project partners: Agua Fria Village Association, Santa Fe County, City of Santa Fe, New Mexico State Land Office, Santa Fe Watershed Association, El Camino Real River Connection (CRRC)

Funding and support: Key funding from voter-approved county conservation finance measures in 1998 and 2000, which together generated approximately $20 million. Additional support from the voter-approved sales tax increase passed in 2002, which helps generate planning, design, and maintenance funding for Santa Fe River projects. Other important support since 2002 has come from the New Mexico state legislature through direct appropriations and from TPL donors.

Accomplishments to date: TPL has assisted Santa Fe County in acquiring open space, parkland, and trail easements over approximately 66 acres of the Santa Fe River corridor in 3 different locations. On the western boundary of the village of Agua Fria, the county in 2002 purchased a conservation and trails easement over about 46 acres of New Mexico State Land Office property, which allows for restoration projects within the river corridor and connects the river trail to the recreation center, ballpark, and open space lands near Highway 599. In 2005, TPL helped the county expand the San Ysidro River Park through the acquisition of about 9 acres of river land at the Community Farm and acquired about 11 acres of river land on the eastern boundary of the village. These river acquisitions leverage other public and protected lands and continue the linking of parks, trails, and open space along the Santa Fe River and sites commemorating the El Camino Real Trail.

CHAPTER 36

Santa Monica, CA, and Other Cities Let Mother Nature Guide New Stormwater Management Practices

Donald Baker, Les Lampe, and Laura Adams

Public desire for open space that includes clean streams and lakes, along with more stringent federal environmental regulations, have prompted many communities to adopt environmentally friendly stormwater management methods. Rather than using the traditional practices of enclosing channels in pipes and draining wetlands, which often permanently alter the ecosystem and destroy habitats, alternative methods mimic natural landscape features to improve water quality and waterside environments.

Traditional stormwater practices typically decrease water quality because they do not include a natural ecosystem to assimilate pollutants. In addition, they tend to shorten flow paths, creating higher peak flows. Many communities face flooding issues as a result.

Environmentally friendly approaches to stormwater management are designed to resemble the natural functions that support habitats and protect water quality. In addition, they slow water flow and often detain it, which results in lower peak flows and less flooding.

Stream Cleaning

Santa Monica, Calif., has adopted new stormwater management methods to improve its water quality. Situated on the Pacific Coast north of Los Angeles, the city is surrounded on all sides by other cities or by Santa Monica Bay, which collects all of the city's stormwater runoff. To protect the water quality of the bay, as well as the beauty of area beaches, the city has begun building additional stormwater treatment facilities to remove pollutants — such as organic compounds, metals and trash — from runoff before it reaches the beach. Because space is limited, the city is building the facilities underground.

One recently completed facility was built under a parking lot in a park owned and operated by Los Angeles. The Westside Water Quality Improvement Project, which treats stormwater runoff from a large portion of Santa Monica, was designed with no moving parts, chemical additives or electrical power requirements. "Urban runoff pollution is a major problem for our coastal waters, and this project is one big step in a long and continual

Originally published as "Clean and Green," *American City & County*, Vol. 122, No. 3, March 2007. Published by Penton Media, Overland Park, KS. Reprinted with permission of the publisher.

process to ensure cleaner water and a healthier coastline, and to safeguard life," says Santa Monica Senior Environmental Analyst Neal Shapiro.

The system is designed to remove chemicals, such as pesticides, as well as organic compounds from automobile emissions and other sources from stormwater runoff. While not its primary purpose, the facility may collect chemicals from accidental spills, preventing them from reaching the bay. Santa Monica currently is identifying other sites for similar treatment systems.

While Lenexa, Kan., is not as confined as Santa Monica and other cities, it has plenty of stormwater and must plan for its proper management now and in the future. In the late 1990s, Lenexa officials began adopting more stringent stormwater design criteria, a stream buffer ordinance, and erosion and sediment control ordinances. To raise money to pay for better stormwater management, the city created a stormwater utility and instituted a capital development charge, and residents approved a sales tax to fund construction of new treatment facilities that also could be used as recreational areas.

The city's stormwater quality efforts are primarily designed to manage nutrients and sediment — the main pollutants from residential areas that comprise the majority of the city's landscape. Nutrients attach to the sediment, and the sediment clogs streams and chokes out aquatic vegetation.

Lenexa is creating multi-use facilities that manage stormwater, prevent floods, improve water quality and provide recreational outlets for residents. The city displays information about watershed protection on signs throughout the park-like areas and uses environmentally friendly construction materials where possible.

Taking a Holistic View

In Kansas City, Mo., as in many large cities, outdated stormwater infrastructure has inadequate capacity to carry runoff from large storms and to adequately treat it to meet current standards. A large portion of the city's stormwater infrastructure is in a combined sewer system that transports both stormwater and sewage. During heavy storms, increased runoff can cause overflows that discharge untreated sewage into area waterways.

To update the system and ensure it can handle future growth, local officials are reviewing the city's entire stormwater management program, including physical components as well as administrative and financial management procedures, to identify areas for improvement. In the months ahead, they will update existing flood control plans to reflect a holistic approach to stormwater management that involves flood control, combined sewer overflow reduction, water quality management and natural resource protection.

As part of the effort, Mayor Kay Barnes kicked off a program in November 2005 to encourage residents to plant rain gardens, which are shallow basins or depressions foliated with native plants that have deep roots that help water infiltrate the soil. The mayor's goal is for 10,000 rain gardens to be planted to demonstrate that if residents and businesses manage their own stormwater, peak flows to the city's infrastructure will reduce — as will costs for infrastructure improvements — and water quality in local streams will improve. The program also is raising residents' awareness of how their daily activities can affect stormwater runoff.

Nearby Mission Hills and Mission, Kan., also are addressing flooding issues, which have been caused by lack of regulations and upstream development that has generated more runoff. Mission Hills is an affluent community in the Kansas City metropolitan area in which residents frequently use public areas for walking, biking, jogging and relaxation. However, recent developments threaten to change the streamside corridors that residents have come to enjoy.

Development upstream of the city over

the years has increased the amount of runoff channeled to area streams. Combined with aging stream channel walls and other infrastructure, the runoff is causing stream banks to fail, jeopardizing adjacent roads, water and gas mains, sanitary sewers, driveways and other property.

Rather than addressing each issue individually, city officials have begun studying the stream network in its entirety and searching for stormwater management practices that can improve large parts of the network at once. Numerous city staff as well as the planning commission, parks board and city council members are involved in the study. "This process has changed people's opinions on how city government manages its streams," says Mission Hills City Administrator Courtney Christensen. "Instead of more limited city government involvement, people feel it is imperative that the city protect our important natural resources."

As a result of the study, city officials will develop stream protection guidelines for buffers, landscaping and channel walls. They also will address land disturbance issues, lawn chemical applications, impervious lot coverage, and develop educational materials for residents. The measures will stabilize runoff from impervious areas and will protect — and eventually improve — the stream corridors by setting back human intervention and activities from streams. The buffers also will filter pollutants from the runoff before it enters the waterways.

Mission, Kan., began changing its stormwater management practices approximately three years ago, when costly floods prompted the city to complete large-scale flood control improvements and to redevelop its downtown area. As the city continues making improvements, it is incorporating environmentally friendly practices and stream restoration projects where they are feasible. City leaders now are looking for methods to decrease runoff and improve water quality citywide.

The city is conducting a study funded by the U.S. Army Corps of Engineers to identify locations for new treatment facilities and stream restoration projects. The project will provide a plan for constructing facilities and stream restoration projects that will improve the environment and the water quality of area streams. In addition, the study includes the development of a geographic information system tool that will identify suitable locations for the projects based on land use, topography and stream connections. The tool will select appropriate projects based on those parameters and on the stream quality. From there, cost estimates for project construction will be developed, and improvements will be prioritized for construction.

The city is working with Kansas State University to monitor the effects of the improvements. It also is constructing demonstration projects that will be monitored for their effects on water quality and will be used to help educate residents about the importance of managing stormwater in an environmentally friendly way.

Like Santa Monica, Kansas City and Mission Hills, many communities throughout the country are embracing environmentally friendly stormwater management methods because of the ecosystem improvements and social benefits they provide. Such holistic and "green" approaches aim to ensure that the natural beauty that residents enjoy does not disappear in the future.

CHAPTER 37

Scottsdale, AZ, and Other Cities Reclaim, Recycle, and Reuse Their Wastewater

David Mansfield, Paul Shoenberger, James Crook, and Karen DeCampli

For most of this summer, residents of much of the Midwest, Central Plains and Texas held onto the hope that it would rain. But because the rain usually evaporated before it hit the ground, little relief came from the series of hurricanes that bombarded the Southeast and Hurricane Katrina that later hit the Gulf Coast. As a result, communities were put on sprinkler watering restrictions and residents were urged to conserve water at home. Meteorologists declared it one of the worst regional droughts since 1988.

As droughts and population booms continue to stress fresh water supplies, municipal wastewater reclamation and reuse increasingly will help alleviate the country's water deficits. Reclaimed water was formerly used in the United States mainly for purposes that did not require high-quality water, such as pasture or nonfood crop irrigation. Today, highly treated wastewater is valued as a resource that, in recent years, has been used for urban irrigation, toilet flushing, industrial needs and indirect potable reuse. Reclaimed water also is used to prevent seawater intrusion and to recharge local underground aquifers. Additionally, industrial users purchase reclaimed water to use in cooling towers, boiler feed and other manufacturing processes. Currently, the United States produces the most reclaimed water in the world, averaging about 2.6 billion gallons daily.

However, some state regulatory agencies have just begun to recognize the value of reclaimed water. Many states recently have developed their first water reuse and reclamation regulations or are in the process of doing so.

Most water reuse projects are located in Arizona, California, Colorado, Florida, Nevada, New Mexico and Texas. California and Florida account for nearly half the total annual reclaimed water use in the nation. Other states — including the Carolinas, Georgia, Virginia, Washington and even relatively water-rich states in the Northeast — also are starting to adopt water reuse programs.

Although the drought spared most of the West this year, many municipalities in the re-

Originally published as "Water, Water Everywhere...," *American City & County*, Vol. 120, No. 10, October 2005. Published by Penton Media, Overland Park, KS. Reprinted with permission from *American City & County* magazine. Copyright 2005, Penton Media, New York, NY.

gion have become accustomed to — and prepared for — water shortages. While some continue to purchase water from private utilities or pay penalties for exceeding their water extraction limits, they realize those are only short-term, and rather expensive, options. Others seeking long-term relief, such as the Scottsdale, Ariz., Water Resources Department and the West Basin Municipal Water District in southern Los Angeles County, Calif., have pioneered water reuse and other conservation programs.

Located in states that have strict water allocation and discharge regulations, West Basin and Scottsdale have two of the nation's strongest conservation and sustainable environment programs. The utilities' reuse programs conserve water and reduce operating costs, and also encourage residents to conserve through incentive programs such as low-flow toilet installation, and rebates for low water-using landscapes and high-efficiency clothes washers. To date, West Basin and Scottsdale's reclamation programs have saved more than 90 billion gallons of potable water.

Promoting Sustainability

Located in the middle of the Arizona desert, Scottsdale has been planning for droughts for many years. Burdened by increasing wastewater disposal costs, the city implemented a water reuse program more than 20 years ago. To treat its reclaimed water, the Scottsdale Water Campus facility uses a membrane technology as a pretreatment to reverse osmosis (RO), producing high quality processed water suitable for landscape irrigation and groundwater recharge.

"Although we've been reclaiming our water since 1984, it wasn't until 1998 that we actually started reusing it," says Art Nunez, acting water/wastewater treatment director at the Scottsdale Water Campus. "Up until then, we had just poured usable water down the drain — and we paid to dispose of it."

Scottsdale began effluent reuse on its golf courses in 1984 and expanded its use in 1998, saving an estimated 25 billion gallons of potable water. In fact, the Scottsdale Water Campus is one of the largest municipal facilities in the world that treats raw wastewater to potable quality for aquifer recharge. It does so by injecting highly treated reclaimed water directly into an underground aquifer via wells. Recharging excess effluent allows the city to store accumulated withdrawal credits until needed during peak periods, reducing the city's water demand from the Colorado River as well as its water treatment requirements.

Scottsdale currently draws more than 65 percent of its drinking water from the Colorado River and pumps another 30 percent from city wells. Other surface water sources supply the rest of the city's drinking water. "Our goal is to replace any pumped groundwater with groundwater recharge," says Beth Miller, an advisor to Scottsdale Water Resources. "We'll only use [groundwater supplies] if surface water supplies are unavailable."

To help offset additional surface water purchases, the city assesses a water resources acquisition fee for all new housing developments. The city has used the money to more than double its available surface water supplies. "We have invested a lot of time, effort and money in creating a long-term water supply," Nunez says. "We expect this water solution will help sustain our continued population growth for years to come."

Golf courses use much of Scottsdale's reclaimed water; 23 of the 42 area courses use it for irrigation and pay all reclamation fees. New golf courses must provide their own renewable surface water supply. "Scottsdale has a reputation for having lots of golf courses, but residents are not aware that those golf courses are using reclaimed water and are not using drinking water [for irrigation]," Miller says. "One of our challenges is educating our general public about that reuse and how important it is."

Miller says that between 60 and 80 percent of Scottsdale's water is used for landscape watering, so the city holds workshops that advocate landscaping with drought-resistant plants, trees and shrubs. "We offer workshops on everything from rejuvenating existing landscapes to designing a new landscape," Miller says. "Interest is definitely growing. In the newer neighborhoods, the ethic is much more toward [planting] low-water-using landscapes."

The city also rebates residences and businesses for replacing grass with low water-using plants and for installing water-efficient plumbing fixtures. It conducts residential irrigation water audits and recommends ways to conserve water. Residents that add greywater piping to their homes beginning in 2007 will receive a $200 state tax credit.

Leading by example, Scottsdale uses rain-sensor irrigation systems in its parks and re-circulating pumps in its main fountains. The city also has started replacing older plumbing fixtures in its buildings with water-efficient devices.

"The Scottsdale Water Campus, with its ability to reclaim water for landscape irrigation and groundwater recharge, was a giant step forward in the wise use of Scottsdale's water resources," Miller says. "Scottsdale must continue to build on its history of environmental stewardship and conservation to leave a legacy for future generations."

Setting Standards

The West Basin Municipal Water District in Southern California was one of several water supply agencies that enacted conservation regulations in the 1990s because of water extraction restrictions and high water import fees. The district imports water to 17 cities in the South Bay and unincorporated areas of Los Angeles County. It produces five different types of reclaimed water: tertiary, nitrified tertiary, softened RO, pure RO and ultra-pure RO — all state-approved for various municipal, commercial and industrial applications.

West Basin was one of the nation's first water agencies to create large-scale wastewater reclamation systems, and its Water Recycling Facility is the largest reclamation plant of its type in the United States. In 2002, the facility was named one of six National Centers for Water Treatment Technologies by the Fountain Valley, Calif.–based National Water Research Institute.

West Basin's first water reclamation plant opened in 1995. Capable of eventually treating 23 billion gallons of wastewater per year, West Basin's Water Recycling Facility currently treats 9 billion gallons of wastewater yearly from Los Angeles' Hyperion Wastewater Treatment Plant (WWTP). After completing its next expansion in May 2006, the facility will increase its reclaimed water production by 15 million gallons per day — 5 million for seawater barrier injection and 10 million for landscape irrigation. To date, West Basin's reclamation program has saved more than 65 billion gallons of potable water — enough to fill about 200,000 football stadiums.

The district purchases 10 percent of its secondary treated sewage water from the Hyperion WWTP, which decreases the volume the plant discharges into the Santa Monica Bay by 25 percent. In addition, the district has reduced its imported water by nearly 20 percent. "West Basin is committed to expanding the use of reclaimed water to safeguard the limited water supply and to achieve new milestones in water conservation," says West Basin Board President Carol Kwan.

The district uses reclaimed water to augment the groundwater as a potable supply source. It also combines 50 percent imported water with 50 percent reclaimed water to inject into a series of wells that serve as a hydraulic dam between the ocean and the groundwater aquifer.

The Water Replenishment District of Southern California purchases reclaimed water from West Basin to use for seawater barrier injections. Many local municipalities and universities also use the treated water for irrigation. Inglewood, Calif., uses it for street sweeping, and Torrance, Calif.–based Toyota Motor Sales USA buys it for toilet and urinal flushing.

Industrial users in South Bay, Calif., including Chevron, ExxonMobil and BP, use the high-quality reclaimed water for cooling towers, boiler feed and various refining processes. To accommodate those industrial users' needs, West Basin built satellite treatment facilities at or near the refineries. Connections to the main pipelines eventually will provide reclaimed water to low-quantity users, such as garden nurseries and schools. By using high-quality processed water for their industrial applications, local refineries and other area industries, such as the Home Depot National Training Center and Goodyear, save billions of gallons of potable water annually for use by the more than 1 million residents within the West Basin service area. "We continue to establish valuable partnerships and strive for innovation to make this program one of the largest in the country," Kwan says.

West Basin also offers a variety of incentives to encourage its residents and businesses to conserve water, including rebates for installing high-efficiency clothes washers and ultra-low-flush toilets. Businesses also receive incentives for installing cooling tower conductivity controllers, water-saving toilets and urinals, pre-rinse kitchen sprayers and water-pressurized brooms. Hospitals and other health care facilities receive rebates if they retrofit x-ray machines with film processor recirculating systems as do hotels and motels that use do-not-wash guest towel and bed linen placards. "Our goal is to remain in the forefront of water resource planning and management to ensure a reliable supply for today and the future," Kwan says.

Affected by drought, increasing pollution and development, communities likely will depend more on water reuse to relieve dwindling water supplies. Potable and nonpotable water reuse programs that use a variety of conventional and advanced water treatment technologies have proved they are a reliable way to provide water for various residential, commercial, municipal, industrial and agricultural purposes.

This year's drought was proof that all utilities must be prepared for the unusual and even the inevitable. By putting water reuse and conservation measures in place, Scottsdale, West Basin and other water agencies have provided their customers with a steady supply of safe, high-quality water for years to come.

CHAPTER 38

Seattle, WA, Uses Smart Growth
Practices to Improve Water Quality

Lisa Nisenson and Jennifer Molloy

Stormwater used to be one of the least exciting subjects in city and county governance, but those days are over. A convergence of new Environmental Protection Agency (EPA) rules, unprecedented rates of growth, and water-quality concerns have brought stormwater management to the fore.

The search for solutions has extended not only across city and county boundaries but within them as well. Almost every city or county department, from public works to transportation, has had to turn attention to stormwater control. Given the changes, what should managers look for to effectively manage the departments that are, in turn, managing stormwater?

Some answers just might lie in programs and projects already underway. This chapter looks at some of these programs, as well as areas where decisions in one department might be working against stormwater management goals.

The Links to Stormwater
and Water Quality

The first step in looking at solutions is to look at what generates stormwater-related

problems. Stormwater runoff is generated when excess rain water cannot be absorbed into the ground and thus flows over the ground toward a receiving waterbody. Certainly the magnitude of a storm event, which cannot be controlled, plays a role in whether a storm will spur flooding or sewer overflows.

At the same time, stormwater generation is related to development and decisions on how and where it takes place. As the number of impermeable surfaces — such as roads, rooftops, and compacted surfaces — increases, less water soaks into the ground to feed groundwater and river base flows. This situation can greatly reduce in-stream flows during dry periods, and some streams essentially dry up.

When less rain water gradually soaks in, large pulses of stormwater enter streams, scouring once-stable streambanks and increasing the possibility of flooding. As stormwater flows to streams and lakes, it picks up oil, fertilizers, animal waste, litter, and even heat. Water quality and quantity problems associated with stormwater are further exacerbated by the development patterns that have prevailed over the past 50 years. While land development necessarily involves creation of

Originally published as "Hidden Credits: Using Smart Growth Techniques to Manage Stormwater Under Phase II," *Public Management*, Vol. 87, No. 9, October 2005. Published by the International City/County Management Association, Washington, DC. Reprinted with permission of the publisher.

impervious surfaces, how and where development takes place can influence the ultimate degree of environmental impact from the streets, rooftops, and yards.

Conventional development patterns of the past several decades are exemplified by separation of uses (e.g., housing, retail, and office uses in separate development pods), a dispersal of development projects, and highly engineered roadways and access routes. This separation of uses typically relies on travel that can be accessed only by automobiles. This, in turn, dictates parking lots, roads, and driveways that are engineered to meet the needs of auto-only travel.

Looking for Stormwater Solutions in Smart Growth

As the links between development patterns and water quality have been more clearly defined, environmental officials, local government planners, and engineers have begun to look for strategies to prevent flooding and property damage while also minimizing the amounts of pollutants flowing into water. Local governments increasingly are looking to the use of comprehensive plans and smart-growth principles to manage a host of city or county goals, which often include stormwater management.

Your locality or state may have smart growth (or in some areas, quality growth or sustainable growth) plans. Simply put, smart growth is development that serves the community, the economy, and the environment. According to the Smart Growth Network (*www.smartgrowth.org*), there are 10 guiding principles of smart growth:

1. Mix land uses.
2. Take advantage of compact building design.
3. Create a range of housing opportunities and choices.
4. Create walkable neighborhoods.

5. Foster distinctive, attractive communities with a strong sense of place.
6. Preserve open space, farmland, natural beauty, and critical environmental areas.
7. Strengthen and direct development toward existing communities.
8. Provide a variety of transportation choices.
9. Make development decisions predictable, fair, and cost-effective.
10. Encourage community and stakeholder collaboration in development decisions.

While better stormwater management is not explicit in the principles, the water-quantity benefits are, quite literally, built in. Compact building design, including building and parking footprints, can reduce the amount of impervious surface associated with each development unit of housing or commercial space. Directing development toward existing communities makes better use of existing infrastructure and provides an economic base for ongoing maintenance and repair of pipes and treatment facilities.

Your city or county may already be engaged in planning and zoning ordinance revisions that have stormwater benefits. The sections here look at some of those efforts and how you can include them in meeting goals for water quality and regulatory requirements. By coordinating across departments, using programs already in place, and integrating those efforts in your environmental programs, you can save money and time.

Regional Planning

Watersheds may be an entirely new organizing feature for managers who are used to working within jurisdictional boundaries, or at most with metropolitan planning agencies. Planning at the watershed scale is gaining attention not only because of stormwater regulation but as a way to manage other water-quality and -quantity problems, such as protection of source water and flooding. Governing at the watershed level requires cooperation across new sets of political boundaries.

This is not to say that managers in neighboring cities and counties have not worked cooperatively before. In fact, if your community is affected by the stormwater rules, you are likely to also be in a fast-growing part of the country dealing with housing, emergency response, transportation, and economic development issues. Existing cooperative agreements on these issues might also serve as partnerships for watershed and stormwater planning.

Your locality, for example, may have a memorandum of understanding (MOU) or memorandum of agreement (MOA) with a local soil conservation district, university, or metropolitan planning organization for planning efforts initiated before the stormwater rules came into effect. Provisions on cost-sharing, enforcement, resource allocation, or data generation might be in place; these can be a good starting point for working with those entities for a watershed-wide planning effort. In addition, determine if there are existing MOUs or MOAs on water-quality monitoring, floodplain mapping, or other water-related activities.

There are other activities that may not occur through a formal organization but that can be used to meet stormwater requirements. States are increasingly creating and modifying land use legislation that allows cities and counties to work together creatively. Managers are likely to be familiar with local and regional efforts to set aside land for preservation. These land preservation deals may have aspects that deal with water quality or quantity — aspects that can be counted in comprehensive stormwater regulations.

What should a manager look for? See if your local government is involved in efforts to establish transfer or purchase of development rights. The areas to be preserved may also be areas that are part of a sourcewater protection plan or important forest cover, and therefore play a role in regional stormwater control. (See more information in this article for areas designated to receive development rights.) You can also check to see if your jurisdiction has special overlay zoning to protect sensitive waterbodies or wetlands. If so, they could be important elements in meeting the requirements of stormwater regulations.

There are also emerging policy innovations that could be included in your plan. Water-quality trading programs are emerging to control nutrients and a few other pollutants but are also being used for water quantity and stormwater. The Charles River Watershed in Massachusetts was one of the first communities chosen to pilot a water-quality trading program sponsored by EPA. While the foundation of the program is pollutant-based, it was sparked by the alteration of water flow to the river caused by increased development in the watershed. For more information, visit the Web site at *www.crwa.org.*

Another emerging tool in watershed programs is that of impervious surface caps. Research indicates that water-quality problems show a marked increase once 10 percent of a watershed is covered by such impervious surfaces as development, roads, and parking lots. This could encourage impervious surface trading among jurisdictions in a watershed for a balance of developed and preserved land.[1]

Streets and Street Design

Two aspects to street design and stormwater have implications for stormwater management: the retrofit of existing streets for better stormwater performance and the layout of new streets. Since many departments of transportation are now required to obtain stormwater permits, there is a growing body of information on best management practices (BMPs) for roadways. Common mitigation techniques include obtaining buffer strips between roadways and streams, and creating bioinfiltration areas or other stormwater management measures.

Seattle, Washington, is a leader in retrofitting existing streets to catch excess stormwater. Its "Green Streets" program uses both structural and nonstructural techniques for retaining and infiltrating rainwater that would otherwise travel along curbs and drain into waterways.

In addition to street surfaces, street layout can have a great impact on stormwater generation, though in complex ways. Certainly, streets create obvious connected, impervious cover by way of parking lots, driveways, curbs, and gutters. For most water-quality professionals, connected impervious surfaces have traditionally been associated with poor water outcomes because the cumulative volume of water, and the pollutants that flow with it, are led uninterrupted to receiving waterways. This begs the question of whether the converse is better for water quality: Does a disconnected and dispersed road system serve the watershed better? The answer lies both in road design and the design of development projects served by those roads.

In most growing areas, site development is governed by subdivision codes or zoning codes that establish discrete areas for housing and commercial activity. Most new development relies on the automobile as the sole viable travel option. As a result, parking spaces, drive lanes, and wide roads are built to meet a system where almost every trip is made by car.

The route to getting better watershed and stormwater performance from better street designs is complex, but you should look for such design aspects as new codes that reduce the number of parking spaces and a mix of uses to better link commuting, shopping, and other activities.

According to the U.S. Department of Transportation's Bureau of Transportation Statistics, on average, people travel 40 miles per day, 88 percent of it (35 miles) in a personal vehicle such as an automobile. Americans take 411 billion daily trips annually. People average about four trips per day.[2] These numbers translate into standards for road design, building design, and parking for individual car trips.

Your planning office, however, may be considering plans that call for a more connected and multi-use transportation system. These systems look at a better mix of development uses, a more compact form, and new development standards that recognize the opportunities for reducing both the length and number of auto trips. These designs may be listed as "new urbanist plans," "traditional neighborhood designs," or "conservation designs." Depending on your zoning and planning system, these may be separate plans or incorporated in "planned unit development" zones or subdivision codes.

At the core of these plans should be a new pattern of street design that allows a more compact form and connects the new development to existing development and activity areas.

One other aspect of street design that local government managers need to consider are standards that govern street design and width for emergency response and safety. In some areas, overly wide streets are required to meet an emergency response model that allows two emergency vehicles to pass in opposite directions. Some emergency responders note that safety is actually compromised under this model because the wide streets encourage higher speeds.

In addition, they note that disconnected cul-de-sacs have a greater effect on hampering response times than narrower streets. The key for a manager is to include emergency responders, public works officials, and stormwater managers in revisions to street codes to find solutions to fit multiple objectives. The Local Government Commission (*www.lgc.org*) has developed fact sheets and research to help localities design multi-objective street design.

Parking

In the past, rarely used, excess parking spaces were seen as a development feature that came with little or no extra cost. The costs, however, are becoming more apparent as localized flooding increases, infiltration is diminished for aquifer recharge, and local water quality decreases. For stormwater managers, this extra impervious surface presents a real challenge — but one that can be tackled by reviewing and fine-tuning development regulations.

Local governments and developers typically plan the number of parking spaces for a particular development project based on published standards. These standards suggest a given number of spaces per 1,000 square feet or per housing unit, and tend to overestimate

the number of spaces needed. An analysis conducted by the Institute of Transportation Engineers in 1987 found that while the recommended parking ratio for shopping malls is five spaces per 1,000 square feet, the actual demand is only four spaces per 1,000 square feet. In conducting the research, ITE found the typical range of spaces provided at shopping malls to be from four to six spaces.

There are several policies that communities can adopt to better manage parking and, consequently, the stormwater that flows through parking lots. These can include:

Resource Information

The Environmental Protection Agency (EPA) and other organizations are developing a growing number of Web sites and publications to help communities develop plans and policies that consider both smart growth and stormwater. EPA's Web site on smart growth (*www.epa.gov/smartgrowth*) contains links to many free publications, including upcoming publications on street design, parking, and using smart growth techniques as stormwater best management practices.

In 2004, EPA published "Protecting Water Resources with Smart Growth," a good introduction to thinking about joint water and smart growth policies and programs. EPA's Office of Water sponsors the Watershed Academy, which contains educational materials that can be downloaded for free. Visit the Web site at *www.epa.gov/owow/watershed/wacademy/*.

ICMA has also developed expertise and resources on smart growth. For communities looking for specific policies and implementation strategies, the primers "Getting to Smart Growth" and "Getting to Smart Growth II" offer information, examples, and additional resources. To join the Smart Growth Network and gain access to information on smart growth, e-mail Dan Emerine at *smartgrowth@icma.org* or call 202/962-3623. For additional materials on smart growth, go to the Smart Growth Network's Web site at *www.smartgrowth.org*.

Shared Parking Arrangements Among Several Building Owners or Tenants

Different types of businesses can have different demands for parking throughout a day. Spaces used by office workers during the day, for example, can be used for restaurant parking at night. Shared arrangements are usually based on an agreement signed by the users so that liability, patrol, and cleanup are agreed upon ahead of time.

Better Use of On-Street Public Parking Spaces

Parking along public streets might be an overlooked resource for a community that wants to add parking efficiently. Unused travel lanes can be converted to spaces, or parallel parking spaces can be converted to diagonal spaces to add parking. In St. Louis, Missouri, diagonal parking is allowed near churches on Sunday in spaces reserved for parallel parking during the workweek.

Setting Parking Maximums, Not Minimums

Parking standards are usually expressed

as the minimum number of spaces to consider for a particular use (e.g., retail or housing). Parking maximums put a cap on the number of spaces that can be built and give water managers better control over the overall development footprint of building projects.

"Unbundling" the Cost of Parking for Apartments

Renters usually write one check a month for rent, which includes the cost of a parking space. By "unbundling" the cost of the parking into a separate bill, the real costs of a parking space are accentuated. Unbundling the costs of parking can be a good strategy to argue for fewer spaces in locations where land costs are high and other transportation options exist. This can also be a good strategy in college towns where parking pressures are severe and the potential for new or expanded transit is high.

Redevelopment

One of the more overlooked, yet most powerful, stormwater management strategies lies in the redevelopment of existing parcels of developed land. The relationship of redevelopment to stormwater is pretty straightforward: When a building is abandoned and the activity transfers to a new building, the watershed must deal with the impacts of two impervious parcels, even if one is vacant. Thus, efforts to steer development demand toward older downtowns, empty parking lots, vacant properties, and underperforming commercial areas have a powerful stormwater angle.

One example of an explicit tie between redevelopment and stormwater lies in New Jersey's Model Stormwater Control Ordinance for Municipalities. In this model ordinance, projects that qualify in "urban redevelopment centers" are exempt from the state's water recharge requirements.

Among other things, projects in enter-

prise zones qualify. This innovative approach takes advantage of work already completed to delineate neighborhoods for priority redevelopment efforts, and serves as an incentive for redevelopment. The exemption is given because land in the urban areas is not likely to be best suited for recharging aquifers and the most common BMPs for recharge are not the best way to handle stormwater in urban settings.

San Jose, California, developed an ordinance on the municipal level that allows alternative compliance measures where the standard list of BMPs is deemed by the city to be impractical. The ordinance gives the city latitude to find that certain smart growth projects can qualify as water quality benefit projects. These projects are, by their design or location in the watershed, considered to have water benefits.

In the list of definitions, the city lists examples of smart growth projects, significant redevelopment projects in the urban core, brownfield sites redevelopment, and projects that contain affordable housing. To many, this may seem to be an unorthodox approach to stormwater management, but it shows that the city understands the regional implications of dispersed growth.

As a local government manager, you may want to review economic development plans to see where they can also serve within regional stormwater planning. For transfer of development rights, your locality may contain areas designated to receive development rights and density from areas to be preserved.

On a watershed scale, this pairing of land to be preserved with land to be developed may have benefits for the watershed that can be a part of your stormwater management plan. For the transfer of development rights receiving area, this may be counterintuitive, since you may be adding impervious surface. Regional and local stormwater management plans, however, should recognize the benefits of a strategy that both preserves and redirects development.

Stormwater Management and Key Regulatory Elements

The Clean Water Act is the legislation governing stormwater. Point source discharges to waters of the U.S. are regulated using National Pollutant Discharge Elimination System (NPDES) permits. The Clean Water Act provides for the delegation of authority over these permits to the states. Currently, most states have been delegated that authority.[3]

In 1987, the Clean Water Act was amended to require the permitting and control of urban stormwater discharges. In 1990, regulations for the first phase of the NPDES program went into effect for certain local governments with populations of more than 100,000.

New rules published in 1999 extended coverage to operators of regulated small local, separate storm sewer systems (MS4s) serving less than 100,000. MS4s are local governments that have separate (not combined with sanitary sewer systems) storm sewer systems that deliver stormwater directly to rivers, streams, or the ocean. These facilities were required to apply for a stormwater permit by March 2003. NPDES permits are renewed every five years.

The NPDES stormwater permit. States that have delegated authority to carry out the stormwater provisions of the Clean Water Act issue NPDES permits. In the District of Columbia and in states, territories, and tribal lands that are not authorized for the program, EPA issues NPDES permits. The permits are written to comply with minimum requirements issued by EPA. Localities then apply for coverage under the state permit to discharge stormwater. Most states and EPA issue coverage under general permits: a one-size-fits-all approach where all permittees have identical permit requirements. States are also offering the option of permit coverage under individual or customized permits.

Stormwater management plan. Under the NPDES stormwater program, permittees must develop a stormwater management plan that provides the details of how the community (owner or operator of the storm sewer system) will comply with the requirements of the permit. Permits are based on a framework of six minimum measures:

• Public Education and Outreach on Stormwater Impacts
• Public Involvement/Participations
• Illicit Discharge Detection and Elimination
• Construction Site Stormwater Runoff Control
• Post-Construction Stormwater Management in New Development and Redevelopment
• Pollution Prevention/Good Housekeeping for Municipal Operations

Stormwater ordinance. A number of states are encouraging—and in some instances requiring—that localities develop ordinances for stormwater control. These can be stand-alone ordinances or woven into existing land use, preservation, or water regulations.

For more information, visit the Web site at *www.epa.gov/npdes*.

You should also check to see if there are local regulations that serve as barriers to the type of development that delivers better stormwater performance on the site and watershed levels. As mentioned above, limits on the amount of impervious surface have been implemented at the site level in the past. This, however, has turned out to be less protective in some areas because limiting impervious cover at the site level can drive large lot development.

This, in turn, disperses development further, resulting in extended infrastructure requirements, longer roads to serve housing, and less emphasis on connecting jobs and housing. Impervious cover limits can also stand in the way of "main street" and transit district development, where intensive development on each lot is desired.

Summary

As a local government manager, you are in a unique position to identify and coordinate programs to achieve multiple benefits.

For stormwater management, this article has presented several opportunities that exist with common economic development, land development, and public works programs.

At first glance, these existing departments may see new stormwater rules as an intrusion into established programs. The key for city and county managers is to help make the connections, identify hidden opportunities in existing plans, and broker new rules that meet the objectives of a variety of interests, departments, and budgets.

Notes

1. Note that impervious coverage caps on a watershed basis are different from those established within local zoning codes for individual development projects. While site-level impervious surface caps have been shown, in some cases, to exacerbate dispersed development, on a watershed basis, a cap can help watershed managers focus on both land to preserve and land to develop.

2. U.S. Department of Transportation, Bureau of Transportation Statistics and Federal Highway Administration, 2001 National Household Travel Survey, Preliminary Data Release Version 1.

3. Currently, Idaho, New Mexico, Arizona, Alaska, Maine, New Hampshire, Massachusetts, and Puerto Rico have not been delegated the authority to issue the NPDES permits for stormwater.

CHAPTER 39

Streamwood, IL, Takes Measures to Protect Its Rivers and Streams

Steve Gibbs

Like a train leaving the station, the impact of the Federal Water Pollution Control Act of 1972 has gradually gained momentum over the years. After more than a quarter-century the effects of the Clean Water Act, as it is often called, are undeniable: America's surface waters are cleaner than they have been in three decades.

There was a time when the Clean Water Act was not vigorously enforced. A few years ago, the U.S. Environmental Protection Agency turned up the heat on enforcement, with particular attention to rules governing point source pollution control and erosion control. The National Pollutant Discharge Elimination System (NPDES) is the portion of the Clean Water Act dealing with point source pollution control. The NPDES states that facilities such as businesses and housing developments that discharge pollutants from any point source into America's waterways must have a permit.

"The NPDES definitely has more bite these days. There is much greater enforcement and fines are being levied for noncompliance," said Trudy Buehler, P.E., with Mackie Consultants in Rosemont, Ill.

The growing emphasis on point source pollution control has focused increasing attention on stormwater runoff. As a result, public works directors all over the country are now addressing the issue, some more eagerly than others. One of the most ardent clean water proponents in northern Illinois is John White, P.E., director of public works for the village of Streamwood, Ill. (population 36,500), a fast-growing suburb about 30 miles northwest of downtown Chicago. In addition to his duties for Streamwood, White serves on the Poplar Creek Watershed Planning Committee, a group that is the prototype for other regional watershed management organizations in the state. For the past several years, White has been actively involved in researching and designing a new residential stormwater system for his community that will incorporate some of the best new pollution control technologies available.

"It's too early to see the results in our local waters, but we're confident that the steps we've taken in designing this system will clean our stormwater runoff and protect the surface water in the area," said White.

Which Way to Go?

Streamwood's newest stormwater system was designed to transfer rainwater runoff from

Originally published as "Protecting Rivers and Streams," *Public Works*, Vol. 136, No. 8, July 2005. Published by Hanley Wood Business Media, Chicago, IL. Reprinted with permission of the publisher.

an upscale residential housing development to nearby Poplar Creek and then further downstream to the Fox River. The new development covers 120 acres and has almost 325 dwellings. Part of the acreage will be left as wetlands or detention ponds, meaning that some of the stormwater will not leave the site but instead percolate into the groundwater.

When considering this new subdivision, one of the first questions White had to answer was, "which stormwater pollution treatment technology was best for this application?" A studious and careful planner, White was not going to make a snap decision based on any one factor. "I started doing research into the different stormwater treatment systems on the Internet and in various publications," said White. "I went to the annual Water Environment Federation conference and spent a couple of days going to each manufacturer's booth to get specific information about each technology. I tried to be very thorough because this was an important decision for us. My goal is to use the same technology throughout all of Streamwood's storm sewer systems, for the sake of continuity and so that we only have to train our personnel to work on one type of device."

White said that several of the systems he examined do a good job of cleaning stormwater runoff and most are generally in the same price range, but that does not mean that all technologies are created equal.

"Ease of operation is always a consideration. I found that a lot of the systems are very difficult to clean. I don't want something that requires an enormous effort to maintain. We have two Vactor trucks already, so we felt it was important to find a technology that could be cleaned using those ma-

chines," he said. "We wanted to avoid buying new equipment or getting into a complicated maintenance program."

After considering several options, White

Pollution solution—people
The active ingredient in pollution control is people

Streamwood, Ill., is fortunate to have a corps of people who are interested in reducing and eventually eliminating pollution of local surface water. Their efforts will pay off for the next generation of Streamwood residents.

Public works director John White has taken an active role in creating systems to clean stormwater runoff, often a significant contributor to water pollution. White also serves on the Poplar Creek Watershed Planning Committee, which represents the efforts of several local communities to clean up the streams and rivers northwest of Chicago.

The committee has assessed the local surface water pollution problem and made recommendations on best management practices to clean up Poplar Creek and the Fox River. The Illinois EPA will use some of the processes created by the Poplar Creek committee as a template for similar groups across the state. The ultimate result will be cleaner water throughout Illinois.

Another active participant in the project is Elgin High School teacher Deb Perryman. Perryman, the 2004–05 Illinois Teacher of the Year, is playing a vital role in local environmental protection. She and her students monitor the water quality in Poplar Creek and their ongoing research will help public works officials like White make future decisions about treatment needs. She and her students also stenciled some 750 storm drains instructing people not to dump wastewater or pollutants into the storm sewer system. Many of these students, now aware of stormwater pollution issues, will become voters and community leaders in years to come.

The efforts of White, Perryman, and others have been enhanced by the support of local governments and even private business. Residential home builder Pulte Homes, one of the nation's largest developers, embraced a new storm sewer designed by White and Buehler that will remove much of the pollution that used to reach Poplar Creek. The company could have pushed for a cheaper or faster solution, but instead opted for the long-term solution—an effective cleaning system that is easily maintained.

This type of public-private collaboration will have a definite impact on the waterways near Streamwood. Within a few months the streams and rivers near Chicago will be cleaner and safer, thanks to some active ingredients.

zeroed in on CDS Technologies Inc., Morgan Hill, Calif., makers of a continuous deflective separation unit that removes solid wastes and floatables from stormwater. According to White, the technology was not only easy to maintain, it was an effective device for removing debris and contaminants from stormwater.

The CDS system is entirely self-operating, relying on water hydraulics and gravity. Raw stormwater enters the diversion chamber where a weir guides the flow into the unit's separation chamber. A vortex is formed that spins the water. The floatable and most suspended solids settle into the sump at the bottom of the separation chamber. The trash and suspended solids remain in the sump until they are removed, typically once or twice a year. The water that is now free of floatables and suspended solids then passes through a self-cleaning screen that removes any remaining debris and then is discharged to Poplar Creek.

Buehler was the lead designer of the Streamwood system. Working with White and the subdivision's developer Pulte Homes, she created a system design calling for 14 CDS devices, each one measuring 6 or 8 feet in diameter.

"We've become very familiar with the CDS technology," said Buehler. "It is a simple technology with a relatively small footprint, and by all accounts it works very well. We heard a lot of good things about it before using it on this project."

Experienced public works directors know that stormwater runoff from certain areas such as lawns and parking lots may contain high concentrations of nitrogen and phosphorous, as well as trash and suspended solids. Removing these chemicals is important in protecting local surface waters but it is not easy to do. According to Buehler, CDS Technologies worked with her in designing modifications in several of the units, fitting them with additional infiltration chambers to trap nitrogen and phosphorous. These special units were placed in strategic locations to filter out the unwanted contaminants.

The CDS units, each weighing in excess of 20,000 pounds, were manufactured nearby at local precaster Welch Brothers in Elgin, Ill. When the units become fully functional this fall, White and his colleagues can evaluate their effectiveness. White seems relatively confident that his system will deliver stormwater that is free of debris to the area's streams.

CHAPTER 40

Toledo, OH, Takes Steps to Remove Pollutants from Its Rivers to Improve Water Quality

Joshua J. O'Neil and Stephen M. Way

The J. Preston Levis Commons Development is a distinctly unique, top quality, master-planned community built on 400 acres in northern Wood County, Ohio. It is strategically located just minutes from the Dixie Highway (S.R.-25) interchange with U.S.-23/I-475 in the Toledo suburb of Perrysburg. Entrance drives to the development exist on three of its four sides; however, the centrally located signature entrance is the Michael Owens Way Boulevard, which intersects with Roachton Road on the south side of the 400-acre plat.

Michael Owens Way is the main access to Owens-Illinois, Inc.'s (O-I) world headquarters and the backbone for the Levis Commons Development, off which other through streets will intersect, while also intersecting with Roachton Road a short distance from the recently constructed Perrysburg High School and surrounding residential developments.

Background

Nestled within northwest Ohio is a region formerly known as the "Great Black Swamp." The swamp was a glacial lake bottom and consisted of very flat topography with impermeable silt and clay soils with occasional sand ridges. Wet forests of hardwood, shallow lakes and prairies covered the swampland.

Between the water, vegetation, mosquitoes and malaria, and the heavy and sticky mud, European settlers found the swamp an obstacle to development. Settlement and farming eventually came to northwest Ohio and it became one of Ohio's best agricultural regions; however, it required draining of the swamp through an extensive system of ditches. It has been estimated that a total of three miles of man-made ditches to every mile of natural stream exist within the region.

The drainage ditches make productive farming possible, but many of them do not provide fish or wildlife habitat. Many of these ditches lack buffer areas and are farmed right up to the ditch bank, thus providing a direct route for nutrients and sediment runoff to Lake Erie. Despite draining and channelizing streams, the swamp still exists.

Originally published as "Beautification Pollution Control," *Storm Water Solutions*, Vol. 1, No. 3, May/June 2007. Published by Scranton Gillette Communications, Arlington Heights, IL. Reprinted with permission of the publisher.

Lake Erie Water Quality

"Eutrophic" is a term that describes a lake enriched with nutrients (phosphates and nitrates) and organic matter. That enrichment results in an increased rate of biological productivity. Studies in the 1970s and '80s identified phosphate as a critical nutrient for eutrophication. For Lake Erie, "over-nourishment" meant accelerated nuisance growths (blooms) of cyanobacteria. These blooms are still popular and are called "toxic algae."

The immediate effect on Lake Erie was to make it an unpopular recreational location due to cyanobacteria's strong odor. The effect did not end there, however. During the winter season, these blooms would die and sink to the lake floor where they covered fish spawning and feeding locations. Ultimately, the decaying blooms would deplete dissolved oxygen from the water that fish and aquatic life needed to survive; the result was an area within the lake known as a "dead zone."

Water quality continues to be a growing concern throughout northwest Ohio and the Great Lakes region as a whole. Legislative action and proactive changes to the management of surface runoff have resulted in significant improvements in water quality throughout the Great Lakes and the elimination of a majority of the dead zones that were prevalent; however, the improvements realized in Lake Erie have declined since the 1990s.

This condition was noted at the same time that Zebra Mussels spread throughout the lake and impacted the environmental balance. Scientists do not completely understand the ecological impact these creatures had on the system; however, they do believe a change in the nutrient routing through the ecosystem did occur.

In 2002 and 2003, the dead zone within Lake Erie's central and western basins and the toxic blooms returned. It is unclear what happened to cause the reoccurrence, although the intrusion of increased levels of phosphorus into the lake is suspected.

Regional Objectives

In its "Areawide Water Quality Management Plan," the Toledo Metropolitan Area Council of Governments stated:

> Phosphorus is considered the critical nutrient where Lake Erie is concerned, but "algae blooms" also require nitrates. Concern over nitrate usually centers on its drinking water impacts, but does it also control algae growth? The question is important to public policy. Nitrates are soluble in water, so controlling nitrates means controlling water. Phosphorus attaches to sediment, so controlling phosphorus means controlling sediment. What should be the priorities of environmental agencies?
>
> Our conclusion is that our primary focus needs to be reduction of sediment and phosphorus, but in conjunction with stream habitat restoration.... For bays and Lake Erie, research and policy emphasizes phosphorus and sediment reduction to control nuisance "algae blooms" and protect aquatic habitat.
>
> Sediment is a pollutant in its own right. Ecologically, it is important because phosphorus attaches to it and is carried with sediment. Generally speaking, actions that reduce the amount of sediment going into Lake Erie will reduce the amount of phosphorus. When sediment settles out, it covers the bottom of streams, bays and Lake Erie. Doing so, it covers fish feeding and spawning areas.

There continues to be quite a bit of specification development relative to sediment and erosion control within construction sites and the implementation of post-construction best management practices (BMPs) within the industry; however, all involved seem to be in agreement that the long-term control of sediment will have ecological benefits to the Lake Erie water quality.

In Ohio, non-point source programs are managed by the Ohio Environmental Protection Agency (EPA) and Department of Natural Resources; these agencies have typically taken the position that reducing the impacts from non-point sources is a matter of prevention through BMPs. A BMP should:

• Be effective in reducing water pollution from non-point sources;

- Be effective in helping waterways meet Clean Water Act "fishable and swimmable" goals; and
- Be practicable.

Project Development

The project use of storm water pollution prevention techniques during construction, as well as post-construction BMPs, were being monitored by the Ohio EPA. Michael Owens Way was designed as an asymmetric boulevard with multi-use pathways winding their way through more than 3,000 plants and trees to create a calming experience for the traveler within the corridor. The design results in a linear park setting that has characteristics similar to New York City's Central Park.

Further accentuating the calming experience provided by the corridor is the innovative bioswale design used to clean storm water prior to its leaving the project site. The use of this bioswale technique eliminated the need for other more conventional design methods (detention ponds), which would have required more land area and detracted from the corridor's beauty while adhering to all Ohio EPA current regulations.

Design Criteria and Approach

The design team's first objective was to develop a method in which the urban runoff from Michael Owens Way could be "cleaned" prior to entering Perrysburg's storm sewer system without detracting from the architectural theme of the corridor. Perrysburg's storm sewer system in this area of the city outlets into Schaller Ditch and eventually the Maumee River. The solution was a bioswale hidden within the boulevard's center median.

The bioswale was designed to clean runoff resulting from a two-year design frequency storm (first flush). The cross-section and grade were engineered to limit the depth of flow to less than 6 in. and the velocity to a rather slow 1 ft per second. By utilizing this criteria and introducing grasses and aquatic plants that could withstand the pollutants that would be entering the bioswale from the adjacent boulevard, the result was an aesthetically pleasing BMP that adhered to the regional goals of limiting the amount of sediment that is introduced into the Maumee River and Lake Erie. Although the bioswale was designed as a BMP, it also serves as the primary drainage system for Michael Owens Way and meets all local roadway drainage design standards (e.g. 10-year design storm frequency).

The performance of the bioswale is dependent on the boulevard cross slopes set to drain toward the center curb lines where a series of Neenah Foundry R-3165 curb inlet frames, grates and curb boxes were positioned. The use of the curb boxes, in lieu of the more traditional catch basin, allowed a 12-in. outlet pipe to drain directly into the shallow bioswale. The use of this system provided additional benefits to the project overall, the most notable of which was the relative flatness of the site, and the required hydraulic gradient was not going to allow a normal ditch section to drain back into Perrysburg's storm sewer system.

Landscape and Streetscape enhancements are abundant along the roadway and linear park. The trees and low-level plantings were specifically selected to provide four-season attraction in northwest Ohio's climate. Decorative bollards, brick pedestrian ramps, stamped and colored crosswalks, lighting and other features also are present. Levis Commons adheres to strict architectural standards that require all plans to be reviewed and approved by an architectural review committee (ARC). DGL Consulting Engineers worked closely with the ARC to exceed the architectural standards required in the development.

The ribbon-cutting ceremony for the roadway was held on Aug. 18, 2006, in conjunction with the opening of the O-I world headquarters that is located at the head of Michael Owens Way. City of Perrysburg Mayor Nelson Evans and Larry Dillin, president of the Dillin Corp., cut the ribbon at the signature entrance. The pride that Perrysburg has over its Michael Owens Way boulevard and the Levis Commons Development was summarized by Mayor Evans: "I believe Michael Owens Way will set the new standard for roadway design and entranceway enhancements. Certainly it has raised the bar for Levis Commons, if that was even possible."

CHAPTER 41

University Place, WA, Prepares Multi-Agency Master Plan for Water-Sensitive Land Area

Brett Davis

Chambers Creek's master site plan is an ambitious project.

With an estimated $70 million in proposed improvements and a conservative time line of 50 years, the plan seeks nothing less than the transformation of 930 acres in Pierce County, Washington, from a working gravel mine with a wastewater treatment plant into a first-rate public recreation facility.

That transformation is already well under way, with completion of Grandview Trail, a "green" county environmental services building, and ballfields. Planned developments include beach access, 10 miles of trails, two public piers, a boat launch, golf course, arboretum, production nursery, and open space.

The project is a lesson in the benefits of governmental cooperation. The properties are located in the cities of University Place (pop. 30,000) and Lakewood (pop. 58,000) as well as unincorporated Pierce County, so the plan's implementation has required a multi-jurisdictional approach. The plan has also benefited from a planning process that brought public awareness, participation, and financial sup-

port. The Chambers Creek Properties Master Site Plan received APA's 2004 Current Topic Award — Parks and Public Land.

This year's special topic award was designed to recognize a plan, management program, design, or program that makes a significant contribution to the protection, maintenance, aesthetics, or utility of public lands at the local, regional, state, or federal levels. The criteria: broad support and context, transferability, balance, and a significant role for planners and demonstration of the value of planners to a broader public.

Private Land

By the early 1990s, Pierce County (pop. 700,000) had, bit by bit, acquired 930 privately owned acres of land in the Chambers Creek area, a site just west of Tacoma. Surrounded by suburban residential areas, the Chambers Creek Properties, as they came to be known, include two miles of Puget Sound shoreline and three miles of forested creek canyon.

Originally published as "Chambers Creek Properties Master Site Plan, Pierce County, Washington," *Planning*, Vol. 70, No. 4, April 2004. Reprinted with permission from PLANNING, copyright April 2004 by the American Planning Association, Suite 1600, 120 South Michigan Avenue, Chicago, Illinois, 60603, USA.

The largest single purchase was the Lone Star Northwest Gravel Mine, originally bought for expansion of a wastewater treatment plant, but community opposition and lawsuits stymied the county's wastewater proposals.

Purchase of the mine turned out to be the catalyst for a new planning effort, and in 1995 the county consolidated planning for the site. "We kind of blended these all together," says project manager Joseph Scorcio, AICP, special assistant to the director of Pierce County Public Works and Utilities.

The Chambers Creek Properties Master Site Plan was the result. The county council voted unanimous approval in August 1997, and the two city councils endorsed it soon after. In 2000, University Place, Lakewood, and Pierce County adopted a joint procedural agreement outlining the process for implementing the plan in each jurisdiction and streamlining the permitting process for individual projects.

"It wasn't clear and it wasn't easy," says Scorcio. For more than 100 years the land had been privately owned, he explains, and now that it was publicly owned it was possible to develop it. Planners asked themselves, "What could we do?"

A lot, it turns out. The plan is off to a good start and is ahead of schedule. The time line, Scorcio notes, is actually closer to 25 than the specified 50 years. Several projects of the hundreds that make up the plan have been completed, with several others in various stages of development.

The 1.5-mile Grandview Trail, which opened in 2000, provided public access to the site for the first time. A second phase opened in 2002. The trail provides sweeping views of Puget Sound, as well as public plaza overlook points, and is popular with walkers, runners, and bicyclists. "As we build it, it instantly becomes filled up," Scorcio says.

Completion of the county environmental services building in fall 2002 helped set the tone for environmentally friendly structures yet to come. The 50,000-square-foot building makes extensive use of recycled and non-toxic materials, natural light and air circulation, and uses rainwater from the roof to irrigate plants. Two multipurpose ballfields opened for play in October.

Golf and Native Plants

Major projects in the development phase include a world-class golf course and a native plant production nursery. The golf course is designed to be the primary economic engine for the site.

"We have been conducting market and feasibility studies," Scorcio says, "which indicate that based on our location, amenities, and market, a full-service clubhouse, driving range, teaching facility, restaurant, high-end daily fee course capable of hosting championship events are what we should consider." A designer is being selected, with construction to begin next year.

The nursery will focus on native plants. "We need a large quantity of plants specifically bred to use in the rehabilitation of mined-out sites like ours," says Scorcio. "One of the master site plan's projects is to recruit one or more of these specialized nursery companies to the site. This would not only generate a source for our uses here, but would provide the potential for a commercial vendor to generate revenues — trees, leases, taxes — to help provide other master site plan uses."

The trilateral agreement calls for the county to develop the land with the support of University Place and Lakewood. It consolidates the permitting process for individual projects and allows for design standards that supplement and replace general development regulations within each jurisdiction.

"Guidelines are more specific and detailed than general city-wide standards and more than most private development-based guidelines," Scorcio says. "On the reverse side, as an example, we exchanged quantity — fewer trees in landscaped areas — for quality. Each tree is much larger than typically required. We believe that consistency, predictability, and quality over the long term are worth the apparent strictness of our choices."

Community involvement is one reason for the project's success. Residents played a key role in developing the plan and continue to do so, helping to account for the accelerated time line. "The public has been very supportive," says Scorcio. He credits the Chambers Creek Foundation with playing a significant part in making the project a reality, and predicts that "their role is only going to grow over time."

"How Can I Help?"

The nonprofit foundation, established in 2000 by members of the community, is the official clearinghouse for donated funds and projects for the Chambers Creek Properties, and attracts volunteers. When people see the site for the first time, "they are astonished," says Valarie Zeeck, president of the founda-

tion. "To a person, they say, 'What can I do to help?'"

The foundation has helped complete several projects. It worked with the Tacoma Labyrinth Project to help build and donate the $70,000 Chambers Creek Labyrinth, a circle, 45 feet in diameter, made up of two-toned concrete brick pavers, a spot for walking meditation or seated contemplation. Eagle Scouts have worked with the foundation on a number of projects, including clean-up efforts.

Those working on and affected by the project are excited about how far it has come and how far it will go. "You keep all your projects running," says Scorcio. "When money and opportunity come, you take it."

"An opportunity like the Chambers Creek Properties comes around but once in a lifetime," says county executive John Ladenburg. "When finished, the site will be one of the premier recreation areas in the Pacific Northwest. An effort of this magnitude requires a plan that reflects the quality of the location and meets the needs of the community."

CHAPTER 42

Washington, DC, Improves the Quality of Its Drinking Water

Kevin Dixon

When Washington, D.C., discovered elevated lead levels in its drinking water in July 2002, water utilities throughout the country began scrutinizing their practices for controlling waterborne lead. Managers knew that, in sufficient quantities, lead consumption could be dangerous to residents, particularly young children, infants and fetuses.

In most circumstances, lead is not present in the drinking water produced at municipal water treatment plants. It enters the water following contact with lead-containing components in the distribution system, such as lead service lines or in homes where solder containing lead joins copper pipes. Hence, utilities face the task of replacing their lines as well as encouraging, if not requiring, homeowners to do the same.

What Happened in D.C.?

The high levels of lead in Washington's water were attributed to a change in chemical disinfectant and the resulting reactions with lead in the distribution system's components. To address the problem, the District's Water and Sewer Authority (WASA) added orthophosphate — a corrosion-inhibiting chemical — to the water supply, is replacing all lead service lines and began extensive monitoring. WASA also immediately launched a public education program.

The Authority's Board of Directors agreed to replace all of its lead service lines over six years and negotiated special rates so homeowners could replace the private portion of the lead-laced service lines. To date, several thousand lead service lines have been replaced. "Monitoring results indicate that the lead levels in the water supply have substantially dropped, but further analysis is needed," says WASA Water Quality Manager Richard Giani.

Madison, Wis., discovered that treating water to avoid waterborne lead problems could lead to another problem. When the city exceeded EPA's allowable level of lead in drinking water (15 parts per billion), it had to reduce the lead corrosion in its pipes. However, adding orthophosphate — the only compound that would meet EPA lead level standards — to the drinking water would have exceeded the city's wastewater treatment system's capacity

Originally published as "Getting the Lead Out," *American City & County*, Vol. 120, No. 11, November 2005. Published by Penton Media, Overland Park, KS. Reprinted with permission from *American City & Country* magazine. Copyright 2005, Penton Media, New York, NY.

to remove phosphorus. It also would have significantly increased phosphorus loading in area lakes from drinking water entering the stormwater system or by direct runoff from outdoor use of the drinking water (washing cars, lawn sprinkling).

"Those impacts would have affected the whole community, not just those customers with lead service lines," says Madison Water Utility General Manager David Denig-Chakroff. "We needed an alternative to chemical treatment, so we decided to go to the root of the problem and replace the approximately 11,000 remaining lead water service lines in the city over a 10-year period."

The most difficult part of Madison's plan was replacing both the utility's and the homeowners' lead service lines. Because legal and liability issues prevented Madison from working on private property, the city passed an ordinance requiring property owners to replace lead service lines at the same time the city replaces the lead service line adjacent to the homeowner's property.

The city also created an incentive for the homeowners to cooperate. "Madison established a reimbursement program, whereby any customer who replaces a lead water service line on private property in accordance with the city ordinance, can apply for reimbursement of half the cost of replacement, up to $1,000," Denig-Chakroff says.

For low-income customers, Madison pays the entire plumbing cost but places a lien on the property for half the cost. The city started the program to replace approximately 6,000 utility-owned service lines and 5,000 customer-owned service lines in January 2001. By the end of August 2005, Madison had replaced 4,214 utility-owned service lines, and customers had replaced 3,494 lines.

"As of September 2005, we have replaced 70 percent of the lead service lines, and we are over two years ahead of schedule for meeting our 10-year deadline for replacement," Denig-Chakroff says. "With so many utilities now facing difficulties maintaining low lead levels

or needing to change their corrosion control treatment to maintain compliance with federal standards, it's becoming more clear that we made the right choice to target the source of the lead and remove the source from the system," he says.

Denig-Chakroff reports that some lead particulates remain stranded in the plumbing system after replacement. "But our post-replacement sampling program is showing that, over time, without the service line providing a source of lead, stranded particulates are flushed out and lead levels will continue to decline," he says.

Lead Monitoring Is Difficult

Utilities have discovered that complying with the specific monitoring requirements of the Lead and Copper Rule (LCR) — EPA's regulation to control lead and copper in drinking water — can be difficult. For example, a one-liter sample of water must be collected from the homeowner's kitchen sink tap only after the homeowner stops using water throughout the entire home for six to eight hours.

Because it is difficult to gain access to customers' homes to collect the samples, many utilities must rely on residents to collect the samples, which can lead to errors. While errors do not invalidate samples once they have been sent to the laboratory, water utilities cannot ensure samples are collected within the prescribed time or with proper collection procedures.

"We frequently find it necessary to call customers several times to remind them to provide samples or return the associated questionnaire," says Jeff Swertfeger, supervising chemist at the Greater Cincinnati Water Works. "For a system of our size, which collects hundreds of lead samples each year, coordinating and completing the sampling is a big effort."

Swertfeger says utilities also can experience problems when the residential sampling reveals high lead levels in homes with poor plumbing. "Under the current requirements, a municipal utility could exceed the Action Level — requiring drastic action — because of a situation outside its control," he says.

Water Contamination at Schools

The discovery of high lead levels in water at schools and child-care facilities in several large American cities recently has gained national attention. Although each school or child-care administrator is legally responsible for the lead levels in those water systems, water utilities have been assisting the facilities.

The Philadelphia Water Department, for example, has joined with the city's Department of Public Health to help reduce children's lead exposure. "Even though Philadelphia's drinking water is optimized for corrosion control, a percentage of taps in schools were found to have elevated lead," says Gary Burlingame, administrative scientist in the Bureau of Laboratory Services for the Philadelphia Water Department.

Having identified which taps in the public schools needed attention, U.S. EPA Region III, the Philadelphia Department of Public Health (Childhood Lead Poisoning Prevention Program), the School District of Philadelphia and the Philadelphia Water Department shared responsibility for mitigating the elevated levels of lead in the drinking water. "The interpretation of lead sampling results from homes — let alone from buildings with complicated plumbing systems such as schools — can be quite challenging because such buildings have multiple potential sources of lead," Burlingame says. Sources could include rust sediment, solder particulates and brass-containing faucets. "The Philadelphia Water Department brought its technical expertise with tap water sampling and testing, interpretation of water quality data and corrosion control to assist in guiding effective remediation strategies based on sound interpretations of the sampling data," he says.

Burlingame says that the first step toward solving a lead contamination problem is making sure that the utility's water has been adequately tested and optimized for corrosion control before determining if the water quality is stable as it moves through the distribution system and into customers' homes. Otherwise, the efforts taken by the schools to mitigate elevated lead levels will be complicated by variability in water quality. Beyond that, the water utilities' ability to help local health authorities and school managers will vary with their levels of expertise and resources.

"Some utilities can provide extensive assistance, and others do not have that capability," Burlingame says. "Nonetheless, communities need to know that their water utilities are aware of the situation and in agreement with the measures being taken to provide safe drinking water."

The National Picture

In anticipation of new regulations — including one to control harmful compounds formed by the addition of disinfectants, such as chlorine — many water utilities are considering significant changes in their treatment processes, including changing the disinfectant applied to water before it enters the distribution system. Washington's experience has shown that communities must be prepared for the consequences of changing their disinfection strategies.

Successfully managing lead in drinking water requires careful attention to optimum operational and treatment practices combined with diligent monitoring of corrosion control parameters and community outreach. Through such careful consideration and attention, municipal utilities can help provide a plentiful supply of safe drinking water to the communities they serve.

CHAPTER 43

West Des Moines, IA, Turns River and Watershed into Park and Open Space

Sally Ortgies and Edwin Slattery

A 770-acre former sand-and-gravel mine has been transformed into the crown jewel of West Des Moines, Iowa's parks program. It is now the site of Raccoon River Park.

Thanks to the vision of the West Des Moines Parks and Recreation Department and a cooperative effort with the Iowa Department of Natural Resources (IDNR), a variety of recreational opportunities are available to the residents of West Des Moines and to the nearly 500,000 residents of the Des Moines metropolitan area.

Years of planning, followed by a phased development program, have changed this large area that was once primarily disturbed land into a major leisure-time destination for softball, soccer, swimming, fishing, boating, hiking, bicycling, picnicking, nature study, special events, and relaxation.

The Setting

The park site, located in the floodplain of the Raccoon River and inside the city of West Des Moines's corporate boundaries, lies next to expanding West Des Moines neighborhoods

and within minutes of downtown Des Moines. It is bounded by the Raccoon River and a levee on the south and east and by a railroad line along the north and west. Here, the river's meanderings have created rich deposits of sand and gravel in the bottomlands that have formed the park site.

Sand and gravel mining operations started on the site about 1950, ending in 1991. Long-term removal of the sand and gravel created a 250-acre lake and many smaller ponds and wetlands. Most other parts of the site have had their topsoil removed or have had their natural features altered in some way by moving or reshaping the soil. In this way, areas of higher ground have risen from the construction of haul roads, deposits of spoil material, levees, and processing stations.

Before development, open space — comprising a combination of water, landforms, and vegetation — was the dominant characteristic of the site. Mining activities had left vegetated piles of overburden and excavated depressions that created extensive wetlands. The site was heavily vegetated with species normally present in highly disturbed areas.

About a dozen small, shallow, but per-

Originally published as "Underneath It All: Raccoon River Park," *Public Management*, Vol. 85, No. 3, April 2003. Published by the International City/County Management Association, Washington, D.C. Reprinted with permission of the publisher.

manent ponds and wetland areas are located on the site, with no clear pattern of drainage between or among them. Provisions for interconnecting these wet areas by culverts in order to promote free circulation of water within the lake system are included in the park development plan.

Along the edge of the park for more than two miles flows the Raccoon River, whose banks are steep in most places and range from four to 12 feet high. A levee was constructed by the mining company along the shoreline of the river to keep high river water from flooding the site, and though it has deteriorated in places, it still provides an excellent foundation for recreational trails.

As might have been expected on mining premises, there was little mature vegetation on the undeveloped site. Canopy-type trees were virtually absent, except along the river and in other isolated areas.

New growth like small trees and low-growing plants had occurred on the higher ground, along haul roads and spoil banks above the 10-year flood level. Other places featured scrub/shrub vegetation, providing extensive wildlife habitat. A marked absence of aquatic vegetation in the lake and ponds reflected the steepness of the bank, the depth of the water, and the lack of nutrients in the sterile sand bottom.

Waterfowl and deer have been the most frequently found inhabitants. Deer are substantial in their numbers and distributed over the entire park, as they have benefited from sufficient cover and availability of browse (grazing vegetation).

Waterfowl and shore birds are the most conspicuous users of the ponds and lake. Blue heron, double-crested cormorants, and Canadian geese are evident, while mallards, teal, and wood ducks are also abundant. An ecological survey performed in the summer of 1989 by the IDNR reported 44 species of birds seen at the site.

Active Participants in the Development

By earlier arrangements, the IDNR had obtained ownership and responsibility for the lake and adjacent areas from the mining company. The department had conducted studies of the lake and its surroundings and concluded that a valuable recreational resource could be developed. IDNR, however, was unwilling to develop and manage this resource without the support and cooperation of other levels of government. It was at this time that West Des Moines decided to join forces with the state in developing the site.

Even though recreational facilities had shown significant growth in West Des Moines in recent years, demand for organized sports facilities and open space still outstripped supply. The West Des Moines Parks and Recreation Department recognized the potential for developing a major complex for a number of sporting events and general recreational activities. To help bring this potential to reality, the city had bought two tracts of land totaling 112 acres as far back as 1987.

In 1988, an agreement was signed by the city and the IDNR that formalized their common interest in acquiring, developing, and managing land in Raccoon River Park. This agreement recognized the potential public benefit of the park facilities and identified the separate and joint responsibilities of each public participant.

Master Plan

In 1991, to realize the dream of a major recreational facility, a master plan was completed by Stanley consultants to determine:

1. Recreational and reclamation activities appropriate to the site.
2. Circulation, utilities, and services necessary to support these activities.
3. Best sequence and order of site development.

A matching of the characteristics of the site with the recreational needs of the community uncovered some unusual and exciting opportunities for development. An awareness of site constraints, site opportunities, and community needs became the basis for generating a realistic set of goals for the project, which included:

- To develop recreational and educational facilities and opportunities for the residents of West Des Moines and its surroundings.
- To restore and reclaim land disturbed by sand and gravel excavation and make it into an attractive environment.
- To identify land uses and recreational activities compatible with the floodplain character of the site.
- To relate uses of Raccoon River Park with compatible and complementary facilities in nearby Brown's Woods and Walnut Woods, the linear Jordan Creek Park, and countywide greenbelts along rivers and streams.
- To achieve a design that could be developed in stages; would make maximum use of existing features; could be constructed within the financial limits of the project sponsors; could be operated and managed in a cost-effective manner; and would make an aesthetic and functional statement that this was a premier local and regional facility.

Recreational Plan

Among the first park components desired and addressed were soccer facilities. The soccer complex now is located in one of the previously undisturbed sections of the park, which had been pasture land. Because this area was already grassed and relatively flat, it was ideal for immediate soccer use and in fact was used for league play by the West Des Moines Soccer Club after construction of the park facilities.

Ultimately, this portion of the park will be graded by the soccer club to provide improved soccer fields, with the possibility of irrigation. Some of the fields may also be lighted. Adjacent to them are restrooms and a concession stand, with parking for 418 cars.

The softball-field complex contains five ASA-regulation softball fields, each with 10-foot-tall outfield fences 300 feet from home plate. Each field is automatically irrigated and uses a manufactured clay in parts of the infield to minimize rutting. Subdrains are found around the infields. High-mast lighting illuminates each field, with provisions to upgrade each field's lighting level to "tournament" standards. Each field has two dugouts equipped with drinking fountains, plus bleachers for the fans. In the center of the complex are buildings that house maintenance equipment, concessions, restrooms, equipment storage, tournament administration, and an umpire's lounge. Parking is available for 408 cars.

The 250-acre Blue Heron Lake offers high-quality boating and fishing opportunities. A double-lane boat ramp with a central courtesy pier allows boaters with trailers to enter and leave efficiently. Paved and lighted parking accommodates 46 vehicles with trailers. Boats on the lake must be operated at a no-wake speed, while certain areas are restricted to boats with electric motors only.

The beach was developed to offer a variety of waterside activities. With a developed shoreline of 750 feet and a dry-sand area of more than two acres, the beach is ideal for "catching" tanning rays and summer breezes. A beach house is proposed that would house shower and changing facilities, administration, and concessions. Parking for 200 cars is available at this facility.

Substantial grading was required to construct the beach. The preexisting shoreline was steep, with nearly vertical banks in places. More than 37,000 cubic yards of earth was moved into the lake, so that the final beach slope, both above and below water, ranged from 5 to 6 percent. The mining operation had done a thorough job of removing the sand from the lake, leaving little sand for beach development. As a result, nearly 25,000 tons of specially graded sand had to be imported to build a two-foot-deep beach.

In the future, a boating concession will be developed that will rent canoes, sailboats, and paddleboats to park users. And eventually, fishing piers will extend from the shoreline into the lake. Combined with a paved walkway, these facilities will allow fishing access for the physically challenged.

Picnics and Much More

Innumerable sites along the lake can be used for picnicking. Acres of grass, combined with views of the lake, woods, or activities, give ample opportunity to spread out a blanket and relax. Picnic tables will be located throughout the park to provide additional picnicking opportunities. Three shelters have been built that are sized to accommodate groups of up to 200 people and are equipped with lights, electrical outlets, and grills. More shelters are planned.

This project has offered a unique opportunity to demonstrate wetlands management and to illustrate techniques for remaking disturbed and mined lands into high-quality wildlife environments. The presence of a hands-on laboratory with potential for demonstration projects in the midst of an urbanizing area will be a rare asset to the community.

The site provides easy access for students and teachers throughout the metropolitan area for nature study in the field. The Nature Lodge, with a naturalist on staff, is located next to the lake and adjacent to one of the parking lots to afford the physical resources necessary to advance nature study programs. The facility also contains space for community rentals.

A system of asphalt and aggregate-surfaced trails has been developed in the park, with a 3.2-mile loop trail running around the lake as its focus. Important to this trail system will be connections to regional bicycle paths at the Grand Avenue entrance and near the Jordan Creek greenway. Paved trails will be mostly 10 feet wide and will accommodate bicyclists, rollerbladers, and pedestrians.

Development Staging and Costs

The park master plan, which was written in July 1991, intended to guide the development of 770 acres of land from a raw state into a premier park that would serve the entire Des Moines metropolitan area. The scope of the improvements and the magnitude of the costs outlined in the plan have forced the adoption of a staged approach to construction of the park and facilities. This work began in 1994 and continues to this day.

In 1991, the estimated cost to construct the park was $11.6 million, an amount intended to cover the major funding requirements for a park, recreational facilities, and wildlife area that would be ready for public use. As more amenities have been added to the park, more detailed estimates and schedules have been developed as preliminary and final designs were planned and constructed.

As of this writing, more than $12 million has been spent. During the next 10 to 15 years, an additional $7 million is budgeted to develop new facilities and to bring the park site to full development.

CHAPTER 44

Yorklyn, DE, and Other Cities Adopt Plans to Protect Buildings in Floodplains from Water

Michael Powell and Robin Ringler

Even before the devastating floods of 2005, local planning officials and commercial property owners were thinking about flood mitigation in new ways. After all, substantial numbers of established business buildings that support local tax bases stand on floodplain sites. Many buildings predate by decades the Federal Emergency Management Agency (FEMA) and National Flood Insurance Program (NFIP) regulations and were built before we knew what we know today about construction on floodplains.

In addition, we now realize that even entire cities are built on floodplains, and unfortunately they flood — time and again. Grandfathering won't keep anything dry. Relocating such buildings and cities is simply out of the question.

Then came Hurricane Katrina, Hurricane Wilma, record rainfalls in the Northeast, and fresh media coverage about global warming and the shrinking polar ice cap. This quadruple whammy has put the flood mitigation issue front and center as never before. Flooding is inevitable. How can local govern-

ments and property owners more effectively protect their assets already located on floodplains? What safeguards and restrictions should we put on new commercial development in designated floodplains?

Bad News, Good News

The bad news is that, according to all responsible predictions, flooding will get worse, not better, for the foreseeable future. This is true in every corner of the country, not just on the Atlantic and Gulf coasts and in Hurricane Alley. Even today, NFIP gets substantial flood loss claims from every state, every year.

It is inevitable that more existing commercial properties and commercially zoned raw land in flood zones will get flooded more often. This will create more business interruptions and property losses leading to more NFIP loss claims. Some floodplain businesses have been flooded repeatedly, and they file loss claims each time.

Originally published as "Floodplain Strategies for Staying Dry and Staying Put," *Public Management*, Vol. 88, No. 4, April 2006. Published by the International City/County Management Association, Washington, DC. Reprinted with permission of the publisher.

Now the good news. First, flood damage to those buildings and their contents is largely preventable. Second, relocation or elevation (building up on stilts) are not the only options available. FEMA also explicitly allows a third option for nonresidential buildings: flood-proofing in place. In the past, this option has been largely overlooked or even discouraged at the local level, perhaps because it is unfamiliar.

Today, however, in-place floodproofing is winning more favor at the local level. More existing commercial properties are successfully floodproofed right where they are so they can remain dry and stay put. In some cases, federal grants are available to defray the costs. Even without such assistance, in-place flood-proofing often proves to be much more cost-effective than elevating, demolishing, or relocating the building.

Turnaround in Thinking

In-place floodproofing has become the new way of thinking about flood mitigation. Done properly, it really works, and this fact should be reflected in the local permitting process. Despite the devastating power evidenced by a Hurricane Katrina, the vast majority of floods are infrequent, temporary, and minor. Some last only hours; most involve less than one foot of water, once or twice a year. Why give up on a building or a site that's perfectly viable except for two or three days each year?

A decade or so ago, the attitude at the local level was much more negative about floodproofing, even though FEMA has always allowed for it. Local government planners and permitting officials either banned flood-proofing outright, allowed it only as a last option, or made the permitting process so oner-ous that property owners gave up trying.

Floods like this almost closed down the Yorklyn, Delaware, Center for the Creative Arts (CCArts), a community nonprofit organization.

Does floodproofing really work? There's plenty of evidence that it does, for both existing and new commercial and institutional buildings. Containment companies, for example, can point to more than 5,000 successful projects dating back more than 25 years. And when floodproofing does work, it's a win-win for both the locality and the property owner.

Let's look at a few cases.

Recent Delaware Cases

In Delaware, in-place floodproofing recently enabled two enterprises to stay put — and stay dry — despite their floodplain locations. A third project, under way now, is expected to be equally successful. Basically, the buildings are waterproofed and all windows and doors are equipped with quick-deploying flood barriers so that the interiors and their contents are undamaged.

Equally important, an emergency operating plan is in place. In all three cases, the Delaware Department of Natural Resources and Environmental Control worked with the affected businesses and localities to ease their costs and ensure success.

One enterprise is the Center for the Creative Arts (CCArts), a nonprofit community arts center located in a former elementary school built in 1932 in the Red Clay Creek floodplain in Yorklyn, Delaware. First-floor elevation is 172 feet and basement elevation is 162 feet, but the 100-year base flood elevation (BFE), also known as the 100-year flood level, is 176 feet. The flood source is actually heavy rainfall in the Red Clay Creek basin, 50 miles north in neighboring Pennsylvania.

Past floods had been so disruptive and damaging that CCArts considered relocating. But the organization couldn't raise the capital, so there also was talk of closing the doors for good. With help from architects and consultants, the arts center worked on a flood-proofing plan, and the Delaware state government helped secure a FEMA grant to defray the costs. The inside of the facility has been bone dry ever since.

The plan for CCArts involved sealing all exterior walls and installing flood barriers in all exterior doorways to 18 inches above the 100-year BFE, per local building codes. Because the center does not employ a full-time custodian, it selected these specific flood barriers so that even a 60-year-old female volunteer could deploy them in minutes. Two of the barriers swing into place like the lower sections of Dutch doors. The other two slide out like pocket doors.

The plan also included an automatic flood phone alert to key employees, which is triggered by a flood alarm installed in the Susquehanna Basin in Pennsylvania, near the flood source. The total project cost $200,000; a FEMA grant covered $100,280, and CCArts picked up the balance.

Another case in Delaware is the two-step project for Bell's Supply Company in the White Clay Creek floodplain. The business occupies a 24,000-square-foot masonry-walled building with a 13-foot floor elevation in a flood plain with a 14-foot, 10-year BFE; a 17.5-foot, 50-year BFE; and a 19-foot, 100-year BFE. As a result of periodic flooding, the company has collected several millions of dollars of NFIP flood claims since opening its doors in 1970.

The first flood mitigation step, taken in 2001, was to flood protect the structure to 30 inches above the floor, or to about the 25-year BFE. This involved waterproofing the walls, installing a variety of flood barriers (based on type of opening) at all doors, and setting up an automatic telephone flood alarm to call in deployment staff if the building is in danger of flooding when the store is closed.

That project cost approximately $130,000, $97,000 of which was covered by a FEMA grant. This worked fine until 2003, when Hurricane Henri generated floodwaters that overtopped the barriers by six inches, causing interior damage in the millions of dollars. In 2004, the owners raised the flood protection height to 60 inches by reinforcing the walls to

handle five feet of hydrostatic pressure and installing higher flood barriers. The total cost of the additional floodproofing was about $500,000, which will be easily recovered in the first major flood.

The third Delaware project is in progress. Standard Technologies and Machine Company is a small machine shop with a 40.9-foot, first-floor elevation in a flood zone with a 43-foot BFE. The company was substantially damaged during Hurricane Henri but couldn't afford to relocate. Because of the heavy equipment typical of machine shops, elevating the building at the site was not feasible.

The solution was to floodproof the walls to 18 inches and install flood barriers to the same height in all doorways. Of the $320,000 cost, $212,000 is being covered by the same type of FEMA grant that the other Delaware enterprises used.

In all three of the Delaware cases, the enterprises were able to stay put and stay dry, and the communities were able to retain community assets and ratables. The success was the result of proven floodproofing technologies, building and permitting codes that allowed in-place floodproofing to FEMA and NFIP standards, and state and local government cooperation that helped secure the FEMA funds.

... And Elsewhere

There are plenty of successes elsewhere, too, and many have not depended on FEMA financing.

In Colonia, New Jersey, Home Depot is running a successful new store on a site that had been abandoned years ago by another retailer because of flooding as high as three feet. For every year the land remained idle, the town suffered from having an eyesore on a main road and lost out on ratables and economic activity.

Home Depot made the site workable by raising the grade level by 18 inches, building a two-foot floodwall snug against the exterior wall, and providing lift-out flood barriers for all openings. Home Depot was able to take advantage of a high-traffic, high-visibility location, and the town benefited from higher employment and the recovery of a performing tax ratable.

In a 25-year-old strip mall near Scranton, Pennsylvania, Redner's Warehouse Market reopened its doors just two days after a flood — no Redner's layoffs, no loss of economic activity, no interruption in Redner's tax revenues — while its neighbors were still cleaning up two months later. The reason: Redner's had floodproofed its store so almost no floodwater got in. (What little water that did encroach came in through floor drains, not through flood barriers.) A neighboring K-Mart didn't fare as well; it lost more than $1 million in inventory and weeks of selling time. The K-Mart manager saw Redner's success and ordered floodproofing, saying "flood barriers are a minor investment."

What Experience Teaches

What can we learn from these cases?

- In-place floodproofing, done properly, works and is supported by both FEMA and NFIP. Floodproofing protects property, cuts NFIP loss claims, and enables enterprises to get back in business sooner after a flood. It can be a much better solution than forcing a business to elevate its structure or move elsewhere.
- In-place floodproofing should include an emergency operating plan and employee training to ensure that barriers will be deployed as needed. The permitting process should include review of the building's emergency operating plan as well as its structural engineering aspects. The FEMA Web site (FEMA.gov) has good information, especially FEMA Form 81–65 and Technical Bulletin 3–93, on what to look for in emergency plans.

- Today's better flood barriers, installed properly, can keep a building interior dry as a bone. For example, during flash floods that sometimes pile up five feet of water outside, not a drop of water gets into the basements of Houston hospitals equipped with flood doors.
- Flood barriers alone do not necessarily make a building floodproof. Walls need to be waterproofed and sometimes need reinforcement to withstand the hydrostatic forces. An engineer must be involved. The FEMA Web site gives more details.
- Grant money is available from FEMA to local governments for valid in-place floodproofing projects on existing structures in floodplains. This creates an opportunity for local jurisdictions to help retain good businesses that otherwise might move to the next town. FEMA makes these grants only to local governments, not directly to property owners, and will cover costs to communities for administering the projects. FEMA's and NFIP's underlying philosophy is that a one-time investment in floodproofing can be more cost-effective than repeatedly paying loss claims.
- Even without grant money, in-place floodproofing of an existing building in a floodplain makes economic sense. It's much more economical than moving a business or elevating a building on an existing site.
- Not all floods or floodplains are the same. A lot of buildings are on sites that get flooding of just 6 to 12 inches, or even less, for a day or two a year. In-place floodproofing in these instances should be encouraged. It's effective, affordable, and far less intrusive than demolishing and rebuilding up or building elsewhere. In addition, raw land with a mild flood threat might be a perfect candidate for new commercial development and additional ratables if buildings placed on it can be properly floodproofed at the outset.

Above all, floodplain projects need to be evaluated on a case-by-case basis.

Evaluating Flood Barriers

Unfortunately, there are no national standards for flood barriers that can be dropped into local building codes. Under FEMA guidelines, validation for the barriers flows from the licensed professional engineer who signs off on the project design. Code and permitting officials should, however, carefully examine any plan to be sure the flood barriers will work when needed.

- **Installed base of the barrier supplier.** Because of the recent increase in flooding, some unproved suppliers are appearing in the flood-barrier business. By contrast, some trusted providers have installed bases covering 5,000 projects over the past 25 years. These are mechanical components designed to protect against catastrophic property damage from flooding, not a piece of trim.
- **Installation or installation supervision of the barriers by the barrier supplier.** Most failures can be traced to improper installation by contractors unfamiliar with flood barriers.
- **Post-installation testing.** Testing of the floodproofing after installation should be a requirement. Testing adds only 2 percent to 3 percent to the installed cost of the barriers, but it ensures that the barriers will work during an actual flood.
- **Ease and speed of deployment by people who will be available during a crisis.** Different brands of flood barriers show enormous differences in ease and speed of deployment. Some barriers deploy in seconds, with just the swing of a door or turn of a latch. Others can take 10 times as long and require a toolbox or proprietary spanner. Beware of tool requirements and extra parts because they can get lost when needed most. Experience teaches that the best-trained responders may not be able to show up during an actual flood, and mandatory evacuations can curtail available deployment time. Keep it simple.

Outlook

The specter of more flooding comes as good news to nobody, but it seems inevitable. Floodproofing, however, gives local governments and property owners more and better ways to protect property and the local tax base in the face of almost certain flooding. In-place floodproofing is allowed under federal standards, and it is gaining acceptance among local planners and local code and permitting officials. The products and know-how—and sometimes the funding—to make floodproofing a success are available for the asking.

CHAPTER 45

Growth and Water Issues

Michelle Henrie

Viewed from the window of a high-rise office building, Albuquerque, New Mexico, stretches along the Rio Grande Valley and rises up across the mesas into the foothills. This is not the same Albuquerque of ten years ago: it is much, much bigger.

There are those who ask, how can we keep growing? — and by growing they seem to be referring to the expanding footprint of buildings, traffic congestion, consumption of natural resources, and the like. But as the West continues to develop rapidly, one of the most pressing issues it faces is water: Where will people find it? Will it run out? How do people get more of it?

As cities and rural areas continue to grow, developers and government leaders need to find ways to use water resources more efficiently. In the 21st century, solutions to water shortages not only need to be unique and creative, but also to contribute to sustainability so that growth can continue. Just where are we now — and where are we headed in the face of continuing growth?

Today's Lifestyle Takes Up More Space

It is easy to assume that the expanding human footprint is merely a reflection of pop-ulation growth, but it is more than that. The expanding footprint is also — to a significant extent — a reflection of the changing American lifestyle.

Here is why:

- Americans live in more homes per capita than ever before. In 1950, an average household held 3.37 persons. In the 2000 census, the average household held 2.59 persons. According to these averages, in 1950, 100 homes housed 337 persons. In 2000, 100 homes housed only 259 people. To house 337 people in 2000, 130 homes were required — 30 percent more than in 1950.

- The average square footage of a new single-family home has increased substantially. In 1950, the average size of a home was 983 square feet (91 sq m), an average of 291 square feet (26 sq m) per person. In 2000, the average size was about 2,070 square feet (192 sq m), or 799 square feet (74 sq m) per person.

What is behind these changes? In short, the American lifestyle. Seniors are living longer. Young people are marrying later. Families are smaller. People are now less likely to remarry after divorce; after a divorce, parents often share child custody — meaning that both parents' houses must be large enough

Originally published as "The New Frontier," *Urban Land*, Vol. 66, No. 10, October 2007. Published by the Urban Land Institute, Washington, DC. Reprinted with permission of the publisher.

to accommodate the children. Many baby boomers own two or more destination homes. Single, young professionals — including women age 30 to 35, a demographic group that has grown dramatically — are buying homes, which is raising the number of single-person households.

The cumulative impact of changes in the American lifestyle is expanding the human footprint. More development of residential properties is necessary to keep up with this lifestyle, which means further strain on already stretched natural resources, especially water. The good news is that although consumers are expanding their environmental footprint, they are trying to be smarter about their consumption of natural resources in an attempt to contribute to environmental sustainability.

Consumers Want Better Choices

Development responds to the market and preferences of the consumer. Consumers in the current market want to make choices that allow them to participate in environmental sustainability: they want to be able to purchase organic food, work in socially responsible workplaces, fill their cars with alternative fuels, and use energy-saving appliances. Today's consumers may want a larger home or a second home, but they also want to conserve natural resources by minimizing water use around the home, harvesting natural water, and reusing water.

Average indoor domestic water use today is nearly 70 gallons (265 liters) per person per day, with toilets and laundry washing machines accounting for nearly half that use. Pre–1994 toilets used 3.5 to five gallons (13 to 19 liters) per flush. Post–1994 low-flow toilets average about 1.6 gallons (6.1 liters) per flush. More consumers than ever are seeking high-efficiency fixtures and appliances and proper placement of water heaters to allow for less water consumption in the home.

American outdoor water use averages 130 gallons (492 liters) per day per household. In the high-elevation cities of the West, such as Denver at 5,280 feet (1,609 m), and Albuquerque at 5,314 feet (1,620 m), household outdoor water use accounts for more than half the annual residential use. Given the increasing number of American households per capita, management of household outdoor water use is a priority. Tools for minimizing outdoor use include graywater plumbing, which allows reuse of some indoor wastewater in landscaping; "smart" water harvesting and irrigation systems; and xeriscaping, or water-conserving landscaping.

These options seem to be working. Total water use in the United States rose in the 1970s and early 1980s. By 1985, however, total water use across the country dropped to about 1970 figures, and has remained relatively constant despite population growth — a surprising statistic.

Basic Services Are Shifting from Government to the Private Sector

Logically, with an expanding human footprint comes an expanding demand for basic services, specifically water. However, local governments across the country face challenges maintaining the status quo in the face of tightening budgets. Local governments also are severely affected by climate change, which requires planning for and implementation of flood management and wildfire control efforts. Aging, inefficient infrastructure results in unaccounted-for water — leaks and other losses from water systems. These issues exist even without growth.

How can local governments tackle existing problems and also serve new development projects, particularly when high-value homes attract buyers with high expectations? The trend is for them to accept the benefits of new development, such as increased property tax revenues, while shifting to the private sector the burden of development, such as construction of infrastructure. Traditionally, local governments built infrastructure. But over time, rather than condemning the land needed for that infrastructure, local governments required developers to dedicate the needed land. Then governments began requiring developers to build the infrastructure and dedicate the needed infrastructure as well as the land. Now, infrastructure installation and improvements required of developers can extend beyond a project. For example, off-site water system improvements required of developers might include construction or upgrading of treatment plants, creation of new pump stations, and the drilling of new wells.

The shift also now includes operations and maintenance. Today's buyers are rarely surprised when they learn that — in addition to the price tag for a new house and the property taxes — they also have a special assessment fee for repayment of major infrastructure development costs and that their homeowners association fees include wages for a security guard and utility system operator.

On the Horizon

For all these reasons, the world of home development is facing a new frontier. Local governments and private developers are finding new ways to do old things. Among the new approaches to management of water resources are the following:

Conjunctive water management. Water suppliers are finding ways to increase their source options, and to juggle those options in response to nature. For example, the Albuquerque Bernalillo County Water Utility Authority's water system is designed to draw Rio Grande surface water during times of natural high flow, and to rely on aquifer water only during seasonally low flows. These systems promote sustainability by reducing aquifer depletion and saving aquifer water for when it

is really needed. Meanwhile, the vast majority of domestic indoor water used flows down the drain to a wastewater treatment facility, after which the treated water can be restored to the river system or reused, for instance, for the irrigation of public parks.

In addition, water suppliers are now able to augment aquifers. By doing so, depending on the particular needs of the community, water suppliers are able to store water underground where it is not lost to evaporation; build up water reserves for emergencies; naturally blend water to meet drinking water standards governing, for instance, dilute arsenic; and restore the health of natural aquifers. One method of aquifer augmentation involves injecting treated water into an aquifer — a technique also called aquifer storage and recovery. An alternative method involves locating and building reservoirs so that water naturally seeps into an aquifer, as is done at the Sand Hollow Reservoir in southern Utah.

Retrofit strategies. Because pre–1994 toilets use two to three times more water than low-flow toilets, and the average adult flushes a toilet five to seven times per day, an old toilet can waste 23.8 gallons (90 liters) per person per day. With average indoor domestic use today at nearly 70 gallons (265 liters) per person per day, retrofitting three or four toilets would provide enough salvaged water for one person's daily use. Clearly, incentivizing retrofits can produce big water savings.

Using this idea, Santa Fe, New Mexico, developed a toilet retrofit program so that the city's water utility would experience no new loss to the system despite growth. This program requires developers to retrofit existing toilets in existing homes before pulling a building permit. By doing so, the city's utility accumulates enough water savings to meet the new demand created by each newly built home.

Additional burden shifting. Another category shifting from government to the private sector is water acquisition. In Santa Fe, developers of certain types of projects must locate and purchase transferable water rights, then donate them to the city. In other projects in the arid West, developers are now considering long-term water leases from tribes or government agencies, as well as desalination of brackish water in deep aquifers.

Often these projects are driven and built by the developer through reimbursement mechanisms such as public improvement districts, which allow local governments to oversee and comment on the master planning of significant water infrastructure projects without bearing any project costs or risks. The developer provides the footwork and expertise while the local government forms the special district, which is a quasi-governmental entity. The special district raises reimbursement capital by issuing and selling bonds, and the bonds are paid off over time by homeowners living within the district boundaries.

Demand management. In response to drought conditions, local governments have developed mandatory water conservation initiatives such as restricting outdoor watering to certain times or days. These measures have proven effective in saving water in emergencies. However, local governments must balance the potentially disproportionate impact that drastic mandatory water conservation requirements can have on older neighborhoods. Established trees and lawns have a cooling effect, in contrast to the reflective heat created by pavement. Shaded areas experience less evaporation. The loss of established landscaping due to water restrictions or the voluntary use of herbicides can be counterproductive to the environment.

By contrast, where developers of new projects have a blank slate in terms of landscaping, they can go much further than local government with self-imposed mandatory water conservation initiatives. Through restrictive covenants, enforced by homeowners associations, developers can limit landscaping to low-water-use grasses and plants or only allow planting of native plants; limit the amount of turf; require drip irrigation to minimize evaporative losses; limit outdoor irrigation to morning and evening hours to minimize evaporative losses; require timed irrigation systems to be equipped with a rain sensor to shut off the system during or after recent rain; and require that landscaping be watered with harvested rainwater, such as water collected from rooftops by cisterns or rain barrels.

Homebuilders also can plumb homes to salvage graywater — water first used indoors for showering, for bathing, in bathroom sinks, or for washing clothes — and use it outdoors. Water used in toilets, kitchen sinks, and dishwashers is called blackwater and generally is not acceptable for watering outdoor landscaping. Use of rainwater can be maximized through prelandscaping techniques, such as layering water-retaining materials like pumice at root zones, or creating French drains or pumice wicks to trench water from a rain gutter downspout to landscaped areas. Maximizing permeability helps reduce flooding by reducing stormwater runoff. In addition, indoor water use can be reduced through water-conserving appliances and fixtures, alternatives to evaporative coolers, and proper placement of water heaters to allow hot water to reach the tap sooner.

As development continues in the West, evidence of more efficient use of water resources already exists. As technology improves and people become more attentive to water issues and sustainability, new solutions will arise to keep up with the expanding human footprint.

CHAPTER 46

Reclaiming Our Rivers

Nancy L. Fleming

As vital resources that can contribute multiple benefits to our cities, urban rivers must be reclaimed.

Once lined by wildlife habitats or bustling waterfront businesses, many of today's urban rivers have become polluted open-air sewers along which sit derelict warehouses and factories. Others have been reduced to concrete channels that provide engineered flood control during the rainy season but sit empty at other times.

As mere vestiges of their original forms and functions, many U.S. urban rivers contribute little to the surrounding natural or built environment, and often lower nearby property values and inhibit a city's economic growth.

Their potential, however, is immense. The urban river can — and should — be an open space and recreational amenity, a prime location for jobs and tax-boosting real estate development, and a linkage that ties communities together. In short, it can be a healthy, unifying, multipurpose corridor of which a city can be proud. This vision not only is a possibility, it is already being implemented in a number of cities through the concerted efforts of various government agencies, planners, developers, and the public.

Natural First Steps

What does it take for a city to revitalize its long neglected, often-damaged urban river? Riverfront development, no matter how well planned and well intentioned, can only be truly successful when the river and its corridor are healthy. Therefore, the revitalization process needs to start with the reversal of decades of environmental damage and degradation; only then can revitalization achieve its many benefits.

First, city officials and the community need to understand the "big picture" of the entire river and its watershed, which intrinsically are linked. If the watershed is not carefully managed, the river can never reclaim its full potential as a vital urban resource.

Second, the river's hydrology — particularly relative to flood control — must be understood and respected. Every urban river once played many roles, including the vital role of conveying natural floodwater. Over the years, however, many urban rivers have been encroached upon, pumped down, and degraded so that their only function is to carry away stormwater — as much as is produced during a theoretical 100-year storm event — as quickly as possible.

Development in the wrong places has caused much of the problem. Many flood-

Originally published as "Urban Rivers Reborn," *Urban Land*, Vol. 64, No. 5, May 2005. Published by the Urban Land Institute, Washington, DC. Reprinted with permission of the publisher.

plains — which are the natural river overflow areas — have been filled and built up. Development has consisted of building roofs that send rain onto nonpervious pavement that dumps water at an accelerated pace into the closed drainage system. Unabated development significantly reduces the amount of stormwater that filters back into the land, thus taxing the rivers' carrying capacity. Rather than reducing the threat of flooding, many channelized urban rivers actually increase the risk of flooding over time, because they accelerate the speed of the water flow and can lack sufficient capacity to carry away an ever-increasing volume of stormwater runoff. As a result, rivers often require further armoring with higher levees and other mechanisms to maintain their flood control capabilities.

Third, how people currently use the river, and how they could use it in the future, should direct any revitalization plan. Water acts as a magnet — it tends to draw people. But few urban rivers attract people to their banks, as these waterways have become ugly flood control mechanisms or polluted waterways. The ecology of many rivers has been destroyed, decimating the fish population and leaving nothing to attract birds and wildlife — or people. Ironically, there also is nothing left to attract desirable real estate development.

Fourth, because the damage inflicted on an urban river, and its subsequent deterioration, usually occurred over decades, it will also take many years to correct. A city needs to undertake a phased, long-term revitalization plan in cooperation with state and federal agencies to implement the community's vision over time. Strong public and private commitment and participation are imperative throughout the revitalization process, from initial planning and design through ongoing maintenance of what has been created.

A Revitalization Plan

Before any meaningful development can occur, an urban river revitalization plan must address stormwater and water quality, river hydraulics and hydrology, and the environment.

Stormwater and water quality. A crucial role of the urban river is to convey stormwater and prevent flooding of adjacent land. To accomplish this, most urban rivers have been engineered to some degree, and their capacity has been fixed at a finite volume. In a plan for change, the floodwater-carrying capacity of the river cannot be compromised. The river planning process must take into consideration the impact of potential future development on flood control capabilities.

Anything that affects the watershed and upstream tributaries will affect everything and everyone downstream. Thus, stormwater must be addressed at the watershed level — and not just locally. Each community within the watershed must adopt policies that will minimize the amount of stormwater runoff that eventually reaches the urban river so that it is not overburdened. More important, each community must create ways to reduce the amount of stormwater runoff that is sent back into the river and direct it into aquifers, thereby recharging the groundwater, and putting stormwater where it belongs — back into the natural hydrologic system — rather than whisking it away as quickly as possible and wasting it.

There are numerous ways to reduce stormwater runoff. At an individual level, every residence can collect rainwater from its roof and use it for irrigation purposes. Neighborhoods can replace concrete street gutters with "bioswales" to collect the stormwater in landscaped depressions that remove some pollutants and more slowly direct water to a wetland or a detention basin.

Stormwater also can be cleaned as part of an environmentally friendly collection and distribution process. Bioswales can be planted with materials that pull out pollutants. Wetlands offer excellent opportunities to "polish" water before it reenters the river.

River improvements can be made in harmony with good flood control engineering. In less densely developed locations where riverbanks are not lined by buildings, the river might be restored to a more attractive meandering geometry through the application of fluvial geomorphology principles, which restore a waterway to a more natural alignment and cross section. This application results in a more stable river whose floodwaters move more slowly, and it also creates an environment that is more attractive to people and in which fish and other organisms can reestablish themselves. Cities should look for opportunities to acquire adjacent real estate to allow such changes to occur. Another approach is to partner with other public agencies or an adjacent landowner, such as a state park, so that the use of the land not only improves the river but also enhances the park environment and its relationship to the river.

In more constrained locations where vertical walls are necessary to create accessible edges, bioengineering techniques such as planted crib walls can be used. This application will provide vegetation that also can help establish habitat for fish colonies.

Where open space is very limited, the urban character of the river can be celebrated. The Seine in Paris, the Thames in London, and the Allegheny River in Pittsburgh are all lined with constructed walls. However, appropriate adjacent land use and careful design of the public realm along the river yield an attractive urban amenity — and some of the highest real estate values in these cities.

Each community along the river must work to limit or, even better, forbid floodplain development, and to mitigate any floodplain loss by creating natural stormwater management systems, such as wetlands, that can both store and cleanse water. The city of Houston, for example, recently established regulations requiring any new development in the 100-year floodplain to provide stormwater retention facilities that will offset the lost capacity.

Enhancing the natural and physical environment. Wherever possible, native stands of trees and understory plants along the river corridor should be preserved, even sup-

plemented. This can help save wildlife habitat and protect an amenity for the community. If river capacity can be increased by widening the channel and if floodwater conveyance will not be compromised, trees can be planted in the channel itself. The shade will enable fish and aquatic habitat to return, creating a healthier river in the long run.

If the river lacks this capacity, trees can be planted at the top of the banks or along the upper promenades to provide shade, a human scale, and some green landscape. The river corridor itself can provide a place for respite and recreation for the community and its visitors. Depending upon the level of water quality improvement, the revitalized river can offer hiking/biking, fishing, or even water sports such as boating and canoeing.

A river can help provide linkages through the city and enhance the physical environment as well. It can serve as the foundation for an urban greenway — a linear park that connects neighborhoods within the city. This can help establish the river as the social heart of the community, making it a more interesting place for people to live and work, and providing an open-space corridor that connects the neighborhoods.

Developing the Riverfront

Many revitalized urban rivers have improved the future of the city and the region as a whole. The Riverwalk in downtown San Antonio, Texas, is an example. A less-known part of the same river system is the San Antonio River Improvements Project, which stretches both north and south of the downtown Riverwalk. This project is improving two long reaches of the river, providing enhanced wildlife habitat, improved flood control capabilities, a 13-mile-long linear park, and greater opportunities for development on both adjacent and nearby properties.

River revitalization should look beyond the river corridor itself. As part of the planning process, adjacent land uses need to be evaluated and existing land use policies such as zoning may need to be revised. Once the right uses are targeted in the right places, appropriate development can occur, and land values are likely to increase as a result. The effects of this economic benefit can often be felt several blocks beyond the immediate river corridor.

River Revitalization Challenges

Although many problems can arise in revitalizing an urban river, the rewards can be immense.

Regional challenges. From flood control to development, urban rivers should be addressed on a regional basis, with multiple jurisdictions working together. Communities should form regional councils, like the Los Angeles and San Gabriel Rivers Watershed Council, that bring people together to form common strategies that can be undertaken regionally.

Regional efforts can achieve significant progress. In Atlanta, for example, the Chattahoochee River Land Protection Campaign (CRLPC) is working to create a 500-foot-wide greenway along both sides of the Chattahoochee River, running from its Appalachian Mountains headwaters to Columbus, Georgia, a distance of 160 miles. Multiple jurisdictions are working together to make this plan a reality.

Funding challenges. With traditional funding sources drying up, funding an urban river revitalization program is becoming increasingly difficult. The federal government recently announced its interest in eliminating the community development block grant (CDBG) program that has funded urban redevelopment over the last 30 years. Another vital funding source, the Water Resources Development Act (WRDA) of 2000, has not yet been reauthorized.

In this restricted funding environment, cities need to adopt new tools to fund their urban river revitalization efforts. One of the greatest unrealized opportunities lies in public/private partnerships in which a public entity provides incentives to encourage a private developer to make desired improvements to a riverfront. The establishment of a tax increment redevelopment zone (TIRZ), for example, encourages development where it would not normally occur — as in derelict riverfront districts.

A city also can create tax increment financing (TIF) districts to finance economic development projects in underdeveloped and blighted areas — like those along an urban river — to lure new development and raise property values.

A city that already has a business improvement district (BID) in its downtown can expand the jurisdiction of the district to take in the riverfront.

Nonprofit land trusts and alliances can help finance and support urban river revitalization projects. Local organizations like the Greenbelt Alliance in the San Francisco Bay Area can help to create a river revitalization plan, generate broad-based public support, raise funds for land acquisition, and work with multiple jurisdictions to implement the plan. Funding should also be secured for the operation and maintenance of a completed river revitalization project from sources like city tax revenues and private river conservation groups, similar to organizations like the Central Park Conservancy in New York City.

The U.S. Army Corps of Engineers provides river revitalization funds, particularly when enhanced flood control is a key objective, such as the current flood control project being implemented on the Napa River in northern California. Corporate challenge grants, which actively involve the business community in revitalizing a major community resource, can be another source of funding and political support.

Urban rivers are one of our nation's most important natural resources, because they affect so many communities and their residents in multiple ways. Fortunately, the general public has largely been made aware of the importance and economic value of healthy urban rivers, and creative ways are being found to revitalize these critical assets.

CHAPTER 47

The Riverfront Conservation Movement

Greg Breining

Stretching more than 2,500 miles from Lake Itasca in Minnesota to the Gulf of Mexico, the Mississippi River is one the nation's best-known natural features. It is also an essential transportation corridor, rich in historic and cultural resources. More than 12 million people live along its banks, and more than 50 cities draw drinking water from the river. Huge barges ply from Minneapolis to the Gulf, moving agricultural products and other commodities through the heartland.

In one way, however, the Mississippi is underutilized: as a recreational resource for the cities along its banks. In recent years, community groups and government agencies from Minneapolis and St. Paul to New Orleans have been working to reconnect residents to the river. They have protected natural areas, established parks, and built museums and trails — often with the help of The Trust for Public Land, which has negotiated for land, raised money, and helped communities plan a vision for riverfront access and conservation.

We're offering a tour of riverfront conservation efforts in the Mississippi's major cities. So pack your valise and board our paddlewheel steamer at the St. Paul, Minnesota, boat landing for our downriver conservation journey.

River Access for the Twin Cities

St. Paul took root in the mid–1800s as a steamboat landing, with bustling levees, warehouses, industry, and later, railroads and barge landings. In Minneapolis flour mills crowded the prime riverfront real estate to generate power from St. Anthony Falls. These uses long blocked residents from the river, but as industry has departed, citizens and government have moved to restore riverfront access. In 1988, Congress created the Mississippi National River and Recreation Area along 72 miles of the river through the Twin Cities. More recently, the McKnight Foundation launched the Embrace Open Space campaign, a partnership among nonprofit organizations to protect open space in the Twin Cities area and along the Mississippi. "People get inspired by a connection to water and their environment," says Cordelia Pierson, Twin Cities program manager for TPL. "The river is also a core feature of our history. It brings together people and the land in a very central way."

Bruce Vento Nature Sanctuary

Named for the late St. Paul congressman, this 27-acre nature sanctuary will link the river

Originally published as "Back to the Mighty Miss," *Land & People*, Vol. 16, No. 2, Fall 2004. Published by The Trust for Public Land, San Francisco, CA. Reprinted with permission of the publisher.

to underserved neighborhoods of St. Paul while forming a vital link in a 300-mile regional trail network. TPL helped the city acquire the land in 2002 with federal funding secured by Representative Martin Sabo. When fully restored, this one-of-a-kind natural area will feature caves, springs, sweeping city and river views from sandstone bluffs, and restored wetland bird habitat on the Mississippi flyway — all close enough to downtown St. Paul that office workers will be able to walk to the river for a picnic lunch.

Pine Bluffs Scientific and Natural Area

Located just 15 minutes south of St. Paul in one of Minnesota's fastest-growing counties, Pine Bend is a little piece of the old Mississippi in an area where most riverfront is crowded with industry. As much as 1,300 undeveloped acres and three miles of riverfront provide critical habitat for wildlife and a unique opportunity to visit the wild river at the city's doorstep. As part of an effort to help the Minnesota Department of Natural Resources protect key parcels, TPL and its partners recently acquired 67 acres in two transaction parcels to help create a 185-acre natural area. The property includes mature oak forest, deep ravines, 660 feet of riverfront, and a bluff-top prairie offering some of the best river views in the Twin Cities region.

Point Douglas Trail

Where the Mississippi and St. Croix Rivers meet, south of the Twin Cities, the sandy beach at Point Douglas draws people to boat, play in the sand, and enjoy the views. But it is hard for residents of the nearby cities of Hastings, Minnesota, and Prescott, Wisconsin, to get to the beach except by car. So TPL is working with the owner of a nearby abandoned rail corridor to turn it into a hiking and biking trail that not only will link the cities to the popular beach, but will also carry commuters and create pedestrian and bike access to visitor centers, natural areas, and other attractions.

Building the Confluence Greenway

Two hundred years ago explorers Lewis and Clark left the confluence of the Mississippi and Missouri Rivers on their famous expedition to the nation's Pacific coast. Today the bistate Confluence Greenway enables the 2.5 million residents of metropolitan St. Louis to make their own explorations where the two rivers meet.

The greenway was first envisioned almost a decade ago as a way to commemorate this year's bicentennial of the Lewis and Clark expedition along with the centennials of both St. Louis's 1904 World's Fair and its beautiful Forest Park. With more than 9,000 acres protected, the greenway incorporates two state parks, four museums, more than a dozen historic sites, 50 miles of hiking and biking trails, and three natural areas — all beginning just north of the Gateway Arch. In 2000 the project advanced dramatically when voters on both the Missouri and Illinois sides of the river created special funding and park districts to support the greenway.

TPL, which helped pass those measures, is one of five nonprofit partners in the greenway and has helped protect 2,400 acres, using funding from six government agencies and foundations. "This is truly one of the nation's most ambitious efforts to create open space near a major metropolitan downtown," says Larry Levin, director of TPL's St. Louis office. "The collaboration among nonprofits, foundations, government agencies, and civic leaders has been nothing short of spectacular."

Chouteau Island

Set off from the Illinois shore by a navigation channel, Chouteau Island stretches from the confluence to just north of downtown St. Louis. Including TPL's acquisition of 2,000 acres for the Illinois Department of Natural Resources, about two-thirds of the island's 5,500 acres is now protected. With funding mostly from the Army Corps of Engineers, nonprofits and government agencies have created a master plan that envisions multiple recreational uses, including biking, hiking, horseback riding, fishing, and hunting. TPL will work to protect the island's remaining acreage as willing sellers and funding become available.

Columbia Bottom Conservation Area

Located at the junction of the great rivers, this 4,300-acre mosaic of forest, wetlands, and agricultural lands features oaks that were living when Lewis and Clark ascended the Missouri. The Missouri Department of Conservation has already committed over $20 million to conserving land in the bottoms and has started to return parts of it to wildlife habitat. Features include eight miles of hiking and biking trails, a boat ramp, fishing pier, new visitor center, and observation platform with a view of the confluence. TPL recently helped the new regional park district protect 160 acres adjacent to Columbia Bottom.

Chain of Rocks Bridge

Motorists traversing historic Route 66 once crossed the Mississippi on this mile-long bridge that spans the river at Chouteau Island. Today the Old Chain of Rocks Bridge, named for the navigation-impeding rocks in the river below, is the longest dedicated bike and pedestrian bridge in the world and a key link between the Missouri and Illinois sections of the Confluence Greenway. TPL helped its sister nonprofit, Trailnet, acquire the bridge, which already connects 28 miles of the greenway's nearly 50 miles of trails, in-

cluding linkage of the Illinois-side Chouteau Island to St. Louis. Ultimately, 200 miles of trail are planned, including a link to the cross-state Katy Trail.

A Riverfront Park for the Big Easy

"People who visit New Orleans really don't have the opportunity to experience the river that made this city happen, and some neighborhoods have no connection to the river," says Larry Schmidt, director of TPL's New Orleans program. Now a bold new plan envisions a mile-long Mississippi Riverfront Park in the Lower Garden District. TPL has signed a memorandum of understanding with the Port of New Orleans to reserve a stretch of abandoned wharves for the park and is working with the U.S. Army Corps of Engineers to study engineering requirements, environmental issues, and pedestrian access.

By the Numbers: About the Mighty Miss

Rank of the Mississippi River among world's rivers in length: 3rd (behind the Amazon and the Nile)

Depth in feet of the river as it exits Lake Itasca, Minnesota: 3

Depth in feet of the river at New Orleans: 200

Number of natural waterfalls on the river: 1 (St. Anthony Falls, St. Paul, Minnesota)

Percent of the continental U.S. lying within the river's watershed: 41

Number of U.S. states within its watershed: 31

Number of counties and parishes that border the river: 125

Population of those counties and parishes, in millions: 12

Percent of all North American fish species present in the river: 25

Percent of all North American bird species that use the river basin as their flyway: 60

Percent of U.S. agricultural exports grown within the river's basin: 92

Cargo moved by river between St. Louis and the Twin Cities each year, in millions of tons: 90

When the park is finished in about six years, visitors will be able to stroll the riverside and watch oceangoing ships pass on the mile-wide Mississippi. The park will include bike trails and perhaps public performance spaces such as an amphitheater. Several museums are being planned near the park site.

CHAPTER 48

Smart Growth and Water Benefits

U.S. Environmental Protection Agency

Communities around the country are adopting smart growth strategies to reach environmental, community and economic goals. Environmental goals include water benefits that accrue when development strategies use compact development forms, a mix of uses, better use of existing infrastructure and preservation of critical environmental areas.

Regulations under the National Pollutant Discharge Elimination System (NPDES) storm water program offer a structure for considering the water quality benefits associated with smart growth techniques. Compliance with federal, state and local storm water programs revolves around the use of best management practices (BMPs) to manage storm water. Given the water benefits of smart growth at the site, neighborhood and watershed levels, many smart growth techniques and policies are emerging as BMPs.

One such technique is redevelopment. The NPDES storm water requirements — in particular the Post-Construction Minimum Measure — have focused attention on how development projects, both individually and collectively, impact a watershed after projects are built. Although this article is geared toward the post-construction measure under Phase II, any city or county renewing a permit under Phase I can use them. Additionally, cities,

counties and townships that are not regulated, but are proactively developing storm water, flooding or watershed plans, can utilize smart growth techniques such as redevelopment to meet water quality goals.

Redevelopment

Redevelopment is development of a site that has been previously developed and is typically covered with an impervious or compacted surface. For purposes of this article, the reader can assume that the lot is covered with a compacted or impervious surface and has minimal to no value in handling storm water. These projects can include development of vacant buildings, lots where a building has been torn down and replaced with gravel parking lots or older malls.

In most instances, redevelopment is left to market forces. Developers and real estate investors seek out available property and either redevelop by right or petition for a variance or rezoning. In other jurisdictions, special entities are formed to foster redevelopment. There are often barriers, including complex approval processes and the perception from lenders that the deal will pose more risk than new development projects.

Originally published as "Smart Growth," *Storm Water Solutions*, Vol. 4, No. 2, April 2007. Published by Scranton Communications, Arlington Heights, IL. Reprinted with permission of the publisher.

Thus the best resources for learning about redevelopment plans can be private-sector organizations or public/private partnerships. Economic entities, such as redevelopment authorities, "Main Street" programs and brownfields offices, often work to line up financing, zoning reforms, shared parking arrangements and other incentives to overcome the barriers and perceptions that suppress market interest. An economic development director, chamber of commerce or city manager would know if there are established redevelopment districts that can be added to storm water management plans. A head of a redevelopment agency can talk to local land development experts to develop scenarios of watershed growth. This way not only the economic benefits of redevelopment, but also the regional water benefits can be presented. Commercial real estate brokers also are a good resource for information on why a commercial district, mall or older downtown is underperforming, and what steps are likely to revive interest.

Vacant property reform, greyfields and renovation codes are examples of programs useful to redevelopment projects.

Vacant property reform. According to the National Vacant Properties Campaign, vacant and abandoned properties occupy about 15% of the area of a typical large city — more than 12,000 acres on average. Vacant property reforms are designed to encourage the redevelopment of vacant properties, allowing the utilization of existing buildings in potentially desirable urban and suburban locations. For more information, visit www.vacantproperties.org. The International City/County Managers Association has researched and reported on successful local efforts to bring vacant commercial and residential properties back into use. For more information, visit www.icma.org/vacantproperties.

Greyfields. Greyfields, a subcategory of vacant or underperforming properties, are large, previously developed properties, such as older shopping malls and warehouses. These sites tend to be large and well served by transportation and storm water infrastructure.

These properties differ from brownfields in that they are not contaminated or perceived to be contaminated.

To see if a community is working on a redevelopment strategy for old malls or other greyfield sites, contact the department of economic development or the local chamber of commerce. This strategy may include mixed-use rezoning, enhanced transportation on the site and/or redevelopment incentives. Because these sites are so large and are not contaminated, better control of storm water on site may be negotiable, which will increase the storm water benefits of the redevelopment project. The Congress for New Urbanism published *Greyfields into Goldfields*, which presents information on common reasons behind the decline in malls and large properties and development options for reusing the sites. For more information, visit www.cnu.org.

Renovation Codes. Renovation, or rehabilitation, codes are commonly developed to replace inflexible building codes with a set of coordinated standards for renovation and rehabilitation in older areas. For example, renovation of an old downtown might be prohibitively expensive, or impossible, under building codes created for new development. Renovation codes meet safety objectives while setting workable standards for renovation. Renovation codes also help towns revitalize the economies of their downtowns while relieving development pressure on greenfield sites (and thus retaining the storm water benefits of open space).

The U.S. Department of Housing and Urban Development published a report, Smart Codes in Your Community: A Guide to Building Rehabilitation Codes, describing various redevelopment codes and examples of rehabilitation codes from across the country. For more information, visit www.huduser.org/publications/destech/smartcodes.html. If a community or state offers support for renovation and rehabilitation, also check to see if historic tax credits are allowed, and count this toward storm water credit for redevelopment.

Historic preservation offices and local non-profits that deal with historic preservation are good resources for this type of information.

Typical Costs

The costs of redevelopment are distributed among several stakeholders. For a city or county, fostering redevelopment can include: 1) the costs of redevelopment planning and stakeholder outreach; 2) the costs of any incentives provided; 3) upgrading and repairing of existing street and water infrastructure; and 4) staff time if specific programs have been established. These costs, however, cannot be appraised without looking at the costs associated with vacant or underused commercial and residential properties. The Vacant Properties Campaign has compiled information on these costs that is available on its website.

For developers, redevelopment projects in already-developed areas are typically more complex, and thus can be more expensive. These developers must work with existing street and circulation patterns, building configurations, and zoning and regulatory codes, many of which are decades or even centuries old. Developers look at the time and cost involved to see if projects "pencil out" economically. Local incentives and regulations play into cost, including storm water management. Smart growth plans and state programs may offer funding mechanisms, open space and park funds, tax incentives or permit review incentives. When packaged strategically, these incentives may serve not only as economic development incentives, but storm water program incentives as well.

Measurable Goals

Because redevelopment projects are discrete and are typically tracked through permits, storm water managers may be able to use databases that are already in use. Because many storm water consultants are establishing tracking software, they can help establish new fields to track the impervious surface reused through redevelopment. One example of a measurable goal would be to create an inventory of vacant properties and set goals for redeveloping them.

The amount of impervious surface avoided through redevelopment programs also may be trackable. This approach would translate how the square footage, building footprint, parking and associated infrastructure would compare under conventional development standards elsewhere in the watershed. As a first step, the storm water or planning office would need to estimate: 1) where the development might go were it not for redevelopment programs; 2) the average parameters for conventional development (e.g., likely number of parking spaces, new roads and access designs); and 3) any other secondary impacts that might come from new growth.

Case in Point

A comparison of build-out scenarios was used to assess the transportation and water and air quality impacts of Atlantic Station, a brownfields redevelopment project in Atlanta. The site design for Atlantic Station, located on a former steel factory, includes several storm water improvements. The developer, Jacoby Development, Inc., built storm water handling features on the site, upgraded the storm and sanitary sewer network for the project and addressed groundwater contamination.

As part of the Environmental Protection Agency's analysis, the agency compared how the same intensity of development would perform if built according to conventional development standards in other parts of the Atlanta metropolitan region farther from the urban core. Compared with a greenfields site, the redevelopment scenario had lower total phosphorous and nitrogen loadings as well as reduced volume. In some cases, the comparative reductions were orders of magnitude lower.

CHAPTER 49

Restorative Development

Storm Cunningham

At last, some good economic news: There's a mushrooming new global economic sector that already exceeds a trillion dollars per year — and even restores natural resources. It's called restorative development, defined as socioeconomic revitalization based on the restoration of our natural and built environments. And it will dramatically reshape our economies, communities, and environments throughout the twenty-first century.

Turning an old-growth forest into a farm, or demolishing a historic building for a shopping mall, is the kind of development we're most familiar with: new development. Decontaminating abandoned industrial property and turning old factories into apartments and stores is another kind of development, one that builds without destroying: restorative development. Returning a distressed old farm to productivity by rebuilding topsoil, removing accumulated salts, and restoring surrounding watersheds is another example of restorative development.

Nations around the globe have accumulated backlogs of needed restoration projects worth trillions of dollars. Meanwhile, hundreds of billions of dollars of new restoration needs are added annually, creating perhaps the largest new growth sector of the world economy. What's more, most of the other so-called "new economies," such as hydrogen, biotech, nanotech, and digital, are either a direct outgrowth of the restoration economy, or will find their greatest markets in restorative development.

Restoration Industries

Our current restoration economy comprises eight industries. Four involve the natural environment: ecosystem restoration, fisheries restoration, watershed restoration, and agricultural restoration/rural development. The other four industries, which restore the built environment, are:

- **Brownfields remediation and redevelopment.** Brownfields are lands that are not being used productively as a result of real or perceived contamination. The U.S. Environmental Protection Agency's Brownfields Initiative has awarded more than $140 million in nationwide grants to help communities clean up abandoned, lightly contaminated sites and restore them to productive community use. For example, in Concord, New Hampshire, officials are working to identify contamination in a 440-acre (178-hectare) industrial corridor and develop a remediation and redevel-

Originally published as "Restorative Development: Economic Growth without Destruction," *The Futurist*, Vol. 37, No. 4, July-August 2003. Published by the World Future Society. Bethesda, MD. Reprinted with permission of the publisher.

opment plan with the potential to create more than 2,500 new jobs — or 8% of the city's total unemployment.

- **Infrastructure refurbishment and reconstruction.** This aspect of restorative development deals with the flows that connect our built environment: power, sewerage, traffic, water, even garbage. One major infrastructure refurbishment project is the London Underground with an estimated budget of $42 million (£27 million).
- **Heritage restoration.** A community's physical heritage comprises aspects of the built environment that lasted long enough to be a source of community attachment — or where an event occurred that the community considers intrinsic to its identity. Heritage can also be environmental (fisheries) or cultural (indigenous languages).
- **Disaster/war restoration and rebuilding.** Three categories of disasters make up this restoration industry: war, manmade disasters (such as oil spills, nuclear power accidents, and even mudslides due to deforestation), and natural disasters (such as volcanic eruptions and earthquakes). The cost of rebuilding wartorn Afghanistan is estimated at $15 billion. The cost of restoring worldwide disasters is roughly $52 billion per year.

Some of these industries, such as disaster and war restoration, have been around for millennia. Others, such as brownfields restoration, just appeared in the past decade. (New regulations in 1990 made it possible for business people to buy contaminated lands.) But the sudden growth of restorative development and its emergence as a collective economic force can be traced to the convergence of three global crises:

1. The Constraint Crisis: We are out of room. This doesn't mean there are no more wide-open spaces fit to develop, but rather that virtually every developable acre of land — whether it's a farm, a historic battlefield, or a recreational greenspace — already serves a vital purpose that people will fight to protect from developers.
2. The Contamination Crisis. Chemical, organic, and radiological contamination from industrial, agricultural, and military activities have affected ecosystems and supplies of water, food, and air.
3. The Corrosion Crisis. We've been building practically nonstop since the beginning of the Industrial Revolution, and many of the world's cities are getting very old. In the United States, much of the infrastructure is decrepit: The American Society of Civil Engineers has documented a $1.3 trillion backlog for restoring infrastructure.

The Money in Restoration

The following selected initiatives come with a hefty—and worthy—price tag, author Cunningham notes. Total projects exceed $1 trillion in expenditures to revive environments, economies, and aesthetics. Here are 10 current (or recently completed) restorative projects worldwide.

1. $100 million in dam restoration or removal worldwide.

2. $225 million to restore site around Stonehenge.

3. $450 million to restore Reagan National Airport in Washington, D.C.

4. $500 million to restore Istanbul's Golden Horn Waterfront.

5. $700 million rebuilding of a single highway interchange in Springfield, Virginia.

6. $2.5 billion to replace the Washington D.C., area's Wilson Bridge.

7. $3.1 billion to launch first phase of Russian railway rehabilitation.

8. $12 billion restoration of a single watershed in China.

9. $15 billion to rebuild and restore Afghanistan.

10. $52 billion per year to restore natural disasters, not including human-caused disasters or terrorism.

Source: *The Restoration Economy* by Storm Cunningham

These are the same three crises that have brought down civilizations throughout history — and that have sometimes triggered their renaissance. However, we now face all three crises simultaneously on a global scale.

Beyond Sustainability

Restorative development, while benefiting the environment, is not an "environmental message" per se. Rather, restorative development is a strategic path for leaders of businesses, nonprofits, and government agencies that wish to grow economically, or that want to revitalize themselves.

Since the beginning of the Industrial Revolution, our growth assumptions have been based on exploring new geographic frontiers and exploiting new natural resources. Now that the greatest new growth frontier is behind us, we need to reexamine what developed in the past three centuries — and all the natural places we've damaged in the process.

For instance, many cities have no remaining greenfield areas (i.e., land that has never been developed) that they can use for expansion. Some cities, such as Niagara Falls, New York, have discovered that 100% of the buildable land they still possess is contaminated. Meanwhile, cities that do have greenfields are finding increasing resistance to developing them. To grow economically, both types of architecturally challenged cities must redevelop their brownfields instead.

In fact, some of the largest opportunities for restoration industries involve revitalizing the cities we've created during the past 300 years of unfettered growth. That's why developers worldwide are shifting their focus to restorative development. Now when they propose to restore ugly, abandoned property that generates no tax revenues, the same citizens' groups, historic preservation societies, and environmental agencies that used to fight their new developments are instead supporting them.

However, restorative development should not be confused with sustainable development. Sustainable development — which has yet to be properly defined or measured — usually requires a decade or more to produce an attractive bottom line. Restorative development pays off big, and pays off now.

What's more, the field of sustainable development emerged in reaction to uncontrolled new development, but it doesn't solve the problem. Sustainable development is simply a greener form of new development; it can't repair the accumulated corrosion and contamination, which will only exacerbate the Constraint Crisis. Sustainability is a great concept, but the world needs restoration first. After all, who really wants to sustain the mess we're living in now?

Restorative development should also not be confused with the maintenance/conservation mode of development. Though highly essential, conservation has largely lost the battle against new development. This is why most of the largest conservation groups, such as The Nature Conservancy, have embraced ecological restoration. They're not just preserving our last few pristine ecosystems; they're buying and restoring the damaged land around them so they can actually expand.

We've moved from an unsuccessful attempt to slow the decrease of wildlife habitat to a successful strategy of increasing wildlife habitat. That's a very different, and much more hopeful, dynamic. Of course, as with any new field, standards are still being set, and not all early attempts are successful. But that, too, is part of the opportunity for academics, engineers, and scientists.

Tomorrow's Restoration Economy

Restorative development is fully capable of replacing new development as the dominant economic growth mode. It's every bit as profitable as new development (often more so), so it offers an attractive path, a natural evolution, away from the old model. In a corporate world that demands dramatic quarterly profits, and a political world that demands results during an election cycle, only restorative development can deliver the goods with bipartisan support.

Integrated partnerships among the public sector, private industry, and nongovernmental organizations may be the best long-term vehicles for complex, large-scale restoration projects. They will also likely be the entities that restore nations in decades to come.

With a new economic sector that delivers strong economic, aesthetic, and environmental returns, many new legal tools and investment products will emerge. This will likely include a broad spectrum of restorative real estate investment trusts (REITs). What's more, the opportunities for inventors, entrepreneurs, programmers, and consultants are virtually unlimited: Almost any industry or profession that existed in the dying new development economy will have its analog in the restoration economy.

This is the greatest new frontier for hardware, software, the sciences, economics, art, philosophy, architecture, engineering, academia, and policy makers: Nothing is more urgent, nothing is more important, and nothing is more economically productive than restoring our world. Virtually every major trend and discipline of this century either will be rooted in restorative development or will converge with it in a way that will transform and revitalize it.

Every city that is currently being touted as a model of rebirth, sustainability, or economic health has already embraced restorative development projects in their new model. For most of them, this was an intuitive, emergent transition: Until recently, they didn't possess the terminology or theoretical structure to talk about or plan for restorative development in a coherent manner.

Now, the dialogue has begun, and this first phase of the restoration economy is about to enter a period of maturation. The concepts and lessons of the past decade must start to be formally incorporated into public policy, university curricula, and business strategies.

Restorative development has already reversed several trends that are taken as gospel by many futurists. Desertification is a good ex-

---

The Truth about Brownfields

In the early 1990s, few people had heard of brownfields. Now they're in the dictionary—and already widely misunderstood. Here is the truth about five common brownfield misconceptions:

1. The purpose of brownfields remediation is not simply to clean the environment. Unlike Superfund sites—the largest, most-contaminated sites in the United States, selected for cleanup by the Environmental Protection Agency to keep the public safe—the chief goal of brownfields remediation is turning a profit.

2. Brownfields comprise more than just ground and groundwater. Buildings can also be highly toxic with contaminants such as lead paint, asbestos insulation, and mercury that fall under the "hard costs" of brownfields cleanup.

3. Most brownfields are not heavily contaminated. Contamination is often minimal, yet perceived as serious. Abandoned industrial sites, for example, have sat idle for decades because the public falsely assumes they're toxic.

4. Most brownfields are not abandoned. Many contaminated sites are in use, but their contamination has not been assessed. When 30% of industrial acreage in Hartford, Connecticut, was abandoned between 1986 and 1997, much of it was found to be contaminated—which means workers toiled in toxic environs.

5. Brownfields are not restricted to large industrial sites in urban locations. Many are small and rural, such as rural gas stations (abandoned and operational) with leaky underground storage tanks. Further, in 27 states, the EPA cannot prevent a company from putting fuel or chemicals into underground storage tanks that are known to be leaking.

Source: *The Restoration Economy* by Storm Cunningham.

The Sudden Rise of Restorative Development

Technology, business, politics, and academic study are all being affected by the restoration economy—yet this dramatic and lucrative shift in development focus has gone largely unreported. How could an economic sector possibly grow to over a trillion dollars annually without being noticed? Four reasons:

1. It has emerged very quickly (some of its component industries didn't even exist in 1990).

2. Rather than putting old companies out of business (which would be newsworthy), existing firms—many of which used to earn most of their money from new development—have quietly moved into the new markets of restoration.

3. Restorative development is not being measured or reported as a discrete economic sector. Planning and budgeting processes are still based on the old "frontier" model of growth, so they only address new development and maintenance/conservation, largely ignoring the critical third phase of all natural development life cycles: restoration.

4. Lack of standardized terminology: Government reports use a bewildering number of synonyms for restoration, including modernization, capital improvement, regeneration, retrofit, reclamation, and many other terms.

Source: *The Restoration Economy* by Storm Cunningham.

ample: We all know that the Sahara has been expanding for decades, right? Wrong. Recent analysis of satellite images shows it's been shrinking for about 15 years. Why? The primary mechanism has been restorative agriculture, which was taught to farmers 15 to 20 years ago in about a dozen nations on the edge of the Sahara.

Restorative development already accounts for a major portion of the good economic news on the planet, yet it seldom gets the credit, because we don't measure it. Within the next five to 10 years, it will dominate most development budgets, and will continue to do so for the rest of the twenty-first century.

CHAPTER 50

Cities, Water, People, and the Future

Martha Sutro

Walk through the thicket of worlds in Williamsburg, Brooklyn, heading west, and you'll encounter a hundred different neighborhoods. Pass by Senegalese dry cleaners and Hasidic day care centers. Listen to Ukrainian spoken by a baker and the chatter of Hispanic teenagers just getting out of school. Meet Italians on one block and Orthodox Jews on the next. Where a rise in the street allows a view, glimpse the towering skyscrapers of Manhattan, looming.

At the edge of this famous borough, at the western brink of this historic neighborhood, cross Kent Avenue, the pot-holed, industrialized route that runs north-south. Slip through a hole in the chain-link fence and follow a bumpy, well-used path through the mugwort. Cross over makeshift skateboard ramps, dip down to a cobbled, half-buried streetbed, and follow it out to the shoreline. There is Manhattan, seeming close enough to touch. At your feet is the East River, running between this margin of land and that. You can feel, for a moment, as if you're standing at the very center of New York City.

"It's empty, it's open, and it's free," says Brooklyn photographer Lynn Bell, explaining why this waterfront land has inspired so many

different dreams for its potential use. Wiry, pig-tailed, independent, Bell, who has an appetite for bygone industrial architecture, has catalogued the Williamsburg site in hundreds of photographs over the past decade. "Just personally for me," she says, pointing to an image of the twin towers of the World Trade Center dwarfed in the distance between the remaining bars of a wrought-iron fence, "that skyline with all of this roughness around it is what makes this place beautiful." Bell, who moved to Williamsburg 20 years ago, knows the preciousness of open space in this city: Brooklyn is framed by two miles of East River shoreline, but until now its residents have had little access to the water. Bell chose Williamsburg for its neighborhood charm; part of that charm, she found, was living among hundreds of people whose notion of home embraced an abandoned, rubble-strewn, seven-acre lot with access to the river.

Those seven treasured acres have sparked a lot of dreaming. One man in the early 1990s envisioned homeless shelters; another imagined a multiplex entertainment center on the land; before that, plans for a 16-story housing complex were drawn up by a developer. Last year, a 2012 New York City Olympic Com-

Originally published as "Taking Back the Waterfront," *Land & People*, Vol. 13, No. 1, Spring 2001. Published by The Trust for Public Land, San Francisco, CA. Reprinted with permission of the publisher.

mittee claimed this would be the ideal spot for archery and beach volleyball events. But it is the people closest to this land — Williamsburg neighborhood activists, craving open space in New York City's most densely populated borough — who will see their dream materialize.

Erik Kulleseid, The Trust for Public Land's New York State director, has worked since 1995 to draw together public and private interests in the effort to see this land become New York's 160th state park. Kulleseid says the diversity — and unity — of this community are at the center of the project's success. "This is a story of individuals gathering together across various lines of difference and showing what they can do for the public good."

A Waterfront with a Past

Kulleseid is talking about folks like Michelle Rodecker, who's lived on the same Williamsburg block all her life and — like Bell and dozens of others — has links to the waterfront through work and relationships. For Rodecker, it's land that's as close as family. "It's almost like a baby, watching it change," she says, referring to the site's checkered history and the passions it has inspired. Among the hip, young SoHo and East Village artists who have recently come to this part of Brooklyn in search of cheap rents, Rodecker is an old-timer, a woman whose life is entwined with the institutions that have shaped the streets, the commerce, the community, and the waterfront.

Brooklyn Eastern District Terminal. The name evokes the industrial heritage of the East River waterfront, where a rail-to-barge terminal operated on the proposed park site for almost a hundred and fifty years. In its heyday, freight agents who worked at the terminal, like Rodecker's husband, Jim, would load as many as 1,400 railroad cars a month onto barges and pull them across New York Harbor to the Greenville yards in Jersey City, New Jer-

sey. Rodecker, a woman with vivid red hair and a flame of passion in her voice when she talks about the old terminal, was inextricably linked to it through her father, a tugboat captain there. "I remember the day he retired," she recalls. "I watched him walk off the terminal. In those days, when someone retired, all the tugboats would line up and blow their horns. It was so emotional, I cried my eyes out."

After the old terminal closed in 1979, the buildings and lands lay empty. Nostalgic for their waterfront past, Williamsburg residents bribed each other for the old BEDT sign that used to grace the terminal building. In the 1980s, homeless encampments sprang up on the site, and fires burned the buildings to empty shells where the sky showed through. Lynn Bell took her camera down on sunny afternoons and photographed the rusted auto parts, roofless shanties, and a fellow artist's spontaneous industrial sculpture displays. But for people like Jan Ruszczyk, veteran Williamsburg resident, Polish immigrant, and liquor store owner, those were the bad old days. "We didn't go down there then," he says from his snug and popular store a few blocks from the water. "It was far too dangerous."

NAGing About Garbage

In that same decade a citizen appeared on the waterfront scene who ultimately became its most heroic advocate. Peter Gillespie, another longtime Williamsburg resident, describes what it was like in 1988, when the homeless left and a garbage transfer station started operating at the abandoned terminal by the water. "Rats and seagulls were everywhere. It smelled horrible, and there were no regulations in place."

A dusty, dirty clean fill operation followed the garbage transfer station, sprawling over the southern end of the site in 1994. "There were a lot of complaints from the community because there was a fear that this operation — or others like it — were really going to take over," says Gillespie, a soft-spoken former artist and videographer. Out of that fear, Gillespie, Michelle and Jim Rodecker, and other concerned residents founded a neighborhood organization and environmental group called Neighbors Against Garbage — NAG — and fought successfully to close the clean fill operation. That success taught its members, as Gillespie puts it, "that when the community makes a lot of noise, the agencies regulating this industry have to wake up and obey the rules."

It was no accident that an organization like NAG, and other concerned neighborhood groups, arose in North Brooklyn. The district had an uncomfortable familiarity with garbage. Community Board 1— which includes Williamsburg and its northern neighbor, Greenpoint — is populated by 19 waste transfer stations, second only to the South Bronx. In a herculean, two-year effort, NAG joined forces with State Assemblyman Joseph Lentol and forced USA Waste, a national commercial waste company, out of its 1996 bid for a permit that would have made way for the largest trash transfer station on the East Coast.

Brooklyn's Community Board 1 had another unenviable distinction: less open space per resident than 48 of the city's 59 community boards. "There was always this idea that we wanted to integrate the waterfront back into the neighborhood," says Gillespie, leaning back in his swivel chair at the Kent Avenue NAG office, "but it wasn't until we succeeded in stopping the waste transfer station that we had the courage to try to make it open space." NAG, with Gillespie leading, gathered a chorus of north Brooklyn voices, from churches to schools, merchant associations to temples, and cultural centers to firehouses. NAG started with community workshops and, with the help of Assemblyman Lentol and TPL, resurrected a community plan that held a vision for the waterfront. The dream of a park was at hand.

The State Steps In

Coincident with Williamsburg's open space vision was that of New York Governor George E. Pataki and Bernadette Castro, commissioner of the Office of Parks, Recreation and Historic Preservation. In his 1996 Clean Water/Clean Air Bond Act, the governor had allotted support specifically for underserved communities. Williamsburg certainly qualified, but at first the terminal site property wasn't appealing to Pataki as a state park acquisition — the property was in foreclosure, and there were environmental remediation issues to contend with. Around that time, however, New York University turned its gaze to the site. Only a few stops from Williamsburg on the L train, NYU had operated among the closely huddled buildings of lower Manhattan for nearly 30 years without playing fields of its own, and envisioned practice and competition space on the East River.

The State Parks department and NYU, with the encouragement of Lentol, Kulleseid, and Pataki, met several times with community leaders in Brooklyn. With the creation of public open space and parkland clearly defined as a community priority, NYU was able to hear out and address the concerns of the Williamsburg community. Other participants in the complex process of reaching consensus on NYU's move to north Brooklyn included the community board; city, state, and federal political representatives; the owners of the site; city and state parks departments; and the State Department of Environmental Conservation.

With the backing of Assemblyman Lentol and Williamsburg's NAG, TPL purchased the land in August with an $8.3 million loan from NYU. Grants from the Deutsche Bank Americas Foundation and support from the J. M. Kaplan Fund provided funds to help defray TPL's costs of liability and ownership. In January, the state purchased the land from TPL using money from its Environmental Protection Fund, thus allowing TPL to repay the loan to NYU. The university ultimately will invest $10 million to develop playing fields and sports facilities to be used equally by its teams and the public. In exchange for use of the property during the 49-year agreement, NYU also will manage the park on behalf of the state.

Taking Back the Waterfront

"This public-private mix was very interesting to the governor," says Assemblyman Lentol, who claims that revitalizing the waterfront is the most important work of his legislative career. "It's unusual to have a university that's interested in partnering with the state and involving itself in the upkeep of the land. That really made a difference. This administration saw it as a golden opportunity. Of course," he laughs, "the gods of open space were working with us, too."

"Throughout New York City, communities are trying to get to their rivers and can't," says Rose Harvey, TPL's senior vice president and Mid-Atlantic regional director. "On the neighborhood level, borough level, city level — on all fronts — there's a critical need for waterfront access." One of the greatest hurdles is mollifying public agencies, which are often scared by the high costs and perceived environmental risks of former industrial properties. "This project shows us that when it comes to waterfront in urban areas, you gotta get it early, accept the risk, and find private dollars," says Harvey. The Williamsburg project, with its bold funding partnership, can serve as a model for opening waterfronts from the Harlem River to the Hutchison River to the Bronx River.

Another challenge lies in successfully appealing to communities that are often suspicious of private institutions. Certainly NYU's presence in Williamsburg has had its critics. Many locals who regularly use the dilapidated piers from which to fish, for example, are fearful that the proposed waterfront promenade — part of the state's design for the park — will restrict their access to the water. Even some community activists who helped fight against garbage were stunned to find they'd made way for NYU's ballfields instead of public open space. NYU will use the fields primarily from September to May, which may preclude spontaneous community use of the site for activities like dog walking and for Williamsburg's Hungry March Band, which practices there on Sunday afternoons if it's not raining or snowing.

No one better appreciates the mixture of personalities in Williamsburg and the importance of listening to local voices than TPL's Erik Kulleseid, who suggests that the real "biodiversity" of this plot of land is its strong and varied local character. "This was a dream project for me," he says, "because it was a victory for the underdog. It got the local people involved when the stakes were high. They've had to cross such incredible distances to get here."

Currently in the works are more than 100 proposals for parks on New York City's 578 miles of waterfront. For communities that have been sealed off from the water for generations, the chance to reclaim their riverfronts is now. They are responding to a clear and uncomplicated need — attaining a more intimate connection to the rivers they live beside. Michelle Rodecker, amazed at what she's seen happen to the old barge terminal site, says, "This project can help show the way for other communities on the river." Ever hopeful, she heads out the door with Jim, their dogs, and four nieces and nephews. They're slipping through the hole in the fence and walking down to the water.

Appendices

Containing A. Abbreviations and Acronyms; B. Glossary of Terms; C. Periodical Bibliography; D. Water Webliography; E. Regional Resource Directory; F. National Resource Directory

A. Abbreviations and Acronyms[*]

AAEE — American Academy of Environmental Engineers

AAG — Association of American Geographers

AARC — Alliance for Acid Rain Control

AASHTO — American Association of State Highway & Transportation Officials

ABES — Alliance for Balanced Environmental Solutions

ADA — Americans with Disabilities Act

ADT — Average Daily Traffic (or Average Daily Trips)

ADU — Accessory Dwelling Unit

AFT — American Farmland Trust

AICP — American Institute of Certified Planners

ALI — American Law Institute

AM — Automated Mapping

AOP — Airport Overlay District

APA — American Planning Association

APFO — Adequate Public Facilities Ordinance

APTA — American Public Transit Association

APTS — Advanced Public Transportation System

APWA — American Public Works Association

ARB — Air Resources Board

ASCE — American Society of Civil Engineers

ATC — Automated Toll Collection

ATM — Advanced Traffic Management System

AVR — Average Vehicle Ridership

BID — Business Improvement District

BLM — Bureau of Land Management

BMP — Best Management Program (or Practice)

BOCA — Building Officials and Code Administrators, International

BP — Building Permit

BTS — Bureau of Transportation Statistics

CA — Citizen Act. Competition Advocate. Cooperative Agreements. Corrective Action

CAA — Clean Air Act

CAD — Computer Aided Design

CBD — Central Business District

CDBG — Community Development Block Grant

CDC — Community Development Corporation

CHAS — Comprehensive Housing Affordability Strategy

CIP — Capital Improvements Plan (or Program)

CMAQ — Congestion Mitigation and Air Quality Program

CMSA — Consolidated Metropolitan Statistical Area

CO — Certificate of Occupancy

COD — Corridor Overlay District

COG — Council of Governments

DOE — Department of Energy

DOT — Department of Transportation

DRI — Developments of Regional Impact

EC — Enterprise Community

EDA — Economic Development Administration

EIR — Environmental Impact Report

EIS — Environmental Impact Statement

EMF — Electromagnetic Field

EPA — Environmental Protection Agency

ETC — Employee Transportation Coordinator

EZ — Enterprise Zone

FAA — Federal Aviation Administration

---

[*]Source: U.S. Environmental Protection Agency (USEPA), USEPA National Headquarters, Ariel Rios Building, 1200 Pennsylvania Avenue, N.W., Washington, DC 20460.

FCAA— Federal Clean Air Act

FEMA— Federal Emergency Management Agency

FGDC— Federal Geographic Data Committee

FHA— Federal Housing Administration

FHWA— Federal Highway Administration

FIRE— Finance, Insurance and Real Estate

FIA— Fiscal Impact Analysis

FM— Facility Mapping

FNMA— Federal National Mortgage Administration

FTA— Federal Transit Administration

GDP— General Development Plan

GM— Growth Management

GIS— Geographic Information Systems

GPS— Global Positioning System

HA— Health Advisory

HAD— Health Assessment Document

HAP— Hazardous Air Pollutant

HAPEMS— Hazardous Air Pollutant Enforcement Management System

HAPPS— Hazardous Air Pollutant Prioritization System

HATREMS— Hazardous and Trace Emissions System

HAZMAT— Hazardous Materials

HAZOP— Hazard and Operability Study

HOD— Highway Overlay District (also Historic Overlay)

HUD— US Department of Housing and Urban Development

I/A— Innovative/Alternative

IA— Interagency Agreement

IAAC— Interagency Assessment Advisory Committee

IADN— Integrated Atmospheric Deposition Network

ICMA— International City/County Managers Association

IDA— Industrial Development Authority

IDO— Interim Development Ordinance

ITE— Institute of Transportation Engineers

ISTEA— Intermodal Surface Transportation Efficiency Act

JAPCA— Journal of Air Pollution Control Association

JCL— Job Control Language

JEC— Joint Economic Committee

LDR— Land Disposal Restrictions

LDRTF— Land Disposal Restrictions Task Force

LDS— Leak Detection System

LEPC— Local Emergency Planning Committee

LBCS— Land-Based Classification Standard

LOS— Level of Service (traffic flow rating)

LRV— Light Rail Vehicle

LUI— Land Use Intensity

LUR— Land Use Ratio

MF— Multifamily

MGD— Millions of Gallons per Day

MH— Manufactured Housing

MPO— Metropolitan Planning Organization

MSA— Metropolitan Statistical Area

MTS— Metropolitan Transportation System

MXD— Mixed Use Development

NAHB— National Association of Home Builders

NAHRO— National Association of House & Redevelopment Officials

NAICS— North American Industrial Classification System

NARC— National Association of Regional Councils

NEPA— National Environmental Policy Act

NGO— Nongovernmental Organization

NFIP— National Flood Insurance Program

NHPA— National Historic Preservation Act

NHS— National Highway System

NIABY— Not in Anyone's Back Yard

NIMBY— Not in My Back Yard

NIMTOO— Not in My Term of Office

NRCS— National Resources Conservation Service

NRI— Natural Resources Inventory

NTHP— National Trust for Historic Preservation

OAQPS— Office of Air Quality Planning and Standards

OCD— Offshore and Coastal Dispersion

ODP— Ozone-Depleting Potential

ODS— Ozone-Depleting Substances

OECA— Office of Enforcement and Compliance Assurance

OECD— Organization for Economic Cooperation and Development

PCD— Planned Commercial Development

PDR— Purchase of Development Rights

PHT— Peak Hour Traffic (or Peak Hour Trips)

PID— Planned Industrial Development

PRD— Planning Residential Development

PWS— Public Water Supply

PUD— Planned Unit Development

QAC— Quality Assurance Coordinator

QA/QC— Quality Assistance/Quality Control

QAMIS— Quality Assurance Management and Information System

QAO— Quality Assurance Officer

QAPP— Quality Assurance Program (or Project) Plan

QAT— Quality Action Team
QOL— Quality of Life
RACM— Reasonably Available Control Measures
RFP— Requests for Proposals
RFQ— Requests for Qualifications
ROW— Right of Way
RPA— Regional Planning Agency
RPC— Regional Plan Commission
RTPA— Regional Transportation Planning Agency
SAD— Special Assessment District
SCPEA— Standard City Planning Enabling Act
SEPA— State Environmental Protection Act
SEPC— State Emergency Planning Committee
SEQA— State Environmental Quality Act
SIC— Standard Industrial Classification (Code)
SIG— Street Index Guide
SLAPP— Strategic Lawsuits Against Public Participation
SMSA— Standard Metropolitan Statistical Area
STP— Surface Transportation Program
STPP— Surface Transportation Policy Project
SZEA— Standard (State) Zoning Enabling Act
TAZ— Traffic Analysis Zone
TDM— Transportation Demand Management
TDR— Transfer of Development Rights
TIF— Tax Increment Financing
TIP— Transportation Improvement Program
TMA— Transportation Management Association
TOD— Transit Oriented Design
TRO— Trip Reduction Ordinance
TSM— Transportation System Management
UAC— User Advisory Committee
UAM— Urban Airshed Model
UAPSP— Utility Acid Precipitation Study Program
UAQI— Uniform Air Quality Index
UARG— Utility Air Regulatory Group
UCC— Ultra Clean Coal
ULI— Urban Land Institute
UMTA— Urban Mass Transit Administration
URPL— Urban and Regional Planning
USDA— US Department of Agriculture
USDI— US Department of the Interior
USFS— US Forest Service
USFWS— US Fish and Wildlife Service
USGS— US Geological Survey
USPLS— US Public Land Survey
VCP— Voluntary Cleanup Program
VE— Visual Emissions

VEO— Visible Emission Observation
VSI— Visual Site Inspection
WCED— World Commission on Environment and Development
WHO— World Health Organization
WHP— Wellhead Protection Program
WHPA— Wellhead Protection Area
WHWT— Water and Hazardous Waste Team
WICEM— World Industry Conference on Environment Management
WMD— Watershed Management Program
WQMP— Water Quality Management Plan
ZBA— Zoning Board of Adjustment (or Appeals)
ZEV— Zero Emissions Vehicle
ZHE— Zero Headspace Extractor
ZLL— Zero Lot Line
ZO— Zoning Ordinance
ZOI— Zone of Incorporation
ZRL— Zero Risk Level

Note: Another excellent source of information on planning-related issues and topics, including acronyms and organizational titles, is the website of the American Planning Association (http://www.planning.org/).

B. Glossary of Terms[*]

acequia: important forms of irrigation in the development of agriculture in the American Southwest. The proliferation of cotton, pecans and green chile as major agricultural staples owe their progress to the acequia system.

acid: a substance that has a pH of less than 7, which is neutral. Specifically, an acid has more free hydrogen ions (H^+) than hydroxyl ions (OH^-).

acre-foot (acre-ft): the volume of water required to cover 1 acre of land (43,560 square feet) to a depth of 1 foot. Equal to 325,851 gallons or 1,233 cubic meters.

alkaline: strongly basic substances with pH value above 7.0; can be harmful to the growth of crops.

alkalinity: the capacity of water for neutralizing an acid solution.

alluvium: deposits of clay, silt, sand, gravel, or other particulate material that has been deposited by a stream or other body of running water in a

*Source: U.S. Geological Survey (USGS), Department of the Interior (DOI), USGS National Center, 12201 Sunrise Valley Drive, Reston, VA 20192.

streambed, on a flood plain, on a delta, or at the base of a mountain.

appropriation doctrine: the system for allocating water to private individuals used in most Western states. The doctrine of Prior Appropriation was in common use throughout the arid west as early settlers and miners began to develop the land. The prior appropriation doctrine is based on the concept of "First in Time, First in Right." The first person to take a quantity of water and put it to Beneficial Use has a higher priority of right than a subsequent user. Under drought conditions, higher priority users are satisfied before junior users receive water. Appropriative rights can be lost through nonuse; they can also be sold or transferred apart from the land. Contrasts with Riparian Water Rights.

aquaculture: farming of plants and animals that live in water, such as fish, shellfish, and algae.

aqueduct: a pipe, conduit, or channel designed to transport water from a remote source, usually by gravity.

aquifer: a geologic formation(s) that is water bearing. A geological formation or structure that stores and/or transmits water, such as to wells and springs. Use of the term is usually restricted to those water-bearing formations capable of yielding water in sufficient quantity to constitute a usable supply for people's uses.

aquifer (confined): soil or rock below the land surface that is saturated with water. There are layers of impermeable material both above and below it and it is under pressure so that when the aquifer is penetrated by a well, the water will rise above the top of the aquifer.

aquifer (unconfined): an aquifer whose upper water surface (water table) is at atmospheric pressure, and thus is able to rise and fall.

artesian water: ground water that is under pressure when tapped by a well and is able to rise above the level at which it is first encountered. It may or may not flow out at ground level. The pressure in such an aquifer commonly is called artesian pressure, and the formation containing artesian water is an artesian aquifer or confined aquifer.

artificial recharge: an process where water is put back into ground-water storage from surface-water supplies such as irrigation, or induced infiltration from streams or wells.

base flow: sustained flow of a stream in the absence of direct runoff. It includes natural and human-induced streamflows. Natural base flow is sustained largely by ground-water discharges.

bedrock: the solid rock beneath the soil and superficial rock. A general term for solid rock that lies beneath soil, loose sediments, or other unconsolidated material.

capillary action: the means by which liquid moves through the porous spaces in a solid, such as soil, plant roots, and the capillary blood vessels in our bodies due to the forces of adhesion, cohesion, and surface tension. Capillary action is essential in carrying substances and nutrients from one place to another in plants and animals.

commercial water use: water used for motels, hotels, restaurants, office buildings, other commercial facilities, and institutions. Water for commercial uses comes both from public-supplied sources, such as a county water department, and self-supplied sources, such as local wells.

condensation: the process of water vapor in the air turning into liquid water. Water drops on the outside of a cold glass of water are condensed water. Condensation is the opposite process of evaporation.

consumptive use: that part of water withdrawn that is evaporated, transpired by plants, incorporated into products or crops, consumed by humans or livestock, or otherwise removed from the immediate water environment. Also referred to as water consumed.

conveyance loss: water that is lost in transit from a pipe, canal, or ditch by leakage or evaporation. Generally, the water is not available for further use; however, leakage from an irrigation ditch, for example, may percolate to a ground-water source and be available for further use.

cubic feet per second (cfs): a rate of the flow, in streams and rivers, for example. It is equal to a volume of water one foot high and one foot wide flowing a distance of one foot in one second. One cfs is equal to 7.48 gallons of water flowing each second. As an example, if your car's gas tank is 2 feet by 1 foot by 1 foot (2 cubic feet), then gas flowing at a rate of 1 cubic foot/second would fill the tank in two seconds.

desalination: the removal of salts from saline water to provide freshwater. This method is becoming a more popular way of providing freshwater to populations.

discharge: the volume of water that passes a given location within a given period of time. Usually expressed in cubic feet per second.

domestic water use: water used for household purposes, such as drinking, food preparation, bathing, washing clothes, dishes, and dogs, flushing toilets, and watering lawns and gardens. About 85 percent of domestic water is delivered to homes by a public-supply facility, such as a county water department. About 15 percent of the nation's population supply their own water, mainly from wells.

drainage basin: land area where precipitation runs off into streams, rivers, lakes, and reservoirs. It is a land feature that can be identified by tracing a line along the highest elevations between two areas on a map, often a ridge. Large drainage basins, like the area that drains into the Mississippi River, contain thousands of smaller drainage basins. Also called a "watershed."

drip irrigation: a common irrigation method where pipes or tubes filled with water slowly drip onto crops. Drip irrigation is a low-pressure method of irrigation and less water is lost to evaporation than high-pressure spray irrigation.

drawdown: a lowering of the ground-water surface caused by pumping.

effluent: water that flows from a sewage treatment plant after it has been treated.

erosion: the process in which a material is worn away by a stream of liquid (water) or air, often due to the presence of abrasive particles in the stream.

estuary: a place where fresh and salt water mix, such as a bay, salt marsh, or where a river enters an ocean.

evaporation: the process of liquid water becoming water vapor, including vaporization from water surfaces, land surfaces, and snow fields, but not from leaf surfaces.

flood: an overflow of water onto lands that are used or usable by humans and not normally covered by water. Floods have two essential characteristics: The

inundation of land is temporary; and the land is adjacent to and inundated by overflow from a river, stream, lake, or ocean.

flood, 100-year: a 100-year flood does not refer to a flood that occurs once every 100 years, but to a flood level with a 1 percent chance of being equaled or exceeded in any given year.

flood plain: a strip of relatively flat and normally dry land alongside a stream, river, or lake that is covered by water during a flood.

flood stage: the elevation at which overflow of the natural banks of a stream or body of water begins in the reach or area in which the elevation is measured.

flowing well/spring: a well or spring that taps groundwater under pressure so that water rises without pumping. If the water rises above the surface, it is known as a flowing well.

freshwater: water that contains less than 1,000 milligrams per liter (mg/L) of dissolved solids; generally, more than 500 mg/L of dissolved solids is undesirable for drinking and many industrial uses.

gauging station: a site on a stream, lake, reservoir or other body of water where observations and hydrologic data are obtained. The U.S. Geological Survey measures stream discharge at gauging stations.

geyser: a geothermal feature of the Earth where there is an opening in the surface that contains superheated water that periodically erupts in a shower of water and steam.

glacier: a huge mass of ice, formed on land by the compaction and recrystallization of snow, that moves very slowly downslope or outward due to its own weight.

greywater: wastewater from clothes washing machines, showers, bathtubs, hand washing, lavatories and sinks.

groundwater: (1) water that flows or seeps downward and saturates soil or rock, supplying springs and wells. The upper surface of the saturate zone is called the water table. (2) Water stored underground in rock crevices and in the pores of geologic materials that make up the Earth's crust.

groundwater, confined: groundwater under pressure significantly greater than atmospheric, with its upper limit the bottom of a bed with hydraulic conductivity distinctly lower than that of the material in which the confined water occurs.

groundwater recharge: inflow of water to a ground-water reservoir from the surface. Infiltration of precipitation and its movement to the water table is one form of natural recharge. Also, the volume of water added by this process.

groundwater, unconfined: water in an aquifer that has a water table that is exposed to the atmosphere.

hardness: a water-quality indication of the concentration of alkaline salts in water, mainly calcium and magnesium. If the water is "hard" then more soap, detergent or shampoo is necessary to raise a lather.

headwater(s): (1) the source and upper reaches of a stream; also the upper reaches of a reservoir. (2) the water upstream from a structure or point on a stream. (3) the small streams that come together to form a river. Also any and all parts of a river basin except the mainstream river and main tributaries.

hydroelectric power water use: the generation of electricity at plants where the turbine generators are driven by falling water.

hydrologic cycle: the cyclic transfer of water vapor from the Earth's surface via evapotranspiration into the atmosphere, from the atmosphere via precipitation back to earth, and through runoff into streams, rivers, and lakes, and ultimately into the oceans.

impermeable layer: a layer of solid material, such as rock or clay, which does not allow water to pass through.

industrial water use: water used for industrial purposes in such industries as steel, chemical, paper, and petroleum refining. Nationally, water for industrial uses comes mainly (80 percent) from self-supplied sources, such as a local wells or withdrawal points in a river, but some water comes from public-supplied sources, such as the county/city water department.

infiltration: flow of water from the land surface into the subsurface.

injection well: refers to a well constructed for the purpose of injecting treated wastewater directly into the ground. Wastewater is generally forced (pumped) into the well for dispersal or storage into a designated aquifer. Injection wells are generally drilled into aquifers that don't deliver drinking water, unused aquifers, or below freshwater levels.

irrigation: the controlled application of water for agricultural purposes through manmade systems to supply water requirements not satisfied by rainfall.

irrigation water use: water application on lands to assist in the growing of crops and pastures or to maintain vegetative growth in recreational lands, such as parks and golf courses.

leaching: the process by which soluble materials in the soil, such as salts, nutrients, pesticide chemicals or contaminants, are washed into a lower layer of soil or are dissolved and carried away by water.

lentic waters: ponds or lakes (standing water).

levee: a natural or manmade earthen barrier along the edge of a stream, lake, or river. Land alongside rivers can be protected from flooding by levees.

livestock water use: water used for livestock watering, feed lots, dairy operations, fish farming, and other on-farm needs.

lotic waters: flowing waters, as in streams and rivers.

maximum contaminant level (MCL): the designation given by the U.S. Environmental Protection Agency (EPA) to water-quality standards promulgated under the Safe Drinking Water Act. The MCL is the greatest amount of a contaminant that can be present in drinking water without causing a risk to human health.

mining water use: water use during quarrying rocks and extracting minerals from the land.

municipal water system: a water system that has at least five service connections or which regularly serves 25 individuals for 60 days; also called a public water system.

nephelometric turbidity unit (NTU): unit of measure for the turbidity of water. Essentially, a measure of the cloudiness of water as measured by a nephelometer. Turbidity is based on the amount of light that is reflected off particles in the water.

NGVD: National Geodetic Vertical Datum. (1) As corrrected in 1929, a vertical control measure used as a reference for establishing varying elevations. (2) Elevation datum plane previously used by the Federal Emergency Management Agency (FEMA) for the determination of flood elevations. FEMA currently uses the North American Vertical Datum Plane.

non-point source (NPS) pollution: pollution discharged over a wide land area, not from one specific location. These are forms of diffuse pollution caused by sediment, nutrients, organic and toxic substances originating from land-use activities, which are carried to lakes and streams by surface runoff. Non-point source pollution is contamination that occurs when rainwater, snowmelt, or irrigation washes off plowed fields, city streets, or suburban backyards. As this runoff moves across the land surface, it picks up soil particles and pollutants, such as nutrients and pesticides.

organic matter: plant and animal residues, or substances made by living organisms. All are based upon carbon compounds.

osmosis: the movement of water molecules through a thin membrane. The osmosis process occurs in our bodies and is also one method of desalinating saline water.

outfall: the place where a sewer, drain, or stream discharges; the outlet or structure through which reclaimed water or treated effluent is finally discharged to a receiving water body.

oxygen demand: the need for molecular oxygen to meet the needs of biological and chemical processes in water. Even though very little oxygen will dissolve in water, it is extremely important in biological and chemical processes.

particle size: the diameter, in millimeters, of suspended sediment or bed material. Particle-size classifications are: clay, silt, sand, and gravel.

pathogen: a disease-producing agent; usually applied to a living organism. Generally, any viruses, bacteria, or fungi that cause disease.

peak flow: the maximum instantaneous discharge of a stream or river at a given location. It usually occurs at or near the time of maximum stage.

per capita use: the average amount of water used per person during a standard time period, generally per day.

percolation: (1) The movement of water through the openings in rock or soil. (2) the entrance of a portion of the streamflow into the channel materials to contribute to ground water replenishment.

permeability: the ability of a material to allow the passage of a liquid, such as water, through rocks. Permeable materials, such as gravel and sand, allow water to move quickly through them, whereas unpermeable materials, such as clay, don't allow water to flow freely.

point-source pollution: water pollution coming from a single point, such as a sewage-outflow pipe.

polychlorinated biphenyls (PCBs): a group of synthetic, toxic industrial chemical compounds once used in making paint and electrical transformers, which are chemically inert and not biodegradable. PCBs were frequently found in industrial wastes, and subsequently found their way into surface and ground waters. As a result of their persistence, they tend to accumulate in the environment. In terms of streams and rivers, PCBs are drawn to sediment, to which they attach and can remain almost indefinitely. Although virtually banned in 1979 with the passage of the Toxic Substances Control Act, they continue to appear in the flesh of fish and other animals.

porosity: a measure of the water-bearing capacity of subsurface rock. With respect to water movement, it is not just the total magnitude of porosity that is important, but the size of the voids and the extent to which they are interconnected, as the pores in a formation may be open, or interconnected, or closed and isolated. For example, clay may have a very high porosity with respect to potential water content, but it constitutes a poor medium as an aquifer because the pores are usually so small.

potable water: water of a quality suitable for drinking.

precipitation: rain, snow, hail, sleet, dew, and frost.

primary wastewater treatment: the first stage of the wastewater-treatment process where mechanical methods, such as filters and scrapers, are used to remove pollutants. Solid material in sewage also settles out in this process.

prior appropriation doctrine: the system for allocating water to private individuals used in most

Western states. The doctrine of Prior Appropriation was in common use throughout the arid West as early settlers and miners began to develop the land. The prior appropriation doctrine is based on the concept of "First in Time, First in Right." The first person to take a quantity of water and put it to beneficial use has a higher priority of right than a subsequent user. The rights can be lost through nonuse; they can also be sold or transferred apart from the land. Contrasts with riparian water rights.

public supply: water withdrawn by public governments and agencies, such as a county water department, and by private companies that is then delivered to users. Public suppliers provide water for domestic, commercial, thermoelectric power, industrial, and public water users. Most people's household water is delivered by a public water supplier. The systems have at least 15 service connections (such as households, businesses, or schools) or regularly serve at least 25 individuals daily for at least 60 days out of the year.

public water use: water supplied from a public-water supply and used for such purposes as firefighting, street washing, and municipal parks and swimming pools.

rating curve: A drawn curve showing the relation between gauge height and discharge of a stream at a given gauging station.

recharge: water added to an aquifer, for instance, rainfall that seeps into the ground.

reclaimed wastewater: treated wastewater that can be used for beneficial purposes, such as irrigating certain plants.

recycled water: water that is used more than one time before it passes back into the natural hydrologic system.

reservoir: a pond, lake, or basin, either natural or artificial, for the storage, regulation, and control of water.

return flow: (1) That part of a diverted flow not consumptively used and returned to its original source or another body of water. (2) (Irrigation) drainage water from irrigated farmlands that re-enters the water system to be used further downstream.

returnflow (irrigation): irrigation water that is applied to an area and not consumed in evaporation or transpiration and returns to a surface stream or aquifer.

reverse osmosis: (1) (Desalination) The process of removing salts from water using a membrane. With reverse osmosis, the product water passes through a fine membrane that the salts are unable to pass through, while the salt waste (brine) is removed and disposed. This process differs from electrodialysis, where the salts are extracted from the feedwater by using a membrane with an electrical current to separate the ions. The positive ions go through one membrane, while the negative ions flow through a different membrane, leaving the end product of freshwater. (2) (Water Quality) An advanced method of water or wastewater treatment that relies on a semi-permeable membrane to separate waters from pollutants. An external force is used to reverse the normal osmotic process resulting in the solvent moving from a solution of higher concentration to one of lower concentration.

riparian water rights: the rights of an owner whose land abuts water. They differ from state to state and often depend on whether the water is a river, lake, or ocean. The doctrine of riparian rights is an old one, having its origins in English common law. Specifically, persons who own land adjacent to a stream have the right to make reasonable use of the stream. Riparian users of a stream share the streamflow among themselves, and the concept of priority of use (Prior Appropriation Doctrine) is not applicable. Riparian rights cannot be sold or transferred for use on nonriparian land.

river: A natural stream of water of considerable volume, larger than a brook or creek.

runoff: (1) That part of the precipitation, snow melt, or irrigation water that appears in uncontrolled surface streams, rivers, drains or sewers. Runoff may be classified according to speed of appearance after rainfall or melting snow as direct runoff or base runoff, and according to source as surface runoff, storm interflow, or ground-water runoff. (2) The total discharge described in (1), above, during a specified period of time. (3) Also defined as the depth to which a drainage area would be covered if all of the runoff for a given period of time were uniformly distributed over it.

saline water: water that contains significant amounts of dissolved salts.

secondary wastewater treatment: treatment (following primary wastewater treatment) involving the biological process of reducing suspended, colloidal, and dissolved organic matter in effluent from primary treatment systems and which generally removes 80 to 95 percent of the Biochemical Oxygen Demand (BOD) and suspended matter. Secondary wastewater treatment may be accomplished by biological or chemical-physical methods. Activated sludge and trickling filters are two of the most common means of secondary treatment. It is accomplished by bringing together waste, bacteria, and oxygen in trickling filters or in the activated sludge process. This treatment removes floating and settleable solids and about 90 percent of the oxygen-demanding substances and suspended solids. Disinfection is the final stage of secondary treatment.

sediment: usually applied to material in suspension in water or recently deposited from suspension. In the plural the word is applied to all kinds of deposits from the waters of streams, lakes, or seas.

sedimentary rock: rock formed of sediment, and specifically: (1) sandstone and shale, formed of fragments of other rock transported from their sources and deposited in water; and (2) rocks formed by or from secretions of organisms, such as most limestone. Many sedimentary rocks show distinct layering, which is the result of different types of sediment being deposited in succession.

sedimentation tanks: wastewater tanks in which floating wastes are skimmed off and settled solids are removed for disposal.

self-supplied water: water withdrawn from a surface- or ground-water source by a user rather than being obtained from a public supply. An example would be homeowners getting their water from their own well.

seepage: (1) The slow movement of water through small cracks, pores, interstices, etc., of a material into or out of a body of surface or subsurface water. (2) The loss of water by infiltration into the soil from a canal, ditches, laterals, watercourse, reservoir, storage facilities, or other body of water, or from a field.

septic tank: a tank used to detain domestic wastes to allow the settling of solids prior to distribution to a leach field for soil absorption. Septic tanks are used when a sewer line is not available to carry them to a treatment plant. A settling tank in which settled sludge is in immediate contact with sewage flowing through the tank, and wherein solids are decomposed by anaerobic bacterial action.

settling pond (water quality): an open lagoon into which wastewater contaminated with solid pollutants is placed and allowed to stand. The solid pollutants suspended in the water sink to the bottom of the lagoon and the liquid is allowed to overflow out of the enclosure.

sewage treatment plant: a facility designed to receive the wastewater from domestic sources and to remove materials that damage water quality and threaten public health and safety when discharged into receiving streams or bodies of water. The substances removed are classified into four basic areas: [1] greases and fats; [2] solids from human waste and other sources; [3] dissolved pollutants from human waste and decomposition products; and [4] dangerous microorganisms.

sewer: a system of underground pipes that collect and deliver wastewater to treatment facilities or streams.

sinkhole: a depression in the Earth's surface caused by dissolving of underlying limestone, salt, or gypsum. Drainage is provided through underground channels that may be enlarged by the collapse of a cavern roof.

specific conductance: a measure of the ability of water to conduct an electrical current as measured using a 1-cm cell and expressed in units of electrical conductance, i.e., Siemens per centimeter at 25 degrees Celsius. Specific conductance can be used for approximating the total dissolved solids content of water by testing its capacity to carry an electrical current. In water quality, specific conductance is used in ground water monitoring as an indication of the presence of ions of chemical substances that may have been released by a leaking landfill or other waste storage or disposal facility.

spray irrigation: an common irrigation method where water is shot from high-pressure sprayers onto crops. Because water is shot high into the air onto crops, some water is lost to evaporation.

storm sewer: a sewer that carries only surface runoff, street wash, and snow melt from the land. In a separate sewer system, storm sewers are completely separate from those that carry domestic and commercial wastewater (sanitary sewers).

stream: a general term for a body of flowing water; natural water course containing water at least part of the year. In hydrology, it is generally applied to the water flowing in a natural channel as distinct from a canal.

streamflow: the water discharge that occurs in a natural channel. A more general term than runoff, streamflow may be applied to discharge whether or not it is affected by diversion or regulation.

subsidence: a dropping of the land surface as a result of ground water being pumped. Cracks and fissures can appear in the land. Subsidence is virtually an irreversible process.

surface tension: the attraction of molecules to each other on a liquid's surface. Thus, a barrier is created between the air and the liquid.

surface water: water that is on the Earth's surface, such as in a stream, river, lake, or reservoir.

tertiary wastewater treatment: selected biological, physical, and chemical separation processes to remove organic and inorganic substances that resist conventional treatment practices; the additional treatment of effluent beyond that of primary and secondary treatment methods to obtain a very high quality of effluent.

thermal pollution: a reduction in water quality caused by increasing its temperature, often due to disposal of waste heat from industrial or power generation processes. Thermally polluted water can harm the environment because plants and animals can have a hard time adapting to it.

thermoelectric power water use: water used in the process of the generation of thermoelectric power. Power plants that burn coal and oil are examples of thermoelectric-power facilities.

transpiration: process by which water that is absorbed by plants, usually through the roots, is evaporated into the atmosphere from the plant surface, such as leaf pores.

Tributary: a smaller river or stream that flows into a larger river or stream. Usually, a number of smaller tributaries merge to form a river.

turbidity: the amount of solid particles that are suspended in water and that cause light rays shining through the water to scatter. Thus, turbidity makes the water cloudy or even opaque in extreme cases. Turbidity is measured in nephelometric turbidity units (NTU).

unsaturated zone: the zone immediately below the land surface where the pores contain both water and air, but are not totally saturated with water. These zones differ from an aquifer, where the pores are saturated with water.

wastewater: water that has been used in homes, industries, and businesses that is not for reuse unless it is treated.

wastewater-treatment return flow: water returned to the environment by wastewater-treatment facilities.

water cycle: the circuit of water movement from the oceans to the atmosphere and to the Earth and return to the atmosphere through various stages or processes such as precipitation, interception, runoff, infiltration, percolation, storage, evaporation, and transportation.

water quality: a term used to describe the chemical, physical, and biological characteristics of water, usually in respect to its suitability for a particular purpose.

water table: the top of the water surface in the saturated part of an aquifer.

water use: water that is used for a specific purpose, such as for domestic use, irrigation, or industrial processing. Water use pertains to human's interaction with and influence on the hydrologic cycle, and includes elements, such as water withdrawal from surface- and ground-water sources, water delivery to homes and businesses, consumptive use of water, water released from wastewater-treatment plants, water returned to the environment, and instream uses, such as using water to produce hydroelectric power.

watershed: the land area that drains water to a particular stream, river, or lake. It is a land feature that can be identified by tracing a line along the highest elevations between two areas on a map, often a ridge. Large watersheds, like the Mississippi River basin contain thousands of smaller watersheds.

well (water): an artificial excavation put down by any method for the purposes of withdrawing water from the underground aquifers. A bored, drilled, or driven shaft, or a dug hole whose depth is greater than the largest surface dimension and whose purpose is to reach underground water supplies or oil, or to store or bury fluids below ground.

withdrawal: water removed from a ground- or surface-water source for use.

xeriscaping: a method of landscaping that uses plants that are well adapted to the local area and are drought-resistant. Xeriscaping is becoming more popular as a way of saving water at home.

Note: For a more detailed glossary of water-related terms please refer to the U.S. Geological Survey (USGS), Department of the Interior (DOI), website (http://ga.water.usgs.gov/).

C. Periodical Bibliography

American City & County
Penton Media, Inc.
Website: http://www.americancityandcounty.com

APWA Reporter
American Public Works Association
Website: http://www.apwa.net/

California Planner
California Chapter
American Planning Association
Website: http://www.calapa.org/

Flood & Stormwater Management Update
National Association of Flood and Stormwater Management Agencies
Website: http://www.nafsma.org/

Governing
Congressional Quarterly Inc.
Website: http://www.governing.com/

Industrial Wastewater
Water Environment Federation
Website: http://www.wef.org/

Journal of Ground Water
National Ground Water Association
Website: http://www.ngwa.org/

Journal of the Air & Waste Management Association
Air and Waste Management Association
Website: http://www.awma.org/

Journal of the American Planning Association
American Planning Association
Website: http://www.planning.org/

Journal of the American Water Resources Association
American Water Resources Association
Website: http://www.awra.org/

Journal of the American Water Works Association
American Water Works Association
Website: http://www.awwa.org/

Land & People
The Trust for Public Land
Website: http://www.tpl.org/

Land and Water Magazine
Land and Water, Inc.
Website: http://www.landandwater.com/

Planning
American Planning Association
Website: http://www.planning.org/

Planning and Environmental Law Journal
American Planning Association
Website: http://www.planning.org/

Public Management
International City/County Management Association
Website: http://www.icma.org/

Public Works
Hanley Wood Business Media
Website: http://www.pwmag.com/

Stormwater Solutions
Scranton Gillette Communications
Website: http://www.estormwater.com/

Urban Land
Urban Land Institute
Website: http://www.uli.org/

Water Conditioning & Purification Magazine
Publicom, Inc.
Website: http://www.wcponline.com/

Water Environmental & Technology
Water Environment Federation
Website: http://www.wef.org/

Water Environmental Regulation Watch
Water Environment Federation
Website: http://www.wef.org/

Water Environmental Research
Water Environment Federation
Website: http://www.wef.org/

Water Policy
Institute for Water Resources
U.S. Army Corps of Engineers
Website: http://www.iwr.usace.army.mil/

Water Practice
Water Environment Federation
Website: http://www.wef.org/

Water World Magazine
Water and Wastewater International
Website: http://www.pennet.com/

Western Water Magazine
Water Education Foundation
Website: http://www.water-ed.org/

World Water & Environmental Engineering
Water Environment Federation
Website: http://www.wef.org/

D. Water Webliography

AQUASTAT
Land and Water Development Division
Food and Agricultural Organization
United Nations
Website: http://www.fao.org/nr/water/

American Water Resources Association
Website: http://www.awra.org/
American Water Works Association
Website: http://www.awwa.org/

Drinking Water Research Information Network
U.S. Environmental Protection Agency
Website: http://www.epa.gov/safewater/

Ground-Water Data for the Nation
U.S. Geological Survey
U.S. Department of the Interior
Website: http://waterdata.usgs.gov/nwis/

Institute for Water Resources
Website: http://www.iwr.usace.army.mil/

International Mine Water Association
Website: http://www.imwa.info/

International Private Water Association
Website: http://www.ipwal.org/

National Ground Water Association
Website: http://www.ngwa.org/

National Association of Flood and Stormwater Management Agencies
Website: http://www.nafsma.org/

National Contaminant Occurrence Database
U.S. Environmental Protection Agency
Website: http://www.epa.gov/safewater/

National Estuaries Restoration Inventory
National Oceanic and Atmospheric Administration
Department of Commerce
Website: http://www.noaa.gov/

National Ground Water Association
Website: http://www.ngwa.org/

National Hydrography Dataset
United States Geological Survey
U.S. Department of the Interior
Website: http://nhd.usga.gov/

National Rural Water Association
Website: http://www.nrwa.org/

National Water Quality Assessment Data Warehouse
U.S. Geological Survey
U.S. Department of the Interior
Website: http://infotrek.er.usgs.gov/traverse/

National Water Quality Standards Database
U.S. Environmental Protection Agency
Website: http://www.epa.gov/wqsdatabase/

National Wetlands Inventory
U.S. Fish and Wildlife Service
U.S. Department of the Interior
Website: http://www.fws.gov/nwi/

National Wetlands Research Center
U.S. Geological Survey
U.S. Department of the Interior
Website: http://www.nwrc.usga.gov/

Publications Warehouse Research Center
U.S. Geological Survey
U.S. Department of the Interior
Website: http://infotrek.er.usga.gov/pubs/

Safe Drinking Water Information System
U.S. Environmental Protection Agency
Website: http://www.epa.gov/enviro.html/

Society of Wetland Scientists
Website: http://www.sws.org/

Stream Statistics (StreamStats)
U.S. Geological Survey
U.S. Department of the Interior
Website: http://water.usgs.gov/osw/streamstats/

Surf Your Watershed
U.S. Environmental Protection Agency
Website: http://cfpub.epa.gov/surf/locate/

UN–HABITAT
Water, Sanitation, and Infrastructure Branch
Website: http://www.unhabitat.org/

U.S. Fish and Wildlife Service
Website: http://www.fws.gov/

Water and Climate Bibliography
Pacific Institute for Studies in Development, Environment, and Security
Website: http://biblio/pacinst.org/biblio/

Water Education Foundation
Website: http://www.water-ed.org/

Water Environment Federation
Website: http://www.wef.org/

Water Quality Association
Website: http://www.wqa.org/

Water Quality Information Center
National Agricultural Library
U.S. Department of Agriculture
Website: http://www.nal.usda.gov/wqic/

Watershed Assessment, Tracking, and Environmental Results
U.S. Environmental Protection Agency
Website: http://www.epa.gov/waters/

Western Waters Digital Library
J. Willard Marriott Library
The University of Utah
Website: http://www.lib.utah.edu/digital/

World Water Council
Website: http://www.worldwatercouncil.org/

World Water Information Center
United Nations
Website: http://www.unwater.org/

World of Water quality
Global Environmental Monitoring System Environment Programme
United Nations
Website: http://www.gemswater.org/

E. Regional Resource Directory

Borough of Bradley Beach, NJ
Website: http://www.bradleybeachonline.com/

Bradley Beach, NJ
See "Borough of Bradley Beach"

City and County of San Francisco, CA
Website: http://www.ci.sf.ca.us/

City of Aurora, CO
Website: http://www.auroragov.org/

City of Baltimore, MD
Website: http://www.baltimorecity.gov/

City of Boston, MA
Website: http://www.cityofboston.gov/

City of Bradenton, FL
Website: http://www.cityofbradenton.com/

City of Charleston, SC
Website: http://www.charlestoncity.info/

City of Charlotte, NC
Website: http://www.charmeck.org/

City of Chicago, IL
Website: http://www.cityofchicago.org/

City of Cleveland, OH
Website: http://www.city.cleveland.oh.us/

City of Delphos, OH
Website: http://www.cityofdelphos.com/

City of Fort Worth, TX
Website: http://www.forthworthgov.org/

City of Houston, TX
Website: http://www.houstontx.gov/

City of Jacksonville, NC
Website: http://www.ci.jacksonville.nc.us/

City of Kansas City, MO
Website: http://www.kcmo.org

City of Lakewood, WA
Website: http://www.cityoflakewood.us/

City of Las Vegas, NV
Website: http://www.lasvegasnevada.gov/

City of Los Angeles, CA
Website: http://www.ci.la.ca.us/

City of Miami, FL
Website: http://www.miamigov.com/

City of Moscow, ID
Website: http://www.moscow.id.us/

City of New Orleans, LA
Website: http://www.cityofno.com/

City of Philadelphia, PA
Website: http://www.phila.gov/

City of St. Augustine, FL
Website: http://www.ci.st.augustine.fl.us/

City of Santa Barbara, CA
Website: http://www.santabarbaraca.gov/

City of Santa Monica, CA
Website: http://www.smgov.net/

City of Scottsdale, AZ
Website: http://www.scottsdaleaz.gov/

City of Toledo, OH
Website: http://www.ci.toledo.oh.us/

City of Salt Lake, UT
See "Salt Lake City"

City of Santa Fe, NM
Website: http://www.santafenm.gov/

City of Seattle, WA
Website: http://www.seattle.gov/

City of University Place, WA
Website: http://www.ci.university-place.wa.us/

City of West Des Moines, IA
Website: http://www.wdm-ia.com/

Community of St. George, ME
See "Knox County, ME"

Community of Yorklyn, DE
See "New Castle County, DE"

County of Santa Barbara, CA
Website: http://www.countyofsb.org/

County of San Francisco, CA
See "City and County of San Francisco"

Halifax Regional Municipality, NS
Website: http://www.halifax.ca/

Harris County, TX
Website: http://www.co.harris.tx.us/

Knox County, ME
Website: http://www.knoxcounty.midcoast.com/

Latah County, ID
Website: http://www.latah.id.us/

Los Angeles County, CA
Website: http://www.lacounty.info/

Manatee County, FL
Website: http://www.co.manatee.fl.us/

Mecklenburg County, NC
Website: http://www.charmeck.org/

Miami-Dade County, FL
Website: http://www.miamidade.gov/

Monmouth County, NJ
Website: http://www.co.monmouth.nj.us/

New Castle County, DE
Website: http://www.co.new-castle.de.us/

Onslow County, NC
Website: http://www.co.onslow.nc.us/

Pierce County, WA
Website: http://www.co.pierce.wa.us/

St. George, ME
See "Community of St. George"

St. Johns County, FL
Website: http://www.co.st-johns.fl.us/

Salt Lake City, UT
Website: http://www.ci.slc.ut.us/

Santa Barbara County, CA
See "County of Santa Barbara"

Streamwood, IL
See "Village of Streamwood"

Tarrant County, TX
Website: http://www.tarrantcounty.com/

Town of Allenstown, NH
Website: http://www.allenstown.org/

Town of Ayer, MA
Website: http://www.ayer.ma.us/

Village of Streamwood, IL
Website: http://www.streamwood.org/

Washington, DC
Website: http://www.dc.gov/

Wood County, OH
Website: http://www.co.wood.oh.us/

Yorklyn, DE
See "Community of Yorklyn"

F. National Resource Directory

Air and Waste Management Association
Website: http://www.awma.org/

Alliance for Regional Stewardship
Website: http://www.regionalstewardship.org/

Alliance for National Renewal
Website: http://www.ncl.org/anr/

American Economic Development Council
Website: http://www.aedc.org/

American Planning Association
Website: http://www.planning.org/

American Public Works Association
Website: http://www.apwa.net/

American Real Estate and Urban Economics Association
Website: http://www.areuea.org/

American Society for Public Administration
Website: http://www.aspanet.org/

American Water Resources Association
Website: http://www.awra.org/

American Water Works Association
Website: http://www.awwa.org/

Association for Enterprise Opportunity
Website: http://www.microenterpriseworks.org/

Asset-Based Community Development Institute
Website: http://www.nwu.edu/IPR/abcd.html

Brownfields Technology Support Center
Homepage: http://brownfieldstsc.org/

Building Officials and Code Administrators International
Website: http://www.bocai.org/

Community Associations Institute
Website: http://www.caionline.org/

Community Development Society International
Website: http://comm-dev.org/

Congress for the New Urbanism
Website: http://www.cnu.org/

Corporation for Enterprise Development
Website: http://www.cfed.org/

Council for Urban Economic Development
Website: http://www.cued.org/

Downtown Development and Research Center
Website: http://www.DowntownDevelopment.com/

Ecological Society of America
Website: http://www.esa.org/

Environmental Assessment Association
Website: http://www.iami.org/eaa.html

International City/County Management Association
Website: http://www.icma.org/

International Conference of Building Officials
Website: http://www.icbo.org/

International Downtown Association
Website: http://ida-downtown.org/

International Private Water Association
Website: http://www.ipwal.org/

Local Government Commission
Website: http://www.lgc.org/

National Ground Water Association
Website: http://www.ngwa.org/

National Association of Counties
Website: http://www.naco.org/

National Association of Development Organizations
Website: http://www.nado.org/

National Association of Flood and Stormwater Management Agencies
Website: http://www.nafsma.org/

National Association of Housing and Redevelopment Officials
Website: http://www.nahro.org/

National Association of Regional Councils
Website: http://www.narc.org/

National Association of State Development Agencies
Website: http://www.ids.net/nasda/

National Association for Environmental Management
Website: http://www.naem.org/

National Association of Local Governmental Environmental Professionals
Website: http://www.nalgep.org/

National Audubon Society
Website: http://www.audubon.org/

National Civic League
Website: http://www.ncl.org/

National Congress for Community Economic Development
Website: http://www.ncced.org/

National Council for Urban Economic Development
Website: http://www.ncued.org/

National Ground Water Association
Website: http://www.ngwa.org/

National League of Cities
Website: http://www.nlc.org/

National Rural Water Association
Website: http://www.nrwa.org/

National Trust for Historic Preservation
Website: http://www.mainst.org/

Sierra Club
Website: http://www.sierraclub.org/

Society of Wetland Scientists
Website: http://www.sws.org/

The Trust for Public Land
Website: http://www.tpl.org/

The Urban Institute
Website: http://www.urban.org/

United States Conference of Mayors
Website: http://www.usmayors.org/

Urban Land Institute
Website: http://www.uli.org/

Water Environment Federation
Website: http://www.wef.org/

Water Quality Association
Website: http://www.wqa.org/

About the Editor and Contributors

Editor and Contributor

Roger L. Kemp, PhD, has been the chief executive officer of cities on the West and East coasts for more than two decades. He is town manager for Berlin, Connecticut, which was founded in 1785. He has also been an adjunct professor at leading universities during his career, including the University of California, California State University, Rutgers University, the University of Connecticut, and Golden Gate University. He holds BS, MPA, MBA, and PhD degrees, and is a graduate of the Program for Senior Executives in State and Local Government from the John F. Kennedy School of Government at Harvard University. He is listed in *Who's Who in America, Contemporary American Authors,* and the *International Who's Who Registry of Outstanding Professionals.* He has been an author, editor, and contributing author to nearly 50 books dealing with America's cities, and their future. He is past-president of the Connecticut City and Town Management Association and the Connecticut Chapter of the American Society for Public Administration.

Contributors

Affiliations are as of the times the articles were written.

Laura Adams, water resources engineer, Black & Veatch, Kansas City, MO.

Tom Arrandale, free-lance writer, Livingston, MT.

Donald Baker, central region water resources practice leader, Black & Veatch, Kansas City, MO.

Greg Breining, free-lance writer, St. Paul, MN.

Michael M. Brodsky, owner and chairman, Hamlet Group of Companies, Salt Lake City, UT.

Laurie Brown, conservation ecologist, Patti Banks Associates, Kansas City, MO.

B.J. Bukata, wetland scientist, Jones Edmunds & Associates, Inc., Gainesville, FL.

John Buntin, staff correspondent, *Governing Magazine,* Washington, DC.

Michael Burger, director of conservation and science, Audubon New York, Ithaca, NY.

Lori Burkhammer, director of public affairs, Water Environment Federation, Alexandria, VA.

JoAnne Castagna, technical writer, U.S. Army Corps of Engineers, New York City, NY.

Amanda Cronin, watersheds program coordinator, Palouse-Clearwater Environmental Institute, Moscow, ID.

James Crook, member, board of directors, Water Reuse Association, and environmental engineering consultant, Boston, MA.

Tony Cubbedge, land management coordinator, real estate division, St. Johns County, St. Augustine, FL.

Storm Cunningham, chief executive officer, RestorAbility Inc., Alexandria, VA.

Brett Davis, editor, *Tacoma Daily Index,* Tacoma, WA.

Karen DeCampli, municipal marketing director, USFilter, a division of Siemens Water Technologies, Warrendale, PA.

Kevin Dixon, senior water quality specialist, B&V Water, Philadelphia, PA.

Nancy L. Fleming, principal, SWA Group, Sausalito, CA.

Steve Gibbs, free-lance writer, Germantown, TN.

Gary J. Goodemote, senior environmental scientist, Kleinfelder Inc., Oakland, CA.

Ray Gordon, septage coordinator, Wastewater Engineering Bureau, Department of Environmental Services, State of New Hampshire, Concord, NH.

Stephen Goudey, CEO, HydroQual Laboratories Ltd., Calgary, Alberta, Canada.

Michelle Henrie, associate, Brownstein Hyatt Farber Schreck law firm, Albuquerque, NM.

Herb Hiller, free-lance writer and chairman, Institute for Travel Writing & Photography, Georgetown, FL.

Cory S. Hopkins, staff writer, *Worcester Business Journal*, Worcester, MA.

Hilary Kaplan, writer, editor, oral historian, and Kaufmann Humanities Scholar, San Francisco State University, San Francisco, CA.

Amy Kimball, Fulbright scholar, McGill University, Montreal, Quebec, CN.

Les Lampe, water resources global practice leader, Black & Veatch, Kansas City, MO.

Guillermo Lopez, vice president, Development Design Group Inc., Baltimore, MD.

Alec Mackie, marketing manager, JWC Environmental, Costa Mesa, CA.

Geoff Manaugh, free-lance writer, San Francisco, CA.

David Mansfield, general manager, Water Resources Department, City of Scottsdale, AZ.

Chris Matthews, senior environmental scientist, HDR Engineering, Inc., Charlotte, NC.

William McCully, director of engineering, Rehbein Environmental Solutions, Inc., Minneapolis, MN.

Jim Miara, free-lance writer, Needham, MA.

Jennifer Molloy, director, Office of Wastewater Management, U.S. Environmental Protection Agency, Washington, DC.

Carole Moore, free-lance writer, Jacksonville, NC.

Lisa Nisenson, director, Office of Policy, Economic, and Innovation, U.S. Environmental Protection Agency, Washington, DC.

Joshua J. O'Neil, project engineer, DGL Consulting Engineers, Maumee, OH.

Sally Ortgies, parks superintendent, Parks and Recreation Department, City of West Des Moines, IA.

John Osborne, principal planner, Manatee County, Bradenton, FL.

Roshi Pelaseyed, associate, Triad Associates, Dresher, PA.

William Poole, editor, *Land & People*, The Trust for Public Land, San Francisco, CA.

Michael Powell, environmental scientist, Department of Natural Resources and Environmental Control, State of Delaware, Dover, DE.

Peter Ralston, executive vice president, Island Institute, Rockland, ME.

Robin Ringler, floodproofing consultant, Presray Critical Containment Solutions, Wassaic, NY.

Peter Romocki, southwest regional engineer, American Excelsior Company, Arlington, TX.

Amara Rozgus, senior editor, *Public Works*, Hanley Wood Business Media, Chicago, IL

Richard Sawey, vice president and client service manager, CDM Consulting, Cambridge, MA.

Debra Segal, wetland scientist, Jones Edmunds & Associates, Inc., Gainesville, FL.

Paul Shoenberger, chief of engineering and operations, West and Central Basin Municipal Water Districts, Carson and Commerce, CA

Jonas Sipaila, director of innovation, Rehbein Environmental Solutions, Inc., Minneapolis, MN.

Gordy Slack, free-lance writer, Berkeley, CA.

Edwin Slattery, principal environmental engineer, Stanley Consultants, Inc., Des Moines, IA.

Richard Stapleton, free-lance writer, NJ.

Martha Sutro, teacher and free-lance writer, Brooklyn, NY.

Laura Tipple, manager of business development and communications, HydroQual Laboratories Ltd., Calgary, Alberta, Canada.

Rich Turnbull, president, Turnbull Environmental, Inc., St. Augustine, FL.

Stephen M. Way, principal and managing director, DGL Consulting Engineers, Maumee, OH.

U.S. Environmental Protection Agency, Washington, DC.

Jon D. Witten, adjunct professor, Department of Urban and Environmental Policy, Tufts University, Medford, MA.

Nancy Zeilig, free-lance writer, Denver, CO.

Index